The Bedside Guardian 2012

The Bedside Guardian 2012

EDITED BY STEPHEN BATES

guardianbooks

Published by Guardian Books 2012

2 4 6 8 10 9 7 5 3 1

Copyright © Guardian News and Media Ltd 2012

Stephen Bates has asserted his right under the Copyright,
Designs and Patents Act 1988 to be identified as the editor of this work

This book is sold subject to the condition that it shall not,
by way of trade or otherwise, be lent, resold, hired out, or otherwise
circulated without the publisher's prior consent in any form
of binding or cover other than that in which it is published
and without a similar condition, including this condition,
being imposed on the subsequent purchaser.

First published in Great Britain in 2012 by
Guardian Books
Kings Place, 90 York Way
London N1 9GU

www.guardianbooks.co.uk

A CIP catalogue record for this book
is available from the British Library

ISBN 978-0852-65379-1

Cover design by Two Associates
Typeset by seagulls.net

Printed and bound in Great Britain by CPI Group (UK) Ltd, Croydon, CR0 4YY

Contents

BILL KELLER Foreword	1
STEPHEN BATES Introduction	7

AUTUMN

CHARLES ARTHUR Steve Jobs: The World Pays Tribute	15
LETTERS Opinion divided on Britain's concrete "treasures"	24
JASON BURKE Delhi's traffic chaos has a character of its own	25
JONATHAN FREEDLAND Liam Fox could defend himself no longer	28
ALEXANDRA TOPPING Dale Farm: "They promised a peaceful eviction. This wasn't peaceful."	31
PETER BEAUMONT Muammar Gaddafi: The "king of kings" dies in his hometown	36
PATRICK KINGSLEY Occupy London: My nights with the St Paul's protesters	40
JOHN VIDAL Ghana's population explosion	47
MAEV KENNEDY Scrabble king celebrates with night on the tiles	58
DONALD McRAE Basil D'Oliveira's desire to return home opened my eyes to inequality	61
LETTER Curry favour	65
ESTHER ADDLEY Leveson Inquiry: Media victims give their side of the story	65
REVIEW: LYN GARDNER Matilda	70
SEVERIN CARRELL Giant Pandas touch down in Edinburgh	72
TANIA BRANIGAN IN BEIJING AND JUSTIN MCCURRY IN TOKYO After Kim Jong-il's death, what next for the people of North Korea?	76
CHRISTINE SMITH Country Diary: South Uist	81

WINTER

HUGH MUIR The Stephen Lawrence Case: How it changed Britain	85
MICHAEL WHITE The Iron Lady portrays a very different Margaret Thatcher from the one I knew	91
MARTIN ROWSON Ronald Searle was our greatest cartoonist – and he sent me his pens	95
HARRY PEARSON Chewing on some long forgotten gems from the terraces	97
PETE SPENCER AND IAN BURDON Letters	100
REVIEW: TERRY EAGLETON Religion for Atheists by Alain de Botton	101
JEEVAN VASAGAR So who is good enough to get into Cambridge?	105
AMELIA GENTLEMAN Below the breadline on Liverpool's workless estates	114
IAN BLACK Syria: Beyond the wall of fear, a state in slow motion collapse	120
REV. GILES FRASER Occupy London's eviction is a failure for the church not the camp	128
CLAIRE TOMALIN A letter to Charles Dickens on his 200th birthday	131
PAUL EVANS Country Diary: When cold strikes the land	134
ALEXIS PETRIDIS Whitney Houston: Squandered talent of a singer who had it all	135
LETTERS Heart of Midlothian	139
NICK DAVIES Leveson witnesses halt tabloid power grab	139
LUCY MANGAN Rage against the Raisins	143
LUKE HARDING Putin has six more years to draw level with Brezhnev	145
PATRICK BARKHAM M25 is UK's newest tourist attraction	149

IAN JACK Printed encyclopedias were once a rare source of knowledge, but no more — 151
STEPHEN MOSS Imagine if you can Richard Littlejohn's worst nightmare — 155
FRANK KEATING Borat's hymn to Kazakhstan not the only anthem to stir emotions — 161
HELEN PIDD Third time lucky: Galloway shakes up Labour relations as Bradford goes to polls — 164

SPRING
JON HENLEY Anders Behring Breivik: The father's story — 171
ANGELIQUE CHRISAFIS François Hollande: From marshmallow man to Sarkozy's nemesis — 178
MIRIAM ELDER The hell of Russian bureaucracy — 184
HADLEY FREEMAN Etan Patz: The tragedy that still haunts me — 188
NANCY BANKS-SMITH A Month in Ambridge — 191
LETTERS Les regles du subjonctif — 193
EMMA BROCKES Maurice Sendak: The fight in him was an expression of life — 195
SIMON HOGGART Queen opens Parliament with a festival of bling — 197
SIMON HATTENSTONE Manchester City fans dare to hope — 200
DECCA AITKENHEAD Christine Lagarde: Can the head of the IMF save the Euro? — 204
REVIEW: JONATHAN JONES A message to Damien Hirst: Stop now, you have become a disgrace to your generation — 214
LARRY ELLIOTT No good options for an economy that flew too close to the sun — 217
MARINA HYDE All Hail Her Majesty — 225
GUARDIAN LEADER The Queen's Jubilee: Diamond is not forever — 228
JOHN HARRIS Back to the workhouse — 230

CHARLOTTE HIGGINS Sound the trumpets: Today's the day for the Cultural Olympiad — 238

JOHN VIDAL Farewell to Lonesome George, who never came out of his — 243

SUMMER

ADITYA CHAKRABORTTY You've been bankered — 249

MICHELE HANSON We don't like the sound of Fifty Shades of Grey — 256

SIMON JENKINS The Shard has slashed the face of London forever — 257

IAN SAMPLE Higgs boson: It's unofficial! Cern scientists discover missing particle — 261

BRADLEY WIGGINS A dream comes true – now it's got to be Games gold — 265

MARINA HYDE Olympic Games opening: Irreverent and idiosyncratic — 268

ANNA KESSEL Usain Bolt takes 100 metres Olympic gold – this time even faster — 271

RICHARD WILLIAMS Mo Farah runs into history — 274

MARTIN REES Since Neil Armstrong's small step space flight has lost its glamour — 278

SANDRA LAVILLE Martine Wright: From 7 July victim to Paralympic athlete — 281

OWEN GIBSON Ellie Simmonds blazes a record trail — 286

KEVIN MITCHELL Ivan Lendl's stony façade cracked as Andy Murray realised his dream — 289

EDITORIAL Our summer of love — 292

EWEN MacASKILL in des moines Obama counting on massive ground campaign to win Iowa's electoral votes — 294

Index — 299

Foreword

BILL KELLER

Isn't this quaint? A book. Ink on cellulose – unlinked, non-interactive, inert, untweetable. Perhaps you've even paid actual money for it. In an age of transient journalism, all aggregated and participatory, what is the point of newspaper articles sandwiched between hard covers and frozen in time? After all, the Guardian prides itself on being in the vanguard of this immediate and hyper-socialised age, where information is fluid and free and the amateur is welcome at the table. "Print is where words go to die," one of the self-appointed priests of new media declared a few years ago (before throwing principle to the winds and writing a couple of books himself.) What would he say about this venture? What's happening here?

In order of diminishing cynicism, what is happening here is a) the Guardian is trying to make a little money and bolster the brand by repurposing journalism that, in its original form, didn't make enough to cover expenses; b) it is creating a souvenir, a chance to relive a year of fresh history before moving on to the next cycle; c) it is demonstrating that good journalism holds up just fine, bears re-reading, and retains the ability to inform, please, arouse, amuse.

I'm pleased to assist in the revenue part, not just because I believe on principle that people who do good journalism deserve to be paid for it (including – full disclosure – my talented wife, who works for the Guardian's American website) but because I think the world would be poorer and stupider if journalism belonged entirely to amateurs. But my main purpose in this preface is to riff on points b) and c), the year we have lived and, especially, the durability of good journalism.

I come from a different, mainstream American journalistic discipline, one that strives to be impartial in its news pages – analytical, tough-minded, but non-ideological, and with the biases of the writers set aside. The Guardian leans proudly left, and does not oblige its writers to suppress their prejudices. But I am a long-time admirer of the Guardian, and was so even before two collaborations with my own paper made the admiration personal. (Those episodes of Times-Guardian complicity – the WikiLeaks saga and the phone-hacking scandal – continued to produce news in the period this volume covers, and the inimitable Nick Davies, whose investigative skill was instrumental in both stories, has a piece herein on the tabloid power dynamics underlying the hacking inquiry.) What our respective journalistic cultures share is a reverence for facts, even inconvenient facts; a respect for the professionalism of a practiced journalist; a conviction that it is generally better to go see for yourself, even if that entails considerable expense or, sometimes, physical risk; and a joy in original writing that evokes, provokes, clarifies and enlightens.

You can be forgiven if you would prefer never to revisit the year measured out in these pages, but you would be mistaken. A colleague of mine, Carl Hulse, who for many years covered our US Congress with distinction, used to say, in the face of one legislative folly or another, "Bad for America. Good for Carl." We can apply his aphorism to the year represented in this volume: not, on the whole, an uplifting year for the world, but rich

Foreword

in material for those of us who covered it. We had persistent crises in the global economy and in the congealing new Arab democracies. We had politics all over the place, some of it sordid and much of it depressing. (My one, admittedly American-centric, complaint about this volume is that I wanted more of the Guardian's take on our presidential campaign – the comic-sad Republican intra-party race to the bottom, the emergence of the Man in the Empty Suit, the disappointment with the Chosen One.) In these dozen months the planet got perilously warmer. The rich left the rest farther behind. Vladimir Putin and Bashar al-Assad – not to mention Rupert Murdoch – continued to elude their comeuppance. Bad for the world. Good for the Guardian.

Stephen Bates, the editor who was tasked with the hard choices, has set an enticing table. The spread is so irresistible that, while I fully intended to follow the conventional preface-writer's protocol – skim and praise – I was seduced into reading, hour upon hour, to the very end.

One of the mighty challenges to news organisations this past decade, as our business was disrupted by the glorious rumpus of the internet, has been to adjust the balance between straight, just-the-facts news reporting, which the news industry gurus tell us is becoming a "commodity", and the deeper, more thoughtful and complex narrative and analysis and comment, which are known in the business-model meetings as "adding value".

What you hold in your hand is a considerable sampling of added value. Fortunately for the survival of our unsettled business, journalism has many ways of adding value, even without the online dimensions of video, dancing graphics, real-time conversation and games. It is satisfying to see so many different traditional genres and sub-genres practiced at such a high level, with such respect for the curiosity and intelligence of the reader, without concession to the hamster metabolism of social media.

The interviews, like Decca Aitkenhead's methodical interrogation of Christine Lagarde, are patient and revealing, worth the time. The sketches, on the other hand, do their magic in a few lines, like Simon Hoggart's observation of the Queen's bling at the opening of Parliament: "It looked as if she had been rolled in jewellery like a chicken nugget in breadcrumbs."

The criticism is not timid. Jonathan Jones's ferocious, finger-waving upbraiding of Damien Hirst is a nasty treat that almost had me sympathising with the subject – almost, but not quite. Simon Jenkins' takedown of Renzo Piano's London megatower, The Shard, which he calls "a cure for erectile dysfunction", is convincingly damning (and I say that as someone who works in a very nice Renzo Piano high-rise.)

I've long had a soft spot for the pieces we used to call "situationers", in which a correspondent takes us to a place where nothing urgent happened today, makes the rounds, listens attentively, and brings us up to date. It is an easy thing to do merely dutifully, but Guardian writers actually make you care about places you weren't aware, when you opened the paper of a morning, that you cared quite so much about. Ian Black's report from Syria, "a state in slow motion collapse", and Larry Elliott's from Athens, "broke and close to being broken", and John Vidal on the population boom in Ghana all made me nostalgic for the days before this genre fell somewhat out of favour.

The responsibility to go to the story applies not just to exotic realms but also to those corners of our own cities from which we instinctively recoil. The Guardian came at the world's enfeebled economies from many angles; I particularly liked Amelia Gentleman's big-hearted but not maudlin coverage of how, exactly, the jobless live their threadbare lives in Liverpool.

Then there is a kind of reportage I think of as the "infiltration", in which a writer insinuates himself into a situation and pays

Foreword

attention. Jeevan Vasagar sat in with the admissions committee reviewing applicants to Cambridge for a piece that, I'll wager, has become a playbook for aspiring students and their parents. Patrick Kingsley pitched a tent at an Occupy London encampment near St Paul's Cathedral, and, in conclusion, rendered this faint praise: "If anything, the camp itself is their demand, and their solution: the stab at an alternative society that at least aims to operate without hierarchy, and with full, participatory democracy. And to be fair, it kind of works."

Well, for a few days of open-air sleep-in, maybe. An American comes to British crime coverage with high expectations, and this collection does not disappoint in range or execution. We have Hugh Muir on how the murder of a black student, Stephen Lawrence, stimulated and reflected a seismic shift in the culture. We have an unnerving visit to the father of the Norwegian racist on trial for slaughtering teenagers at a Labour party youth camp. And we have Julian Borger's chilling dispatch from the war crimes trial of the unrepentant Ratko Mladic, which includes this observation: "And when the furious mother of one of the 8,000 men and boys killed in 1995 in Srebrenica could restrain herself no more and made a dismissive hand signal at him, [Mladic] drew a single finger across his throat."

Another journalistic form at which the best English press excels – in part by being less dainty about passing stark judgment on the newly dead – is the obituary. My paper's send-off of Maurice Sendak was splendid, but it could not include a full account of the querulous author's fight with Salman Rushdie, whom Sendak called a "flaccid fuckhead". On the whole, this year that was good for the Guardian was also good for the undertaker. You will read here of the squandered talent of Whitney Houston, the inglorious end of Muammar Gaddafi, the gentle lift-off of Neil Armstrong, the unlamented death of Kim Jong-il, along with learned reflections on the passing of Steve Jobs, the great media disrupter, and of Lonesome George, the last known member of a subspecies of giant Galapagos tortoise.

And thank heaven we had the Olympics for a chaser. Athletic accomplishment and (mostly) triumphant spirit rise in a strong assortment of reports from the games and the subsequent Paralympics, all prefaced by Marina Hyde's delighted and delightful account of the opening theatrics: "Tonight was Britain's opportunity to speak directly to the world, and – as befits a nation that declines to learn other languages – it did so in English," she wrote.

And, "I'm still reeling that a country that can put on a show that hilariously bonkers is allowed nuclear weapons."

Along the way there are entertainments, asides, "experiences", flashes of serendipity: advice on what sweets to eat at a football match (midget gems, unknown on my side of the Atlantic), and bits of mail from readers – including a five-day exchange on the use of the French subjunctive.

In March the Guardian held an open weekend at its Kings Place offices, a festival of debate and music with stalls offering crepes and Welsh cheese. Stephen Moss, in his account of the festivities, tells us that he bumped into Alan Rusbridger, his editor-in-chief, and proposed that this event become the Guardian's new business model.

"Forget all this digital stuff and concentrate on pancakes, smoothies, mature cheddar laced with whiskey..." Moss urged his boss. "He gave me a slightly quizzical look."

I can picture that look. But herein you will find pancakes aplenty.

Introduction

STEPHEN BATES

On my final day working at the Guardian last March I was called in by the editor Alan Rusbridger for a brief valedictory chat – a sort of pat on the back after 22 years working for the paper, in lieu of a gold watch – and diffidently, as I bowed out of the presence, I asked whether I might be allowed to edit the Bedside Guardian one fine year. I didn't quite touch my forelock and sort-of imagined that I might join the end of a long list of supplicants, each to be dutifully considered in turn, but no. The editor pondered the matter for less than a second and said: "How about now?" I should have known that that is how things are sometimes done on this mighty national news organ, or indeed on most others. I did not realise that he had been being pressed for some time by the publisher to find someone, anyone to do the Bedside – one of a myriad of decisions an editor has to make each day and some way down the list of importance or immediacy. Inadvertently and fortuitously, I had brought him a solution.

That is not to say that the Bedside Guardian is not a significant facet of the paper. As a book it is now in its 61st year of publication: an impressive annual anthology of the paper's articles, reflective not only of some of the great and small events of the previous year but also of its journalists' take on them. It is probably still the most tangible and enduring evidence of the Guardian's most witty, heartfelt and incisive articles, permanently memorialised between hard covers instead of being tossed aside with the paper at the end of the day, or consigned to the ether as the computer mouse clicks on. And, of course, the Guardian is particularly appropriate for anthologising. It has always been a repository for good writing: what is enviously known as a writer's paper. That's probably partly a legacy of its original provincial status and perennial lack of resources, but also of its prevailing and enduring ethos: sometimes a bit hard to discern these days in its chatty, sassy and occasionally sweary coverage of style and pop culture, but still there; as deeply embedded now in its DNA (if a paper can have such a thing) as in the days of its great editor a century ago, C.P. Scott, who was in charge for a staggering 56 and a half years. When I joined the paper as education editor, from the Daily Mail at the end of 1989 – a considerable culture shock in itself – it was something of a surprise to be told by my predecessor that I must insist that my copy went into the paper unaltered and that the view I took on a story must prevail. Such licence would make most journalists on other papers gasp, but, while of course over the succeeding years my copy was edited – and improved in the sub-editing – it was never once changed to reflect a particular editorial line or prejudice. I was not once told what to write, or what to think, on any given subject. They even kept the jokes in, mostly. This is what makes working at the Guardian a particular pleasure, as well as responsibility, for a journalist.

But if I ever thought that editing the Bedside Guardian this year would be simply a matter of leafing through the paper for unconsidered trifles, I was mistaken. The paper, even in its current, slightly truncated state, still fills a hefty new bound volume of about 2,000 pages every fortnight. On an average September weekday as I write this, the paper contains 120 assorted articles and probably about 50,000 words. And that's

Introduction

before you get to the web, which includes at least as many words again, including the comments, considered and otherwise, of readers from Idaho to Isleworth. As the Bedside year runs for publication purposes from October to October these days, I not only had six months of back copies to catch up on by the time I was chosen, but also a considerable selectorial headache. Even someone who reads the paper quite carefully every day is liable to have missed stuff, or to have forgotten the substance, or the date, of articles they enjoyed, or which moved them, made them laugh, or told them things they did not know before. Some of the articles here were ones I looked out for in making my selection, but many more were stumbled across by accident. Even so, distilling a year's worth of pieces into an anthology containing little more than the word count of a single day's newspaper is a near-impossible task to do comprehensively. Don't think I am making excuses (which I am) but the paper's articles are actually getting longer – 2,000 words is common these days and 3,000 not unknown – so that choice and variety is even more constrained. This year's book contains 70 items, compared with Bedside 2008's 89, for instance, or 2004's 123, spread that year over 324 large-format paperback pages.

Having said that, it has been a huge privilege to have the chance to read, and re-read, some very fine writing from Britain and around the world. The calibre and versatility, as well as the numerousness of the paper's journalists, must be greater now than in the days of its most famous names: the Carduses and Arlotts, Shrapnels, Ransomes and Cookes; and the demands made on them are correspondingly higher. I imagine Cooke or Cardus would blench if asked to knock a piece out for the web, or file running tweets in 140 characters, before penning something more considered for the early editions to be updated later, and I suspect I can guess their responses. Of course, their worlds of foolscap and fountain pens, Remington portables and telexes have irrevocably disappeared too: as distant technologically as the flatbed press and the feather quill. Perhaps they would have been intrigued and maybe even enthralled, by the new and limitless possibilities of immediate, global communication and adapted, just as those of us who started our careers as recently as the mid-1970s with typewriters and slips of copy interleaved with carbon papers have had to do.

In making this selection, I have tried, not entirely successfully, to limit each contributor to one item, in order to squeeze in as many writers as possible, particularly from the reporting staff, rather than the star columnists – nothing dates as rapidly as opinion – being well aware in doing so that I am inevitably and haplessly excluding some distinguished and diligent contributors, as well as some readers' favourites: I am afraid I could not take up one suggestion that the selection should be thrown open online for all readers to offer suggestions, or I would never have seen the light of day. These articles are, however, mainly drawn from online versions of pieces which may have appeared, truncated, in the paper. I know that some of my selections will not necessarily represent the best writing of the journalist whose work has been picked, or be the cherished piece that they would have chosen themselves. I was very conscious that some Guardian writers would merit anthologies of their own – no names, but dozens of them are probably aware who they are – and that many articles regretfully omitted could furnish a pretty impressive alternative selection. To those squeezed out this year: apologies.

To give just two regretted omissions: Marina Hyde pertly and characteristically skewering non-Guardian-reading spectators at the Olympics: *"a chap informed me that 'unfortunately, using the military is the only way we can get anything done in this country any more. Now, where are you from? Oh dear...'* (It must be said that a distinctly *non-scientific sample of equestrian ticket-holders were not immensely impressed to peer at your correspondent's media accreditation and see the words 'The Guardian' – though naturally one puts them at their ease by agreeing that one absolutely wouldn't have the paper in the house oneself)."* Or, also, Richard Williams's account of George Osborne, the Chancellor of the Exchequer, being booed at a Paralympic Games medal ceremony: *"The arena has seen a variety of reactions on the faces of winners and losers over the past few weeks but nothing to match the emotions that flickered in quick succession across Osborne's smooth features – feigned joviality giving way to fleeting masks of ruefulness, introspection, fear and humiliation – as the most unpopular member of an unpopular government was forced to listen to the sound of mass disapproval. His range of expressions could have filled a room in the National Portrait Gallery and will join the storehouse of 2012 memories."* These were just throwaway lines, deep in the text, indicative of the sort of serendipitous phrases that can make reading the Guardian such a pleasure. I am relieved to have squeezed these two examples in and, naturally, both Marina and Richard make appearances more fully elsewhere in the book.

As I finalised the selection, I jotted down a list of stories not covered, or only glancingly mentioned. It is a daunting one: nothing on Julian Assange or G4S, little on the US presidential election, government politics or soccer, torture and rendition, women in public life or religion, only one theatre and no film reviews (a real regret), naught on Scottish independence, or the London mayoral election. Not even Lancashire Viagra (black puddings) or sightings of the Beast of Bushey and the Lion of Essex. In my defence, look at what has been included from a busy, but not exceptional, year. Some stories will doubtless resurface when the paper's former editor Peter Preston edits this book next time. As I write, the outcome of the US presidential election is unknown, as it will not be by the time you read this, and for now

I am left only with Alistair Cooke's brilliant solution when he had to record his weekly Letter from America about the denouement of the Watergate scandal before knowing whether President Nixon would resign or not: "The rest you know."

A little while ago in a second-hand bookshop, I picked up a copy of Bedside Guardian number 30, covering 1980-81. It contained some familiar names: Michael White, Simon Hoggart, Frank Keating, Nick Davies, all represented this year too. There was also an article by one Alan Rusbridger, then a young reporter who had been in Lowestoft, stalking that former seaside summer staple "Chalkie White" who (younger readers may need to know) would appear anonymously at resorts and hand over £5 to the first reader of a particular tabloid newspaper who accosted him each day while exclaiming a slogan gleaned from the paper. The book also contained a slightly grumpy introduction by William Golding, the Lord of the Flies author, in which he praised Guardian reports for being comfortably "at two removes from the red hot news... just as well as it was not a year in which you could hear much good" – not, I guess, a sentiment that would be much welcomed by the newsdesk today – and added presciently: "some day we shall have instant bad news (via satellite) from everywhere and cease to look. And so on." He then went on to list the stories of the year: Afghanistan, "the amusingly named Olympic Games", Iran, Iraq, Syria and "England, my England, (which) seemed to break down in a welter of riots that smashed and burned and broke heads and hearts." At least, in the current year under review, we have avoided that.

Autumn

6 OCTOBER

Steve Jobs: The World Pays Tribute

CHARLES ARTHUR

The bunches of flowers began arriving outside Apple stores as morning broke around the world: a potent symbol of the extraordinary outpouring of emotion that greeted the death of Steve Jobs, the co-founder of Apple Inc. His death was announced by his family late in the afternoon on the Californian west coast where he lived most of his life.

"It's a dark day in Silicon Valley," Matt Drance, a former Apple employee, remarked in an email. Anyone who thought that technologists couldn't be moved to tears would soon realise, from the tributes on Twitter and Facebook, that Jobs, who died at 56 from cancer which he had held at bay for eight years, had inspired the strongest feelings.

In Beijing a steady stream of mourners and admirers made their way to lay flowers and light candles at the Apple Store. One corner of the ground floor had been turned into a shrine of sorts with photographs of Steve Jobs, bouquets and messages: "You have enriched our lives. Thank you for changing the world," said one in English. "Go in peace. We love you," said another.

It seemed as though there wasn't anyone who hadn't somehow been touched by his work. The tributes came from everywhere. President Obama called him a visionary and said "he exemplified the spirit of American ingenuity" and that "he transformed our lives, redefined entire industries, and achieved one of the rarest feats in human history: he changed the way each of us sees the world."

Bill Gates, his long-time rival but also friend – born, like Jobs, in 1955 – said that "the world rarely sees someone who has had the profound impact Steve has had, the effects of which will be felt for many generations to come... I will miss Steve immensely."

The fact is that for multiple businesses – computing, film, music, mobile telephony and most recently mobile computing – Jobs overturned the existing order. Again and again he refused to go along with the conventional wisdom, and introduced his own instead. He lived his life by the instruction he gave in a commencement address to Stanford graduates: "Don't let the noise of others' opinions drown out your own inner voice," urging them to keep innocently seeking the new: "Stay hungry. Stay foolish."

Jobs, though, came across as anything but foolish. He was often described as a tyrant able to throw a "reality distortion field" around his immediate area, to make people believe anything that he told them. The reality was simpler, but harder for technologists used to comparing numbers to understand. Jobs was a brilliant negotiator who had the rare ability to visualise exactly what other people – whether singly across a table or by the thousand in an auditorium or by the million in homes and businesses – wanted. He could frame a price negotiation or a product launch to get the maximum benefit at the minimum risk.

The single occasion on which he did this best was in 1996, when he had recently rejoined Apple (the company he co-founded in 1976) – which was on its knees. The management had lost a billion dollars in the previous 12 months. Jobs knew that it was 90 days from bankruptcy. So he flew north to Redmond to see Gates at Microsoft – which was infringing a number of Apple patents. He needed investment, but being confrontational would just make Gates, then richest man in the world, obstinate – and Apple would have to turn the lights out.

Jobs instead turned the discussion into one where the two companies had a common purpose, in computing: "Bill," he told his old friend and rival, "between us, we own 100% of the desktop!" Gates wasn't fooled – he knew that Microsoft had 95% and Apple 5% – but even so was won over. Microsoft bought $150m of non-voting stock; Apple was saved. Gates observed afterwards: "That guy is so amazing. He is a master at selling," recounts Alan Deutschman in his book The Second Coming of Steve Jobs. (Had Microsoft held on to the stock, it would today be worth 130 times more than Gates paid, or $19bn – about a tenth of Microsoft's present market value.)

Jobs could be ruthless. He fired people who let information slip before an event and spoiled the surprise. He was unforgiving of failure: when Apple's first effort at a "cloud" service, MobileMe, suffered flaws in its early weeks he called the team together into a hall and excoriated them for half an hour. Chuq von Rospach, who worked at the company until 2009 (though not on that project), characterised it as: "Imagine Steve walking up and down the corridors with a flamethrower, stopping people at random and saying 'Do you work on MobileMe? How about you?'"

Yet for all the claims of tyrannical behaviour, Jobs also kept staff fiercely loyal. Former employees speak of their devotion to their company with something approaching amazement; they sound almost surprised at how hard they worked and how demanding Jobs was. Yet the staff at the company have stayed almost unchanged since he returned there at the end of 1996, taking over the reins in 1997. Tim Cook, now chief executive; Phil Schiller, head of marketing; Jonathan Ive, head of design. The core of Apple's functionality flows from them.

His beginnings were inauspicious. Jobs was the adopted child of a university lecturer and a student (he was a quarter Syrian) raised by working parents who could barely scrape together the money to send him to college. When he did go to Reed College he soon dropped out, but stayed behind and studied calligraphy and typography – which would later feed into the products whose design he would oversee in microscopic detail.

The first time he overturned the way the world worked was in 1984. In 1979, three years after setting up Apple with Steve Wozniak, Jobs had visited Xerox's Palo Alto Research Center in California and saw its experimental system which used "windows" and a "mouse" – an insane idea at a time when all other computers (including Apple's) communicated via blinking cursors into which you fed obscure commands such as CP: A: B:, rather than by manipulating virtual objects on a screen.

"It wasn't complete," he told Wired magazine later. "It wasn't quite right. But within 10 minutes, it was obvious that every computer in the world would work this way someday. And you could argue about the number of years it would take, and you could argue about who would be the winners and the losers, but I don't think you could argue that every computer in the world wouldn't eventually work this way."

Jobs licensed the system from Xerox (which took payment in Apple stock) and oversaw the development of computers using the new "windowing" system. The first was called Lisa, after his daughter; the next, the Macintosh, which went on sale in 1984, aimed to make windows ubiquitous. Jobs also wanted it to be as simple to use, and as closed-in, as a washing machine or other domestic appliance. Computers, he felt, were just too complicated. Using window systems was much easier.

Microsoft agreed, licensed and then extended the idea, and while Jobs wrangled with John Sculley – hired from his presidency of Pepsi with the immortal line "do you want to sell sugared water for the rest of your life, or do you want a chance to change the world?" – Bill Gates extended the idea of windows to

Windows, which rapidly overtook Apple's products and became the most widely used desktop computer operating system in the world. Jobs was kicked out of Apple in 1985, and over the next 12 years Microsoft infiltrated and then took over personal computing. All the computers used windows – in some form. Jobs had been right.

His next target was the film business. Pixar, the company that he bought from George Lucas (who was selling it as part of a divorce settlement) in 1986, is a classic "people business": the talent walks out of the door every day. It was also cutting-edge, making films entirely with computers – actors, pictures, everything. Jobs was able to keep John Lasseter and other key staff working there through thick and thin. But it was his negotiation genius that pulled off the deal getting Disney, the most powerful force in film, to distribute Pixar's first production, Toy Story – the first feature-length computer-animated film. Pixar never had a flop as an independent company; Disney bought it in January 2006 for $7.4bn (it was stock in Pixar, rather than Apple, which made Jobs a billionaire).

At Pixar, Jobs discovered the importance of managing people. He rehoused it at great expense – personally designing the building with all the toilets in a central location so people would meet there, mix and keep the creative juices flowing.

On returning to Apple (which bought his other post-Apple business NeXT in 1996), Jobs quickly took over and installed himself as "interim CEO" in 1997. From NeXT and Pixar he had learnt the harsh lesson of inventory management – keeping projects under control – and the finesse of recruiting the right person. Tim Cook – now chief executive – may have been the most important single hire he ever made. Cook turned Apple from a bloated manufacturer into a slick one which had less stock tied up in warehouses than its bitter rival Dell.

But as he nursed Apple back to health, the music business – one of his oldest loves – came into his sights. With online file sharing rampant and revenues crashing, record labels needed a saviour. It came in the unlikely form of a cigarette packet-sized white-and-silver object. And so Jobs changed the world again.

The iPod was initially conceived by a team led by then chief of hardware Jon Rubinstein, as a way to get more people buying Apple's Macintosh computers. Jobs drove its designers to distraction, again, and even on the day before the product's launch was complaining that the "click" when he put headphones into the prototypes on display wasn't satisfying. (An engineer had to polish the sockets by hand.) But the iPod changed everything, first because of its tiny size – with 1,000 songs in svelte enclosure – and for its simple, quick synchronisation. There were already music players, but they were bulky, had horrible software, and would take five hours to transfer 1,000 songs. The iPod would take 10 minutes.

Then Jobs pulled off yet another audacious negotiation, and another revolution: persuading the record labels to let him sell music digitally. He did this by playing on Apple's tiny size: with the iPod still limited to Apple computers, making only 5% of the market, he persuaded them that there was little risk if anything went wrong. The labels reckoned they could license their music to someone else if it went right. "Apple's target, believe it or not, was to sell 1 million songs in the first year," the journalist Robert X Cringely – aka Mark Stephens – told me earlier this year. When the iTunes Music Store opened in April 2003 it sold the first million songs in a week. Within a few months it was unstoppable, and Jobs created a version of Apple's iTunes software for Windows which accelerated it. Within a year it had sold nearly 100m songs, and the iPod had 70% of the music player market.

But it was the design of the iPod – small, appliance-like, simple – that most struck people. Jobs had insisted that it should be able to get to any song within three clicks. Design, as he explained in 2000, wasn't about how it looked. It was about how it worked. "In most people's vocabularies, design means veneer. It's interior decorating. It's the fabric of the curtains and the sofa. But to me, nothing could be further from the meaning of design. Design is the fundamental soul of a man-made creation that ends up expressing itself in successive outer layers of the product or service."

In 2006 Microsoft tried to imitate it with the Zune – coloured brown. It was a flop.

Computers? Film? Music? Now Jobs had one of the biggest businesses, the booming mobile industry, in his sights. The iPhone was the result of a two-and-a-half year project to use touchscreens to manipulate a computer. "We have been very lucky to have brought a few revolutionary user interfaces to the market – the mouse, the click wheel [on the iPod], and now multi-touch," he said in January 2007. "Each has made possible a revolutionary product – the Mac, the iPod, and now the iPhone. Today we're going to show you a software breakthrough. Software that's at least five years ahead of what's on any other phone."

Not only was the phone different; Jobs also beat the mobile operators, formerly the rulers of the business, and used Apple's growing brand power to drive deals which offered iPhone owners unlimited data. After the iPhone, everyone needed a touchscreen: Google, and then Microsoft, and then market leaders Nokia and RIM followed suit as quickly as they could. But not fast enough: in mid-2011 Apple became the world's biggest mobile phone maker by revenue, an idea that would have been nonsensical four years earlier. Jobs's revolutions were coming faster and faster.

For Drance, then working at Apple trying to recruit outside developers to write Mac software, the unveiling of the iPhone was a stunning moment: an internal project that had run for two and a half years, yet he hadn't heard about it? "There's a competitive thing to Apple's secrecy, because you want to keep competitors guessing. But also Apple has built so much around the event, around the reveal, the announcement, and you really lose the magic if people know what's coming; if people know what's behind the curtain, it's not as magical an event."

The final candidate for disruption? Computing, once again. Though Bill Gates introduced tablet computers in 2001, they went nowhere – but Apple took them up as a research project, and dusted them off for the January 2010 launch of the iPad. A computer you could carry, operated by touch, with a 10-hour battery life, that ran on "apps" – none of it was like the past. And Apple sold them by the tens of millions, while would-be rivals struggled. "Our competitors are looking at this [tablet market] like it's the next PC market. That is not the right approach to this. These are post-PC devices that need to be easier to use than a PC, more intuitive," he said, pacing the stage in one of his last public appearances in March. "The hardware and software need to intertwine more than they do on a PC. We think we're on the right path with this."

The iPad is changing how people work and play; newspapers and magazines are desperate to find ways on to it and to make money. The latest forecasts suggest Apple will dominate the market at least until 2014 – even with Microsoft, which as in the mobile market and music player market, is following its lead with a new iPad-like "Metro" interface for its next version of Windows, due next year.

All the devices had one crucial thing in common: people fell in love with them. They felt passionately about them, in a way the world had never seen before. "Touch is a very important sense; a lot of human emotion is built around touching objects, other people, touching things," Don Norman, co-founder of Neilsen/Norman Group, said. "I think that we lost something really big when we went to the abstraction of a computer with a mouse and a keyboard, it wasn't real, and the telephone was the same, it was this bunch of menus and people got lost in the menus and buttons to push and it felt like a piece of technology. Whereas the iPhone felt like a piece of delight. It really is neat to go from one page to the other not by pushing a button but by swiping your hand across the page... it is more intimate. Think of it not as a swipe, think of it as a caress."

The one challenge Jobs couldn't beat was life's finite span. "No one wants to die," Jobs told the Stanford graduates in 2005. "Even people who want to go to heaven don't want to die to get there. And yet death is the destination we all share. No one has ever escaped it. And that is as it should be, because death is very likely the single best invention of life. It is Life's change agent."

The cancer that eventually killed him was initially diagnosed in October 2003. At first, the doctors thought it was pancreatic cancer – which typically kills in six to 12 months. "My doctor advised me to go home and get my affairs in order, which is doctor's code for prepare to die." But it was neuroendocrine cancer, a more treatable form. Yet – ironically for someone working in a company working on the most advanced engineering – Jobs, a lifelong pescatarian (eating fish and vegetables) didn't seek medical intervention until summer 2004. That seemed to have quelled the problem – but in 2009 he needed a liver transplant, and the immunosuppressant drugs required appear to have let the cancer back.

In January 2011 he took extended medical leave from the company he had co-founded, saying plaintively in his departure note "I love Apple so much".

The questions now will turn to Apple, and its future – though they are exactly the same as those which were posed when Jobs stepped aside, finally acknowledging his illness, in August. Can it be the same creative force without him? Can those in charge find new industries to revolutionise, in the way that Jobs did with personal computing, films, music, telephony and most recently newspaper and magazine reading through the iPad?

Put like that, it is the tallest of tall orders; in retrospect it seems amazing that it happened at all. Much may depend on whether those inside the company can stay true to Jobs's parting advice to the Stanford graduates. "Stay hungry," he said. "Stay foolish."

9 OCTOBER

Opinion divided on Britain's concrete "treasures"

LETTERS

Jonathan Glancey refers to Preston bus station as "baroque" ("Fashions change, but fine buildings must be saved", 6 October). On this we are as one, assuming his interpretation of baroque is as resembling a public convenience and a harbour for cutpurses. Methinks Mr Glancey does not catch any buses from there.

Andrew Swarbrick
Preston, Lancashire

The purpose of a bus station is to provide bus users with a convenient waiting area to connect with their buses. Preston's station is dark and claustrophobic, and doesn't have very many seats. It would have been much more appropriate to accompany

Glancey's article with images of the insides of the bus station as used by commuters, rather than a pretty image that shows the entrance to the multi-storey car park which sits on top of the library.

Furthermore, the pedestrian underpass from the station to the city centre is so successful that when passengers alight from the buses, many walk along the dedicated bus exit road. Perhaps the kindest thing to be said about Preston bus station is that Steve Jobs didn't use it as a template for the iPhone.

Pascal Desmond
Lancaster

11 OCTOBER

Delhi's traffic chaos has a character of its own

JASON BURKE

The best time to drive in Delhi is at dawn or, even better, around 7am. By then the last of the trucks that cross the city during the night are halted at roadside restaurants with the drivers sipping scalding tea and eating fried parathas and eggs, and there is a short period before the traffic builds up.

Delhi's urban sprawl is now so extensive that entire satellite cities, where several million people live, have disappeared into the mass of the metropolis. Gurgaon, the new town to the south, is still separated by a thin belt of scrubby grassland, but Noida, the vast development to the east, is, to all intents and purposes, part of the city. If these satellites are included, the city's population probably touches 25 million. This is set to increase further as economic growth sucks in villagers from across the country.

Girdling the city's old core is a ring road – an unplanned set of linked chunks of carriageway widened over three decades. Over nearly two years, I have learned to respect, if not necessarily appreciate, its rhythms. Like the city itself, it changes character through the day and night.

At 7am, in the cooler, clearer morning, driving over the crumbling flyovers, there is relative calm. You can look in one direction and see the pristine marble-tiled dome of the tomb of the Muslim Mughal emperor Humayun. In the other, the modern forms of a Bahá'í temple mark the horizon. Kites and crows wheel overhead. Dogs forage in the rubbish at the roadside. A few auto-rickshaws putter straight down the centre of the three- or four-lane carriageway, not much faster than the bicycles ridden by the nightwatchmen returning from their shift.

By 9am this (relatively) bucolic vision is long gone. In 2008, a government report announced that the ring road had reached capacity with 110,000 vehicles a day and predicted the total would reach 150,000 cars, trucks, buses and bikes by the end of the decade. In fact, continuing economic growth, the new middle class's demand for cars and the parlous, if improving, public transport system has meant even more vehicles than feared. Some estimates are as high as 200,000. As "lane driving" is seen as an odd, foreign practice, the result is gridlock.

This gridlock evolves, however. The buses are slightly less empty mid-morning, then refill with schoolchildren and students. The dreaded privately owned Blueline buses, badly maintained and driven as fast as possible to maximise profits, have gone. Those that have replaced them are marginally better, but still often flatten small cars and motorbikes. There is an opening around 2pm when the traffic eases, but by 5pm, the ring road is a strip of snarling, grinding vehicles. The buses, now with passengers packed against doors and windows, loom like ships full of refugees above a choppy sea of jerking cars. The air is black with fumes. The new cars – Audis, BMWs, huge imported SUVs – sit bumper to bumper. Labour is so cheap in India that a minor retired bureaucrat is likely to have a driver, even if the vehicle is a tiny, battered Suzuki. The really wealthy have a uniformed chauffeur.

Vestiges of another India occasionally surface. Over by the badly built, badly designed complex used as athletes' accommodation in last year's Commonwealth Games I saw a bullock cart negotiating traffic around one of the new metro stations. Yesterday there were two tractors hauling trailers full of fodder – for the elephants, which the authorities use for tree pruning? For the zoo? — stuck at the busy crossroad, Ashram Chowk. On the central reservation, entire families sleep.

After rush hour, there is a lull. The day workers have gone home. The buses even have empty seats. There is a new peril however: the minivans used by call centres. They race to get their passengers to their offices as fast as possible, hurtling up inside lanes, jinking between slower vehicles like a footballer dribbling his way through a pack of defenders. Part of their haste is explained by the approaching deadline that heralds the next phase in the life of the road: the trucks.

At 10pm, the police allow the heavy goods vehicles that need to traverse Delhi into the city. With no proper bypass, a small army of honking, overloaded, low-geared, multicoloured road behemoths gathers during the afternoon on all approach roads. These now clank forward, filling two of three available lanes with an apparently inexhaustible convoy carrying construction materials, foodstuffs, manufactured goods, from Udaipur to Chandigarh, from Agra to Amritsar, from Bareilly to Jammu.

By 1am most of the trucks are through and the final phase begins. Road deaths in India reach 140,000 a year. This means that every two years, more people died in accidents in the country than were killed in total in the 2004 tsunami. Most fatal accidents in Delhi occur in the small hours, when fast cars driven by young, wealthy and often drunk men hurtle across the city. These regularly career out of control to hit families sleeping on the pavement, insomniacs, night-shift workers, even traffic policemen. Hit and runs are the rule, not the exception. Those with the means bribe their way out of trouble. The casualties or their families may get some compensation, if the culprit can be traced.

At 5am and 6am, in that small moment of calm, you can hear the horns of the trains leaving the main stations, hauling their packed carriages out into another India and another day.

14 OCTOBER

Liam Fox could defend himself no longer

JONATHAN FREEDLAND

Dr Liam Fox, the Government's defence secretary, resigned following revelations that he gave his close friend, the lobbyist Adam Werritty, privileged access to the Ministry of Defence and allowed him to accompany him on official trips abroad.

In the end, the defence secretary could defend himself no longer. Once he called the claims that his friendship with Adam Werritty had compromised his office "wild" and "baseless". On Friday he had to concede not only that "mistakes were made", as he passively put it last weekend, but that they were grounds for resignation.

A man who once fancied himself a future leader and heir to Margaret Thatcher, with a worldview too important to be constrained by pettifogging civil servants, had to send himself to the backbenches.

The biggest impact is on David Cameron. A man said not to approve of rushed reshuffles was rushed into one, hastily appointing Philip Hammond to take Fox's place. Those around the prime minister have long spoken disparagingly of the way his predecessors handled ministerial scandal.

John Major's problem was that he always held on too long, eventually bowing to the inevitable, thereby looking weak twice over. Tony Blair, meanwhile, overcorrected, hastily dispatching anyone who fell foul of Alastair Campbell's notorious 10-day rule – if you're on the front pages 10 days running, you're toast – including those who really didn't deserve to go, such as Peter Mandelson (the second time around). Cameron would be different.

The Fox episode has surely taught him that that's easier said than done. Yes, he stood firm in the face of a baying media, but that could equally be read as weakness, failing to eject someone who clearly had to go. This week, Cameron learned that there's rarely a right place to stand in the middle of a political storm.

Still, his slowness to act has a substantial upside. It means that no one on the right will now be able to blame Cameron for dumping their standard bearer too hastily; the PM was ready to let due process take its course. Had Fox resigned quickly, his reputation might have been protected. Instead, by letting it go on this long, with day after day of negative stories, he has diminished his own standing permanently. If he does eventually seek to challenge the coalition from the backbenches – and his resignation letter professed loyalty – he will be a much less potent force.

Nor is it just Fox who now stands smaller. He spoke for a Tory right that flexed its muscles to protect him this week – and failed all the same. It was striking that George Osborne and Michael Gove joined Fox in the Commons when he mounted his defence on Monday, the trio all luminaries of the party's Cheney-ite wing. That they could not save their man leaves Cameron, who did not appear in the chamber that day, a tad more comfortable.

The only risk is that a Tory right smarting from defeat will start making its resentment known. They clearly don't feel fully represented by this government – a fact made plain by Fox's obvious belief that he needed to run his own shadow foreign policy – and they have now suffered a bad setback. It will pain many of them that their hero has gone. Not that the opposition can draw sustenance from Fox's agony. What ousted the defence secretary was media pressure – begun, it has to be said, by this newspaper, with the others piling in later.

The shadow defence secretary, Jim Murphy, boasted that he had never once called for Fox's resignation. Nor did he exactly deliver a Robin Cook-style forensic skewering of the minister in the Commons on Monday. Some wonder if Murphy was hobbled by Labour's own declared receipt of largesse from Cellcrypt, one of the companies at the centre of the Fox story. Whatever the explanation, Labour cannot yet be said to have mastered the art of opposition.

19 October

Dale Farm: "They promised a peaceful eviction. This wasn't peaceful."

ALEXANDRA TOPPING

Traveller families, who had occupied an unauthorised site near Basildon in Essex for more than 10 years, were forcibly evicted by the local council in a large-scale police operation

Protesters thought the barricade at Dale Farm was secure. Knowing that bailiffs could arrive at any time, a small band locked themselves to the gates – some with D-locks, others with chains looped through a bar sunk into a concrete-filled barrel – and waited for them to come.

But when the bailiffs did arrive, just as day began to break, they came unannounced, through the barely guarded back of the site.

The eviction Basildon council had spent more than a decade fighting for had finally begun. By the end of it, and after violent clashes, the main barrier to the site had been cleared of protesters, paving the way for bailiffs to begin clearing the site – a process that could now take weeks.

As police first entered the site at 7am, protesters appeared to have been taken by surprise. Some threw missiles at officers, who stormed through barriers and wooden fences that were flimsy against their collective strength. Up to 150 officers in full riot gear charged on to the site, using Tasers against those that stood in their path. "They promised a peaceful eviction, but it wasn't," said Nora Sheridan, one of the residents still refusing to go. "It wasn't peaceful at all."

Others described protesters writhing on the floor due to electric shocks. Some said they had been shoved aside as the highly organised force moved forward.

Police – who confirmed two people had been Tasered in the dawn operation – then made their way to the site's front gate, to which several protesters were locked. About 20 others were on scaffolding, though their numbers diminished throughout the day, with police arresting at least 11 people by the evening.

The eviction has been a long time in coming. After 10 years of legal wrangling, the Travellers finally lost their fight on Monday when a high court judge ruled they could not challenge a decision which said the eviction from the unauthorised area of Dale Farm – part of the site is legal – was proportionate and should go ahead.

Over the summer, this unauthorised area of Dale Farm, once home to 86 Traveller families, became more like a camp of war. Protesters moved in and set up "Camp Constant", and many resident Travellers decided to leave. By the time the bailiffs arrived around 50 protesters remained, and a similar number of Travellers. It was the protesters manning the barricades as the bailiffs arrived, people who had been planning for a siege.

But the force and efficiency of police left many in shock. Electricity supplies were cut early in the morning leaving some elderly residents without crucial medical equipment, according to protesters.

Traveller Mary Sheridan, who brought the original injunction against the eviction that halted bulldozers on 19 September, said an alarm "like an air raid siren" woke her at dawn. She ran to the back gate as police were entering. "They were pushing things out of the way. When the boy was tasered, he was hopping – it was like an electric shock. I didn't think the police could use Tasers, it was terrifying," she said.

"The hardest bit now is going to be seeing the plot that was my home being dug up. We have no address now, we are going to have to go on the road and we will be illegal."

An hour after police and bailiffs had first entered the site, protesters had lit a blazing fire across a main route into the site in an attempt to keep back the line of police. Young men in balaclavas fuelled the blaze with rolled carpets, discarded furniture, parts of chalets that had already been abandoned. A caravan that had been pushed in the path of bailiffs caught fire, sending black smoke across the site. There was panic when a gas canister in the caravan exploded, but no one was hurt.

Two women claimed to have been injured in the skirmishes. The ambulance service said a woman was taken to hospital with a back injury, two people were treated for smoke inhalation, one for a nosebleed and one for chest pains.

It was thought that bailiffs would lead the operation but Essex police said they had received intelligence that bricks, bottles and liquids had been stockpiled, which could put council workers and bailiffs in danger. Inspector Trevor Roe insisted officers had treated those on site with "respect and dignity".

By afternoon the situation had "reached a considerably more calm state than officers faced this morning", said Essex police.

With helicopters circling overhead, Kathleen McCarthy, a spokeswoman for the Dale Farm Travellers, said Basildon council had not provided any alternative pitches in the area. "If they would just offer us a piece of land we would leave now," she said.

Speaking to the assembled press from around the world, the council leader, Tony Ball, said he did not take any satisfaction from the eviction, but it was necessary. "I am absolutely clear that after 10 years of negotiation to try and find a peaceful solution to this that actually what we are doing is the right thing," he said.

Ball thanked police for their support: "I think we have seen from the level of violence put up by the protesters this morning that it was absolutely right that the police led the operation." He said that "alternative bricks and mortar accommodation" offered to the Travellers had been turned down.

"I feel some sympathy for the women and children who have been misled by their own community who said that if they settled on the site they would be granted planning permission and this was never the case."

That argument found little traction among the Travellers. "Was what we've seen today Tony Ball's peaceful resolution?" asked Mary Sheridan, who has been on Dale Farm for 10 years and has four children. "When he goes home tonight will he sleep happy knowing he has put our children on the roadside?"

Travellers were angry at the way they had been portrayed throughout the long battle, she said. "People are saying that we have other places to go. But if I had anywhere else to go do you think I'd be putting my children through this?

"We don't want mansions, we don't want a flat, all we want is a little piece of land where we can park our caravans so we can school our children and look after our elderly. Is that so hard?"

Back on site there were outbursts of anger, and arrests were made. Towards the end of the day, as police advanced slightly further into the site, officers were met with a hail of stones from some protesters.

But the mood at Dale Farm had changed since bailiffs had to plough through an angry crowd to reach the outside of the gates on 19 September. Since then a series of high court judges have ruled that the eviction should, and must, take place and numbers have depleted.

Autumn

Among the Travellers there was a sense of helplessness. Several sick residents, including Cornelius Sheridan, who had asked to be able to die on his plot, had been stretchered from the site by police medics. Those that remained sat in caravans pulled on to legal plots and watched the news unfold on TV.

With her four-month-old son Richard on her knee, 29-year-old Margaret Sheridan said she had little hope left. "We're the main headline today, tomorrow we'll be the second," she said. "But by Friday we'll be a forgotten about race."

She feared for the future of her son, she said: "Our children are never going to be integrated now. If we pull on the road how can they get an education, how do you get a health appointment for your baby? Nobody in England should have to go through what we are going through."

Father Dan Mason, priest at Our Lady of Good Counsel, criticised the way the eviction had been carried out. The police were not due to lead the operation but ensure that there were no breaches of the peace on either side, he said. "Clearly that changed," he said. "Because of an impatience caused by legal delays perhaps there was a sense of let's get on with it and, maybe, let's show them a lesson."

He added: "I'm just so sad it came to this. There were other options – Basildon was offered sites from the Homes and Communities Agency, and it is tragic that they were not taken up."

The implications of the eviction of the wider Traveller community were huge, said Candy Sheridan, vice-chair of the Gypsy Council, who tried to ensure sick residents had access to generators for nebulisers and insulin.

"What this says to every council in the country is that why should you provide for my community, when you can just ignore their needs," she said. "It will mean that it will become even harder to get pitches, and every council will get the message that it is acceptable to ignore this community's needs. But we'll survive, we've got our heritage and we will survive."

There was some optimism too though. "I feel we still had a victory," said Kathleen McCarthy. "If through us being here people have realised that we are human beings, that we have changed some prejudices, then that is something. I think eventually Dale Farm will make things better for Travellers, even if we are out on the road."

20 OCTOBER

Muammar Gaddafi: The "king of kings" dies in his hometown

PETER BEAUMONT

Colonel Muammar Gaddafi was born near Sirte, and when he became the ruler of all Libya, he transformed it from an insignificant fishing village into the country's sprawling second city. On Thursday, after a brutal – and ultimately hopeless – last stand, it was the place where he died.

For the past three weeks, with Gaddafi's whereabouts still unknown, government fighters had been puzzled by the bitter and determined resistance from loyalist fighters. Trapped in a tiny coastal strip just a few hundred metres wide, they had refused to give up, even when a victory by the forces of Libya's National Transitional Council seemed inevitable.

Here at last was the answer: they had been fighting to the death with their once-great leader in their midst.

The emergencies director of Human Rights Watch, Peter Bouckaert, was one of those in Sirte during the final battle. "A very heavy bombardment started at midnight with shelling of the remaining strongholds with Grad rockets that went on until 6am," he told the Guardian. "I went down to the city centre at 9am and went in with the fighters from Benghazi who said the whole city was free.

"I went to the hospital and a fighter arrived with a gold pistol he said he had taken from Gaddafi. He said there had been a fight with a convoy of people trying to flee. Mansour Dhou [Sirte's pro-Gaddafi military commander] was also in the clinic, shot in the stomach. He said they had been trying to flee and were caught in gunfire, which is when he lost consciousness. He confirmed Gaddafi was with him."

It appears Gaddafi was trying to flee the city in a convoy of cars when they came under attack from Nato jets. Last night the French claimed responsibility for the airstrike. The convoy was then apparently caught in a gun battle with fighters loyal to the National Transitional Council, Libya's interim government. Possibly wounded in the shootout, Libya's former ruler crawled into a drain; later he was set upon by revolutionary fighters, one of whom beat him with a shoe. Witnesses said he perished pleading for mercy after being dragged out of a hiding place inside a concrete drain. According to one fighter, the dying Gaddafi demanded: "What have I done to you?" Abdel-Jalil Abdel-Aziz, a doctor who accompanied Gaddafi's body in an ambulance as it was taken from Sirte, said he died from two shots, to the head and chest. "I can't describe my happiness," he told the Associated Press. "The tyranny is gone. Now the Libyan people can rest." Gaddafi's death was a humiliating end for a man once used to surrounding himself with cheering crowds of supporters. Video images showed him being bundled bloodied on to the back of a pick-up truck, surrounded by fighters waving guns and shouting "Allahu Akbar" (God is great). At first Gaddafi was apparently able to walk with assistance before being lifted on to the truck's tailgate. A second clip, however, showed him lifeless. In the second sequence, the tunic over one of his shoulders was heavily bloodstained. Also killed was one of Gaddafi's sons, Mutassim, a military officer who had commanded the defence of Sirte for his father.

After his death, Gaddafi's body was taken – accompanied by a huge convoy of celebrating revolutionaries – to Misrata, two hours away. In Misrata – which itself went through a bitter siege during Libya's eight-month civil war – the body was paraded through the streets on a truck, surrounded by crowds chanting, "The blood of the martyrs will not go in vain."

Bouckaert said: "I followed the convoy with the body to Misrata, where it was displayed. I have seen a lot of celebrations in Libya but never one like this."

Across Libya, as the news broke, there were celebrations. "We have been waiting for this moment for a long time," the Libyan prime minister, Mahmoud Jibril, told a news conference.

In Tripoli there were volleys of celebratory gunfire as vast crowds waving the red, black and green national flag adopted by the NTC gathered in Martyr's Square – once the setting for mass rallies in praise of the "Brother Leader".

Jibril said: "We confirm that all the evils, plus Gaddafi, have vanished from this beloved country. It's time to start a new Libya, a united Libya. One people, one future." In London, David Cameron hailed Gaddafi's death as a step towards a "strong and democratic future" for the north African country. Speaking in Downing Street after Jibril officially confirmed the death of the dictator, Cameron said he was proud of the role Britain had played in Nato airstrikes to protect Libyan civilians after the uprising against Gaddafi's rule began in February.

Cameron added that it was a time to remember Gaddafi's victims, including the policewoman Yvonne Fletcher, who was gunned down in a London street in 1984, the 270 people who died when Pan-Am flight 103 was destroyed by a bomb over Lockerbie in 1988, and all those killed by the IRA using Semtex explosives supplied by the Libyan dictator. Nato commanders will meet on Friday to consider ending the coalition's campaign in Libya.

Gaddafi, 69, is the first leader to be killed in the Arab spring, the wave of popular uprisings that swept the Middle East demanding the end of autocratic rulers and greater democracy. When the end came it was not as his son Saif al-Islam once promised, with the regime fighting to "its last bullet". Instead, the man who once styled himself "the king of the kings" of Africa was cornered while attempting to escape with his entourage in a convoy of cars after a final 90-minute assault on the last few loyalist positions in Sirte's District Two.

Last night the charred remains of 15 pickup trucks lay burned out on a roadside where Gaddafi's convoy had attempted to punch through NTC lines. Inside the ruined vehicles sat the charred skeletons; other bodies lay strewn on the grass. Government troops gave chase, said Salem Bakeer, a fighter who was on the scene at the last moment. "One of Gaddafi's men came out waving his rifle in the air and shouting surrender, but as soon as he saw my face he started shooting at me," he told Reuters. "Then I think Gaddafi must have told them to stop. 'My master is here, my master is here', he said, 'Muammar Gaddafi is here and he is wounded'," said Bakeer. "We went in and brought Gaddafi out. He was saying 'What's wrong? What's wrong? What's going on?' Then we took him and put him in the car." Even as Gaddafi's body was being driven away, the drain where he was found was being immortalised in blue aerosol paint. On it, someone wrote: "The hiding place of the vile rat Gaddafi."

20 OCTOBER

Occupy London: My nights with the St Paul's protesters

PATRICK KINGSLEY

It is seven in the morning in the City of London, and the sun has just risen. A lone jogger glides down Cannon St, across the steps of St Paul's Cathedral, and through the rows of silent tents that constitute Occupy London. "Wake up," he shouts. "Wake up and get a job."

I'm spending a couple of days at the camp, to glimpse what it's like to live here. Most occupiers aren't yet awake, but I couldn't sleep for the cold, so I'm already up. "Twat," notes the jogger as he turns past me towards Paternoster Square, the home of the London Stock Exchange. The occupiers originally tried to take the square last Saturday, but since it's private land, they were foiled by a well-timed injunction. So they settled for the piazza outside St Paul's, with the (short-lived) blessing of the cathedral leaders.

"What do you think of the camp?" I ask after the jogger. He stops, turns around, and realises I'm a journalist. "What do I think of the camp?" he replies. "I think this wishy-washy thinking, this vague thinking – it shows they don't really know what they want. Either they contribute to the debate, or they're just camping." What's his name, I ask. He's a banker, he says. "Or put it this way: I work. I work full stop." The man's a jogging cliche, but he nails the age-old issues some people have with large groups of protesters who hang around longer than the government want them to. Who are they? What do they believe? And what do they want?

Autumn

In the short term, I learn quickly, these guys want to stay here. I arrive on Tuesday, the fourth day of the occupation, and already the place seems staggeringly well organised – and growing fast. Estimates vary, but yesterday some say there were 100 tents lining the steps of the cathedral, and along its northern face. Today there are around 150. A kitchen – compliant with health regulations – has been here since day one. Portable toilets were due to arrive on Thursday. Pallets – to insulate the tent-floors – have been ordered, and the corporation of London has supplied a full gamut of recycling bins. There is a tech tent – filled, one techie tells me, with enough hardware "to host a TV station" – and a library; a welcome tent, and a "university" that holds daily lectures. Where do they get this stuff from? Most of it is donated. So much food has been dropped off by passers-by that it can barely fit in the kitchen. There's enough spare camping kit to fill a designated storage tent. Financial gifts – including a big cheque from one local businessman – top £3,000. "A woman on her way to work wanted to know what she could buy us," says Kai Wargalla, a 26-year-old economics student who first put a Facebook call-out for an occupation. "She said: give me a list!"

Other locals get involved in more surprising ways. Round the north side of St Paul's, five men kick about a football. This is Occupy FC, Occupy London's official football team, and they were founded late on Monday. The funny thing is, the players aren't all occupiers. Two of them are wearing suits, businessmen on their way back from lunch. "It's like that football game they played in no man's land during the first world war," muses one suit, Ian, a management consultant who won't give his surname. "We were just on our way back from our gentlemen's club, the ball rolled in our path, and we thought we'd have a quick match."

Twenty-three-year-old Tom Rodriguez Perez, the club's co-founder, is ecstatic. "This is what it's about," he says. "We're not saying football's going to change everything – but it's starting a conversation, it's bringing people in."

People always impatiently ask what the occupiers' "demands" are, and why collectively they seem unwilling, or unable to provide quick-fix solutions. These questions miss the point. First, there are lots of occupiers, all from different social and political backgrounds, who understandably need time to thrash out what it is they want to achieve together. The camp gives them that time. Second, if there's one thing that does unite almost all of them, it's their rejection of capitalism – although they are wary of how they couch this. Nevertheless, a huge "capitalism is crisis" banner hangs over the entrance to the site; they're not interested in making petty demands on a system they see as irreconcilably flawed. If anything, the camp itself is their demand, and their solution: the stab at an alternative society that at least aims to operate without hierarchy, and with full, participatory democracy. "That's what keeps me going when I'm feeling really tired, when there are threats to the occupation," says 29-year-old Sarah, a community arts worker who asked for her name to be changed. "I feel like what I want to see happening is happening here, right now. A space to speak. A space to be heard." Wail Qasim, an 18-year-old politics student, agrees: "You can go to the ballot box every five years, but politicians don't actually represent your view. So the importance of this kind of space is in the way it brings together people to open up a dialogue about building an alternative." Blogger Steve Maclean, 31, is slightly more pragmatic: "We're forming a space where people can come together and crystallise all of what we think. Out of this more concrete ideas can be formed."

People often criticise gatherings such as this for their lack of social and ethnic diversity. It's true that the protestors here are, more often than not, young, white, and studenty — but this

Autumn

is still a fairly diverse crowd. There are pensioners, people in wheelchairs, and a whole range of professions. The first person I meet is David, a soldier for 10 years. Then there's Lucy, a performance artist. Randy, like several other campers, is unemployed and recently homeless – "for no other reason," he claims, "than the colour of my skin." My neighbour, Duncan, is a middle-aged barrister. Bear, who co-ordinates the kitchen, runs catering at festivals. He, incidentally, as he picked his way over a few crates of donated fruit, gave me the most nuanced view of what he hopes the camp will achieve: "We're not going to create the answer here, but we can effect a change by leading by example, by showing people that an autonomous, democratic community based on social rather than financial cooperation can work."

There are all sorts of political groupings, too. The occupation is the spawn of three or four competing actions called by several different groups (one of which was UK Uncut), which then merged plans. Predictably, there's a forlorn Socialist Workers party stall on the plaza. A few yards away are camped half a dozen Anonymous campaigners, frequently clad in crumpled suits and shiny Fawkes masks. There are people from Climate Camp here, while members of a shop stewards' union rallied in solidarity yesterday. Conversely, a few of the key facilitators in last winter's student protests haven't come down – they're not sure it's radical enough.

For all everyone's best efforts, the camp isn't the most comfortable place. The wind blasts through like a racing car, buffeting the strongest tents and uprooting the weakest. On my first afternoon, it collapses the kitchen marquee, the largest structure on site. At night, until 11, an orchestra of occupiers bang drums on the cathedral steps, others dancing manically around. It's for fun, of course, but it's also to keep warm. The evening I leave, the temperature drops to 4C. Tent pegs can't pierce stone, so some campers have gaffer-taped the guy-ropes to the cobbles. If it rains overnight, the tape will get unstuck, so they'll repeat the process again in the morning. Others weigh their tents down with leftover Evening Standards. Jay Gearing, a 32-year-old graphic designer from Peterborough, uses large bottles of fizz and a sack of potatoes. It's with these groceries that I shelter overnight. Gearing's heading home for a couple of days, and needs someone to man the tent, so he generously lets me house-sit. Good luck sleeping, he says. The cobbled floor is freezing, there is no nearby toilet, while the traffic and police helicopters buzz away all night. And then there are the bells. They'll wake you up on the hour, every hour.

Some people don't sleep at all – the police guarding Paternoster Square, and the techies. Eight of them work through the night, huddled around a long table covered with cables, computers and hard-drives. "Sleep doesn't interest me," says UCL undergraduate Sam Carlisle, at least not when there's so much to do. They're trying to sort a video link-up with parallel occupations in New York and Frankfurt. He and the team have also made a clever e-map of the camp, and now they're creating an online donations wish list, and a wiki that will chronicle events and decisions made at the camp.

The tech team is one of 15 autonomous sub-groups at the camp, each with responsibility for a particular area. There is a group that deals with the camp's donations; there are the food, and "university" teams; the police negotiation group; legal, which has enlisted a friendly QC, in case of future trouble; recycling; outreach, which distributes flyers about the camp, and is planning a politics workshop for schools; music, art, and entertainment; a cathedral liaison team, which is tactfully dealing with its increasingly wary clergy; and a media team, for dealing with people like me.

Almost everyone's involved in something and, crucially, there's no hierarchy – or there's not supposed to be. The teams meet once a day and agree things by consensus, in a discussion "facilitated" (but not led) by a different member of the group each time. Their decisions are announced every lunchtime at a pan-camp logistics meeting – once again ideally facilitated by different people, to avoid anyone gaining too much influence. But the main meeting of the day is the general assembly. Held at 7pm, it's attended by 400-500 people and aimed at political discourse and camp strategy. To avoid people speaking over the top of each other, the occupiers use a series of silent gestures popularised during anti-capitalist protests in Seattle in 1999. To the uninitiated, they look like a satanic version of jazz hands, but they're fairly simple to master. Waving your hands upwards means you agree with something. Waving downwards signals disagreement. Raising your index finger means you want to make a point yourself; rolling your arms suggests you want the speaker to come to a close.

At its best, the system is empowering. But facilitating's a tough job – and even though some of the more visible members of the camp constantly encourage newbies to get involved, sometimes the same people end up mediating discussion. Sarah, the community worker, is one of those who often draw the short straw. She admits it's a slight problem: "I worry that people who have simply got more time to commit themselves are seen to be the people who are the 'organisers'. Some people don't understand that the process is completely open and that we want and need people to get involved in these processes so that we can carry on for a long time and grow our organisational skills."

It's a hard system for newcomers to get their heads around. "Our institutional structures – schools, university, most forms of employment – only involve hierarchical structures where you either do what you're told or tell other people what to do," says Sarah. "Sometimes people want to help and they have a sense that they need to ask permission, or be expressly told how to help so they find themselves asking people who are working if they can do anything to help."

Part of the problem is that not everyone can be here all the time. Around 300 probably sleep overnight, but up to 1,000 supporters drop in over the course of the day. Elaine Williams, 25, comes every day for a few hours with her seven-month-old daughter, Phoenix. With half a dozen other parents, she hosts Tots with a Cause, a play area at the bottom of the church steps. "We don't stay late – we're not bad parents," smiles Williams. "But we don't want other parents to feel they can't come because they have children." Toys are supplied, along with a warm rug, and spare nappies. In fact, it's a bit like the creche that, thanks to the education cuts, was almost scrapped at Goldsmith's university, where Williams studies. If the nursery goes, "I can't complete my degree."

Mid-afternoon on Wednesday, a reporter from the BBC's One Show convenes an informal debate between the occupation and a greying banker. Packed across the cathedral steps, the occupiers surround him and take it in turns to lambast the financial system. Don't blame the bankers, he replies. Blame the regulators who didn't stop them. Surprisingly, this time the occupiers don't slaughter him – and the BBC man can't understand why. "You're letting him off the hook," he cries. But most of the occupiers don't think this is a problem that can be solved by a few tweaks to regulation. They think it's a systemic problem not attributable to a single group. It's a problem with capitalism.

At the back of the crowd, the suit standing next to me leans in to say something. "So what answers have they got?" is what I expect him to say. After all, he's a former investment banker now studying for an MBA. But Nikita – "yes, just call me Nikita" – surprises me. "Even if they don't have a solution, people still have the right to say 'no'," he says, pausing between each word.

"It's only once people start saying 'no' that we will start thinking about what the solution could be."

21 OCTOBER

Ghana's population explosion

JOHN VIDAL

Sometime in 1947 or 1948, King Jorbie Akodam Karbo I summoned one of his young unmarried daughters to the palace at Lawra. The all-powerful ruler of the small kingdom in the far north of what is today Ghana, but was then the Gold Coast, told the girl she must go to Accra, the capital of the colony. She was to learn to be a midwife and return to teach others, so helping to prevent the many childbirth deaths that were taking place in the community.

You can imagine her trepidation at leaving. The journey of around 600 miles south would have taken many days in the weekly post bus. The girl knew no one, none of her family had ever been to a city or seen the sea, and she would have barely seen a car, let alone a white person. She stayed in a boarding house and learned to nurse at the colony's principal hospital, Korle Bu.

At around the same time, another young woman, my mother, set off on what was to be an equally adventurous journey, from Liverpool to Accra by boat. My father was to be the last in a long line of West African colonial administrators, and, like the princess, Mum knew no one in Accra. She had barely met a black person, and knew only that the Gold Coast was a dangerous place because of malaria and other tropical illnesses.

The two women struck up a friendship in January 1949 after my mother, remarkably for the time, chose to give birth not in Accra's private European hospital but at Korle Bu, the public African hospital. Mum never told me the name of her midwife, but used to say I had been born with the help of the "beautiful daughter of the King of Lawra", who "had her teeth filed to sharp points that made me think she was a cannibal". Having me at Korle Bu, she said, was not just an act of faith in the new Africa then emerging with powerful independence movements after the second world war, but also a pragmatic decision. "You got a better standard of care there!" she would say.

The women never met again. Within a few years, we had moved to Nigeria and the King of Lawra's daughter had left Accra.

With the world's population officially hitting 7 billion this week, just 12 years after reaching 6 billion, I went back to Accra to try to understand the massive explosion in human numbers that has been largely responsible for Ghana's development since I was born, and that will, for good or else, determine its future. In those 60 years, the world's population has grown by two new Chinas and an India combined; Ghana has doubled and doubled again from around 4 million people to more than 25 million. It is projected to keep growing to around 50 or even 60 million people by 2050.

How will this small country, which is seen as one of the economic and social success stories of Africa but which is in most parts still desperately poor, cope with twice as many people in just over a generation? Clutching a birth certificate, some old black and white photos of the houses we lived in, a description of the princess with filed teeth who delivered me, and a tourist map, my plan was to find my midwife's family and to trace the roots of Ghana's population explosion through the places that we knew.

Autumn

Clearly, the city to which the two women travelled in the late 1940s is unrecognisable today. Accra was then about the size of Stoke or Shrewsbury. Now it sprawls 30 or more miles from the old town centre, throwing up new slums and suburbs every year. A 1948 census estimated 4,113,345 people and 3,035,125 goats in the whole country. There were fewer than 2,500 Europeans and only 84 doctors, of whom just 17 were Gold Coast Africans.

What hits you hardest, though, is not Accra's size today but the fact that everyone is young. It is rare to meet anyone over 40. Officially, 3% of Ghana's population is over 60, but these are mostly invisible people. In fact, more than one in three people are under 14, and the country is adding nearly 500,000 children a year.

My questions started at Korle Bu hospital, in 1949 a collection of quite grand, colonnaded buildings, these days Ghana's premier teaching hospital. My old maternity ward is still there, now sponsored by Latex Foam, but most births take place in a purpose-built six-storey baby factory built in the 1960s. A young Accravian mother-to-be now has a choice of giving birth in nearly 20 private and public hospitals and clinics in the city. If the family has $5,000, she can stay in what is effectively a five-star hotel. If poor, as the vast majority are, she may have to share a bed or sleep on the floor at Korle Bu. Every day 35 babies are born there.

"That's 12,000 babies a year from this one hospital," says Professor Samuel Obed, head of obstetrics and gynaecology, who says that Ghana's population explosion has been a triumph of modern midwifery, prenatal and maternal care. He puts the success down partly to people such as the young princess of Lawra who learned so well how to deliver babies and teach others. "The vast increase in the number of people in Ghana today is entirely due to the efforts made to stop birth mortalities. I put it down to better education. As more people get a formal education, so they see the need to have proper prenatal care. Many women in the past never went for prenatal care. Now 95% in Ghana do. Back in 1949, it was only available to a very few people.

"In your mother's time here, everything was still left to nature. People used to offer a libation or they would pray when they gave birth. You lived or you died in childbirth. It was very risky. A lot of people died. That is why in Ghana new mothers wear white. Birth is seen as a victory.

"Your nurse probably came here at a very young age. She would have been one of the first generation of northerners to have a formal education."

The population explosion puts immense strains on the health service, he says, with nearly half the hospital's resources being spent on childbirth and the rest on illnesses related to malaria. "Everything comes down to money. We need to re-equip one operating theatre to take care of caesarean births. We need more nurses... The explosion in numbers is not going to go away. Women are having fewer children, but they are surviving and there are more and more families. It's cultural. If a couple have no children, you will have the in-laws round their necks. Pressure to have children is not going to abate."

"Everyone used to have big families in your mother's day," says Felicia Darkwah, a retired teacher born in 1926 and typical of the wealthy, land-owning, educated Ghanaians who took over from the British at independence in 1957.

I met her in the sitting room of 47 Seventh Avenue, the first house we lived in in Accra. Most of the other houses in the street have since been pulled down and rebuilt as embassies, banks or private executive residences. They hide behind high walls and razor wire, are guarded night and day, and can cost as much as anything in Chelsea, London. But number 47 is almost unique. Still owned by the government, its grounds have been divided up for three other houses, but it has barely changed. The rosewood parquet floors are the same but now lifting, the ceiling fans have rusted a bit and been augmented by air conditioning, but the pre-independence bungalow with its tin roof is intact, lived in for the past 24 years by Felicia, her Cambridge-educated agronomist husband and two of their children and their families. (One is now a very high-ranking government official who is fearful of being identified.)

"I am one of 13 children," Felicia says. "That was a small family for the time. My uncle's daughter, Animeh, died the other day and she had 100 children and grandchildren. I've known people with far more."

There seems to be a rule of thumb among educated Ghanaians that each generation has about half the number of children as their parents. Felicia had five children, and her children have two or three each. "I don't think anyone needs to bother about the numbers in Ghana as long as we work hard," she says. "We can produce enough food but the speed of growth is difficult."

I show her the pictures of my father's office, a young white man surrounded by more than 50 Africans. "This face looks familiar... and that one," she says.

Next week the UN will warn that the world population could spiral not to 8 billion or 9 billion people as demographers expected in the 1980s, but to 10 billion, or even 16 billion after 2100 if countries do not control their populations soon. And while it will be the rich whose consumption of goods is likely to destabilise the climate and global food supplies, it will be the very poorest countries of Asia and Africa that will be left to cope with inevitable large-scale environmental degradation, the explosion of slums, pressure on health and education services, and the reality of living in a world without enough food and water for all.

Of all the continents, Africa will see the greatest changes in the next 40 years – 11 countries in the world have fertility rates above six babies per woman and nine of them are there. Sub-Saharan Africa's population was around 100 million in 1900, 750 million in 2005 and the latest UN projections suggest it will level off at over 2 billion after 2050.

West Africa will be at the centre of this tidal wave of births. Nearby Nigeria, now with 150 million people, is expected to have 600-725 million before numbers start to tail off in 40 years. And far from reducing fertility rates, some countries', such as Mali's, are still rising.

Space is not the problem for Ghana or most other African countries. The continent is physically big enough to fit China, India and the US in its boundaries, and it can grow enough food for itself and for others. But a rapid, huge population increase linked to deep poverty in ecologically fragile, nearly landlocked countries such as Chad, Niger, Ethiopia and Mali terrifies planners and demographers the world over.

In Niger, a few hundred miles east of Ghana, two in three people are under 20, women have an average of more than seven children and only 5% of adults use any form of contraception. If its current growth rate of 3.3% per year remains unchanged, by 2050 it will have 56 million inhabitants, from under 15 million today. It is already one of the poorest countries in the world, it is intensely vulnerable to climate change and is experiencing regular food crises.

Other west African countries, such as Burkina Faso, traditionally saw their youths migrating to other countries to relieve pressure on environments, but Ghana, growing at less than 2% a year, is much better off, says Marilyn Aniwa, head of the Union for African Population Studies: "Hunger will not be the problem here. Contraception is still not widely used, but the country has land, water and space enough to double in numbers.

"But population is not about the numbers of children. It's about environment, rapid urbanisation, wellbeing and human rights. These are the areas that have not been addressed in the same way as midwifery and prenatal care. Development has not kept up with the numbers. What has been left behind is the social aspects."

You can't just pin all the problems on African governments, say demographers. Back in the 1970s, family planning was high on their and western political agendas, but in the 1980s countries such as Ghana were treated by the IMF and Britain as laboratories for enforced economic reforms and debt programmes. Contraception and family-planning programmes, just beginning to have an effect, were sidelined. The free market economy pushed on Africa may have worked for the cocoa farm and gold field owners of Ghana, but there was far less money for health and education. The result was a rapidly growing, ill-educated, fast-breeding generation living in a technically richer but more unequal country where people knew how to save children dying at childbirth but were not able to look after their long-term interests.

"The danger is that we now revert to how we were 30 or 40 years ago," says Emmanuel Ekaub, a Cameroonian demographer. "Maternal mortality is worsening across Africa again. Poverty is worsening again, and the cities and planners cannot cope."

Five minutes down the road from 47 Seventh Avenue is 9 Second Circular Road, a brutish two-storey house built by the colonial government in 1950 for my father and his young family. In those days it was exclusively for elites. Nothing changes. Now the road is reserved, it seems, for diplomats, judges, bankers, government ministers and people with £300,000 to spend on an apartment.

But number 9 stands empty behind a concrete wall. A large tree has grown right outside the front door, the gardens, laid out in the English cottage style of the 1950s, are overgrown, and a high court judge and his daughter live in what were the servants' quarters to the side.

Number 9 is still owned by the government but it hides a dark secret. No one wants to live there when they hear that, in 1982, it was the scene of Ghana's most notorious political murder. A military junta, led by Flight Lieutenant Jerry Rawlings, had seized power months earlier and there was a curfew in place, but on the evening of 30 June a death squad called on Cecilia Koranteng-Addo, a high court judge who was living here and, at the time, breastfeeding her baby. She was abducted, along with three others, and their bodies were later found riddled with bullets. The "enemies of the revolution", as Rawlings called them, were never caught.

In fact, number 9 is squatted. Two lads, who call themselves D.Jen and D.Beal from "X-tribe", have stuck their pictures to the wall of the old living room. "Fuck U Mother Fucker" someone has scrawled. There are cigarette butts, bottles of cheap South African wine, and a bedroll and TV in the old cloakroom.

"What Ghana's population explosion has done is suck young people into the city," says Aniwa. "They live in kiosks, old shipping containers, anywhere they can find. Some live in incomplete houses. New suburbs and townships like Gbawe, Sowutum amd Ashiaman are sprouting."

"Urbanisation will inevitably go to another level in the next 20 or 30 years," says Delali Badasi, a researcher at the Regional Institute for Population Studies at Accra University. "The average young person does not want to live in rural areas. They are all leaving to come to the cities. The slums will increase. We can't even house people today. The problem is the speed of change."

Opinions are sharply divided among economists about the advantage of having a younger population and youthful

Autumn

workforce. According to the government, 250,000 young women and men enter the job market every year, but the formal sector is able to employ fewer than 5,000 of them. "A rising population will support local firms and inspire foreign investment, but unless the youth have jobs and social betterment is achieved, the risk of social uprising is profound," says Simon Freemantle, Standard Bank Africa's senior analyst. "There is a real risk of social instability if the disgruntled youth feel left out."

We had sent a message north to tell King Puowele Karbo III in Lawra that we were trying to track down the family of the young princess who had delivered a white baby back in 1949. But that had been several weeks ago and we had received no reply. So, with a long journey ahead, warnings of bandits and no idea of what would greet us at the other end, we, too, set off in some trepidation.

It takes at least two days to reach Lawra from Accra. We flew 400 miles to Tamale, found an old banger and a driver, and travelled the last 200 miles along some of the worst roads in Africa, passing the great Bole national park with its elephants and baboons, villages with names such as Tuna and Ya, and shops called The Forgive And Forget Chemical Drug Store. The land is mostly flat and, this being the end of the rainy season, quite green.

Late in the evening we presented ourselves at the palace, a rambling collection of low buildings, some built underground, a courtyard dominated by two enormous marble graves and several flagpoles. We were greeted by the king's brother, who said he knew we were coming because our car made an unusual sound. We arranged to meet the family the next day.

When you have an audience with King Karbo, you must bring libations, in this case two bottles of gin. He greeted us from his throne, animal skins strewn at his feet and pictures of his ancestors on the walls. "We believe that we have identified the woman your mother knew," he said. "She was one of the first ladies from the north of Ghana to be sent to Accra for training. My father believed we needed a trained midwife because so many children were dying under the traditional childbirth system. It was a very important mission. The whole community depended on her."

The concept of children in a place such as Lawra 60 years ago was pretty relaxed. They defined men's social standing, they were needed to increase wealth, they were assets to work the fields and fetch water, but numbers did not matter. A man did not look after them, and no one actually knew how big families were.

In retrospect, it would seem that King Karbo I, Puowele's father, was on a mission to populate Ghana single-handedly. When he died in 1967, the family tried to count his offspring. "I did a population census of him in 1970," says the king. "We counted about 70 daughters and 35 sons. He left 39 widows. I could not count them all. Our children are many, and traditionally we don't count them. We don't actually know how many he had – he never counted them. He tried keeping records, but it didn't work."

Today, says Puowele, children are no longer seen as an asset. He has eight, his brother, an international athlete and recently retired university lecturer, five. "The trend is downwards. Nowadays the demands [on families] are great. You are in deep shit if you have too many. So you go for quality rather than numbers."

If his father had been responsible for so many births, and his relative had devoted her life to saving children as a midwife, Puowele could be said to have played a major role in Accra's rise from a small town to a megalopolis. He was national director of planning in the city, and devoted a lifetime to trying to control the tide of young people heading to the cities from places such as Lawra.

"Yes, Accra is a mess," he concedes. "We just could not control the population. We created a green belt, we planned reservoirs to stop flooding, we planned for oil, but the [politicians] refused to implement these things." He and his colleagues even considered building a new capital city to take pressure off Accra. "We looked at Abuja, the purpose-built capital of Nigeria. You can build a city from scratch, but if you do not change behaviour, it will be the same as the old one."

Lawra survived by traditionally exporting its youths to Accra and the south, to the gold mines and coffee plantations. "Women here still have eight to 10 children, but these days they are living. We are the stubborn ones, who refused to die."

Even so, Lawra is testament to what happens if people overuse resources and approach their ecological limits as is happening across large parts of west Africa. "Our environment has suffered badly from the pressure of numbers," the king says. "Our natural resources are diminishing. Our forests are being cut down. We can no longer find the herbs we used to use. The riverbed is now silting up because we are farming close to the banks of the river. There used to be a gap between the villages, but now they are joining up. We cannot capture rainfall in the increasingly long, dry spells. Climate change is taking place."

But Lawra's future, he says, is not bleak at all. Like most Ghanaians, he loves children and believes that, if planned better and given a fair wind, the country's burgeoning population will be the key to its future prosperity. "We will have to diversify, yes. We will learn new things. But we are still confident in the future. Lawra will become a city, with all its social problems."

He turns the conversation back to the princess. "I can tell you she is our auntie. Your mother was very observant to see she had chiselled teeth. Her name is Stella Yeru, or Mrs Kuortibo. She had four children, two of whom are living now. The boy is a tax inspector at Tamale. She filled a void. She paid her dues. She worked in Lawra and all the other big hospitals in the region. She would have trained very many people. It was very rare in those days for a woman to work in public service like her. We can think of no other women like her. She was a pioneer. If you worked under her, you had no place if you were lazy."

Out of the blue, the king then asked if I would like to meet her. I was flabbergasted. Stella must now be in her mid-80s and I had not expected her still to be alive, let alone there. "But she is very old. She is bedridden and has forgotten everything," he warned.

We find a very frail old lady lying in her bed on the veranda of the house she had had built just outside the palace walls. She was beautifully, even ceremonially dressed, but was very weak and clearly near the end of her life. Her son, Anthony, had come to be with her.

I held her hand as her helper told her that I had come from London because she had delivered me at Korle Bu hospital in Accra all those years ago.

"Yes, I remember the white woman," she said in a thin voice that spoke loudly across the generations.

6 NOVEMBER

Scrabble king celebrates with night on the tiles

MAEV KENNEDY

At the end of a long grey day, it came down to suet and it was all over: Gary Oliver's enchantingly dull word was worth just 10 points, and meant that Wayne Kelly's lead was unassailable. The audience, which hung on his every word throughout the day, went as wild as was possible for about 50 mainly middle-aged,

Autumn

very polite people, and Kelly was proclaimed British national Scrabble champion.

Kelly, 37, a local government finance adviser who lives with his parents in Warrington, and who will invest a good chunk of his £2,000 winnings in a new computer, does struggle slightly to convey the drama of his chosen sport.

"I'm on a bit of a buzz," he said. "My colleagues will be pleased for me. They know all about it – I've talked about nothing else for weeks. But I know some people see it as a game like Monopoly that doesn't really involve skill."

He conceded that his last high-scoring word, travails, was "a bit of a slog word", but he was proud of caromel, which was immediately challenged: "I wasn't 100% sure of it myself, to be honest." He was allowed the word, then shaken when Oliver came back with the 107-point ergotize (to argue logically).

Many hours earlier it had begun innocuously enough with wox and wee. Two moves later, Oliver laid down eaterie for 85 points, Kelly could only come back with haul for 26, and the grand final of the national Scrabble championships suddenly got personal.

"Most people would only think of spelling it the common way, eatery, but Gary saw immediately that he could get in the ie – nice," said Philip Nelkon, the tournament organiser, who works for Scrabble manufacturer Mattel and used to be a contender. He still glows quietly over the memory of his 293-point muezzins (the criers who lead the call to prayer in a mosque).

"It's not like a family game at home, where everyone is desperate to block the others from getting to the triple word score because that usually decides it. These guys have the vocabulary – they're not scared of the triple score."

When play resumed after lunch at one game each and everything to play for, the board was soon littered with such strange, horrible words as woofy, suq and euoi.

"It is a very specialised vocabulary," conceded Nelkon – his own name adapted by his grandfather from a much more Scrabble-useful central European version.

"You get people who are good at Scrabble who don't even speak very good English."

Kelly and Oliver were locked in combat in a quiet, narrow second-floor room, with an undistracting view of a blank brick wall.

Each won scores of games, including nine in one day in the semi-finals, to get to the finals for the first time.

Every word was relayed to the hall downstairs and followed by the audience, not on a video screen – even though the games were relayed live on the internet – but by real analogue human beings moving oversized tiles on a giant board. The commentator was a former champion, Brett Smitheram, who speaks fluent Scrabble. "This could be where Wayne considers playing unnipple," he warned, to moans of dismay from the audience.

Kelly now has three days off in London before he has to return to his studies for his next exams in public finance accountancy. "I'm going to go wild," he promised.

20 NOVEMBER

Basil D'Oliveira's desire to return home opened my eyes to inequality

DONALD McRAE

Basil D'Oliveira, the Cape Coloured cricketer who played for Worcestershire and England after being denied opportunities in South Africa because of apartheid, whose selection for an England tour of his home country in 1968 caused the series to be banned by the South African government and the rupturing of sporting relations for many years, died on 19 November, aged 80.

In 1968, the year in which a man called Dolly changed the way the world looked at us in white South Africa, I began my first sporting scrapbook. I discovered that memento of my childhood a few years ago when I went home to visit my parents. The scrapbook had faded with age but the yellow cover and dark blue pages reminded me how sport, and Basil D'Oliveira, helped a small boy to become briefly colour-blind in the depths of apartheid.

I had just turned seven in 1968, and I was obsessed by sport. I cut out photographs of great sportsmen and stuck them down with Scotch tape on to the pages which meant so much to me. Most of the photos were of white Springboks – like Frik du Preez, the great lock forward, Graeme Pollock, the world's best batsman, and Paul Nash, the sprinter who was the only white man in the world to have run the 100m in 10 seconds dead. I also pasted in images of my favourite black boxer, Cassius Clay, who, confusingly, had just decided to call himself Muhammad Ali. And then there was Dolly.

In 1967, D'Oliveira had been one of Wisden's five Cricketers of the Year, and he featured regularly in our sports pages. I began a gallery dedicated to Polly & Dolly, Pollock and D'Oliveira, because I was thrilled by the prospect of England arriving in late 1968 for a Test series – where we would prove ourselves the world's best side. But the adults around me were preoccupied by one prickly question: would England select a coloured South African in D'Oliveira?

Eight years earlier, Dolly had left Cape Town to play cricket in England. He was born in October 1931, in the Bo-Kaap, and had been classified as a Cape Coloured. But he played cricket like a dream; and scored 80 centuries in the coloured leagues. He was still not allowed to play against white players, and definitely not at Newlands, the beautiful Test ground in Cape Town.

The sports minister, Frank Waring, warned: "If whites and non-whites start competing against each other there will be such viciousness as never seen before."

Dolly eventually made it all the way to county cricket with Worcestershire and became a British citizen. He took the most radical step of all when, in 1966, he was selected to play for England against the all-black West Indies. I found it odd that a South African, even a coloured cricketer, might want to become English. Dolly had taken the opposite journey to Dimitri Tsafendas – the deranged white man who had assassinated our prime minister, Hendrik Verwoerd, in 1966, because he wanted to be reclassified as coloured. Dolly, my dad explained, was not mad. But the possibility of him playing for England in South Africa turned our politicians purple with anger. Piet Le Roux, the minister of the interior, said: "If this player is chosen he will not be allowed to tour."

Autumn

Apartheid shaped the growing isolation of South African sport. In May 1968 the International Olympic Committee announced an indefinite ban on the country's white team – which meant South Africa was barred from competing in the Mexico City Olympics that year.

I asked Dad why the world wanted to hurt us. His answer made my head hum. Even though they had never met us, people around the world decided we were unfair to black people. It upset me. They knew nothing about our black maid – Maggie Thabang. How could they say we were unkind to Maggie when we made jokes with her every day and gave her food to eat in her room in the backyard? They didn't know how much we loved Maggie, and how much she loved us. Dad said that the outside world didn't quite understand South Africa. They thought things were just black and white when we actually lived in a very colourful country.

Before facing South Africa, England met Australia at home in the Ashes. We pored over the news that Dolly had been picked for the opening Test in Manchester. He scored 87 not out in the second innings but, after England lost, he was dropped for the next three Tests. England's selectors, it seemed, had one eye on the tour of South Africa.

But England were desperate to square the Ashes and so, 1-0 down, they recalled D'Oliveira for the final Test at the Oval. He struck a glorious 158 to set up an England victory.

Dolly was on his way to South Africa. How could they exclude a batsman who had just scored a huge Ashes century? A few more pictures of Dolly, raising his bat shyly at the Oval, were stuck into my scrapbook. I still felt certain he would be put in his place, as a beaten England cricketer, rather than just a coloured South African, when he faced Peter Pollock and Eddie Barlow at the crease – or saw his polite seamers skim to the boundary when bowling at Graeme Pollock.

If I was surprised when England left out Dolly, I was also relieved. The tour was definitely on. Cleverly, England's selectors had saved us a big headache by excluding Dolly.

Dolly was "devastated", which Dad said meant he was very sad. I could imagine how much Dolly must have wished he could be back in Cape Town, with his family, playing at Newlands. But he would be better off staying in England and allowing the rest of us to get on with the cricket. It was simpler that way.

The English newspapers went out of their way to complicate everything. They wrote article after article about the way English cricket had bent over backwards to please our government. Thousands of demonstrators took to the streets in London and waved placards. One of the worst newspapers, the News of the World, stirred up more trouble by inviting D'Oliveira to go to South Africa as their guest columnist.

Soon, there was another twist. Tom Cartwright was injured and had to withdraw from the squad. D'Oliveira would replace him. He was ecstatic and proud.

But, being a coloured South African, Dolly was also less shocked than most by prime minister John Vorster's reaction. On Tuesday 17 September 1968 I came home from school to hear that the tour was off. Mom and I listened to the radio as Vorster confirmed, in his thick Afrikaans accent, that: "We are not prepared to accept a team thrust upon us by people whose interests are not the game, but to gain certain political advantages which they do not even attempt to hide. It is the team of the anti-apartheid movement. They are not welcome."

I felt sorry for Dolly. But I felt even sorrier for Graeme Pollock and his fellow Springboks who would be prevented from thumping England. Most of all, I felt sorry for myself. Summer stretched out ahead of me but, empty of Test cricket, it felt ruined.

Autumn

Our world never seemed quite the same again; and for a long time I was bewildered. But eventually, as the years passed, I began to understand how a man called Dolly had helped change me. I owe him much and now, following his death, I regret never writing to tell D'Oliveira how I loved pasting black-and-white photographs of him into my old yellow and blue scrapbook.

20 NOVEMBER

Curry favour

LETTER

If Eric Pickles wants to create curry colleges (Report, 19 November), shouldn't he change his name to Chutney?
Henry Malt
Huntingdon, Cambridgeshire

25 NOVEMBER

Leveson Inquiry: Media victims give their side of the story

ESTHER ADDLEY

The judicial inquiry into press standards, chaired by Lord Justice Leveson, set up following Guardian revelations about phone hacking at the News of the World, conducted hearings at the Royal Courts of Justice throughout the year

Hugh Grant, as someone noted rather astutely this week, hasn't been in anything this good for ages. Lord Justice Leveson's inquiry into standards in the British media may have been formally sitting since earlier this month, but it was not until this week that the plot of this procedural legal drama twisted, suddenly, into an unmissable blockbuster, played out in as much Technicolor as the crowded confines of court 73 at the Royal Courts of Justice would allow.

It had its moments of drama and at times almost of farce, but this was, in truth, a horror story, dipping into moments of such cruel and terrifying menace that, had the script been pitched to a Hollywood executive, it would have been returned as scarcely plausible.

After he had spent months touring the TV studios, not to mention all three party conferences, there was much about Grant's appearance on Monday that was familiar – pointed, dryly witty, and cross. But this was one occasion the actor was not prepared merely to play the diffident posho. An article in the Mail on Sunday in 2007 had stated that his then relationship with Jemima Khan was "on the rocks", he said, because of his latenight phone calls with an LA studio executive, which was untrue.

"I cannot for the life of me think of any conceivable source for this story in the Mail on Sunday except… voice messages on my mobile phone… Well, I'd love to hear what [their] explanation for that article is, if it wasn't phone hacking."

"You haven't alleged that before, have you, in the public domain?" asked counsel to the inquiry. He hadn't. The celebrities, Grant indicated, were fighting back. In the following day's Daily Mail, however, he had his response: a vehement denial of his "mendacious smears", accompanied by one of the tabloid's routine kickings ("a man consumed by hatred for the media… [with] a colourful and many would say unedifying love life"). "Are we to expect," Neil Garnham QC, for the Metropolitan police, asked on Tuesday, "that everyone who has the temerity to give evidence critical of the press is going to have to face this the following morning?"

It was inevitable, if ironic, that the steady stream of minor celebs and megastars to the Bell Yard entrance to the court building brought with it a four-tiered bank of photographers, past which they had to process before giving evidence. Sheryl Gascoigne, ex-wife of England footballer Paul, told the inquiry of driving in desperation, pursued by paparazzi, into a police station while heavily pregnant, and begging them to help. They could not. Sienna Miller described life as the 21-year-old girlfriend of Jude Law, being chased down a dark alleyway at midnight by "10 big men" carrying cameras, or spat at to provoke a reaction. JK Rowling, who seemed most nervous about giving evidence, said she had, on occasion, smuggled her children out of the house wrapped in blankets to avoid paparazzi.

For some, there was little sympathy. "Garry Flitcroft not really doing it for me," sniffed the singer Lily Allen on Twitter, as the former Blackburn Rovers captain gave evidence about the savage tabloid monstering he received as vengeance, he believed, for taking out an injunction to block details being published of an affair. Philandering multimillionaire footballers do not naturally attract the greatest sympathy – and yet, as Flitcroft continued his evidence, it became clear why he had asked to address the inquiry.

As the taunting in the stadiums, fed by relentless negative press stories, became worse, he said, his father, who suffered from depression, felt unable to watch him play. "His life was coming and watching me play football, and his work, and that took him out of his life," said Flitcroft. His father killed himself in 2008. His death came a long time after the tabloid assault, Flitcroft conceded, "but all I can say is, it affected him a lot".

Over four unedifying days, the stories of lives carelessly ruined kept coming. Max Mosley's 39-year-old son, a drug addict, hadn't killed himself over the press coverage of his father's sex life, Mosley was careful to say, but "the News of the World story had the most devastating effect on him. He really couldn't bear it. He went back on the drugs." Alexander Mosley died in 2009.

Mary-Ellen Field told the inquiry her own story was "like a B movie" – in fact, it was the most terrifying of psychological horror stories. So firmly convinced had her former employer Elle Macpherson become that the highly personal information that routinely appeared in the press originated with Field selling stories, that she persuaded her bewildered former adviser to enter a psychiatric facility in the US, where she was treated under armed guard for "an 'adjustment disorder'". Field was later sacked. The real explanation, of course, was that their phones were being hacked. For all the disturbing tales told by the wealthy and famous of the batterings they had received at the hands of the press, it was Field's story, and those of the other ordinary individuals who gave evidence, that really had power to silence the courtroom. "We're ordinary people so [we have] no experience in a public life situation or controlled media involvement situation," Bob Dowler told the inquiry. He and his wife just wanted the full extent and nature of tabloid malpractice to be known. Sally Dowler described the moment she had realised that some of the messages on Milly's phone had disappeared. "She's picked up her voicemails Bob, she's alive!" Milly was almost certainly already dead.

Gerry McCann's evidence to the inquiry, reliving the savaging he and his wife Kate had received in the aftermath of their three-year-old daughter Madeleine's disappearance in 2007, listed just a handful of the headlines written about them: "MADDY MUM ORGY FURY", "PRIEST 'BANS' MADELEINE", "IT WAS HER

BLOOD IN PARENTS' HIRE CAR". In 2008, the Portuguese attorney general, having reviewed all the evidence of the case, ruled that there was no evidence either parent had committed any crime.

The most compelling testimony of the week, though, came from Margaret and Jim Watson. They were not the victims of hacking, and have not been stalked by paparazzi. Rather, their daughter Diane, 16, was stabbed to death in 1991 in the playground of her Glasgow school by another pupil, Barbara Glover. Days after Glover was sentenced to life in prison, the inquiry heard, an article in the Glasgow Herald suggested that she had been bullied by the dead girl and had acted under provocation, a defence Glover had put forward that had been expressly rejected by the trial judge.

"[The article] tore everything that we had of Diane apart, the essence of her life, the person who she was," said Mrs Watson. She stood outside the office of the newspaper holding a banner every day for six weeks until the journalist responsible and the paper's editor agreed to see her, but they stood by the story, she said.

A similar article appeared in Marie Claire the following year. Shortly after that piece was published, the couple's 15-year-old son Alan, their only other child, killed himself. He had a copy of the magazine article in his hand when he died.

On Tuesday, only 20 years late, the Herald and Times Group, which now owns the Glasgow paper, issued a statement saying it "deeply regrets any action which added to the Watson family's grief over the tragic loss of their daughter and later their son". Asked if she had anything to add to her evidence, Mrs Watson said: "No, just to thank everyone for being so kind and for listening to us."

25 November

Matilda

REVIEW: LYN GARDNER

Those who think that the West End is always dumbing down and that an intelligent musical is an oxymoron will have to stay behind for detention with the diabolical Miss Trunchbull.

Writer Dennis Kelly and composer and lyricist Tim Minchin go to the top of the class with this anarchically joyous, gleefully nasty and ingenious musical adaptation of Roald Dahl's story about a girl, Matilda, played tonight by Sophia Kiely, who scoffs Dickens and Dostoevsky like other kids eat sweets.

Sadly for the loveable moppet, her TV guzzling parents think she is just a jumped-up germ. Mum knows her brainy daughter is the best argument yet for population control. Dad thinks you don't need to be clever if you can sell.

This classy and ultimately touching addition to the West End proves him wrong. It wears its learning and wit proudly, but has undoubted box office appeal too: it is likely to do for the RSC for the next 25 years what Les Mis has done for the past 25.

If anything, it is actually richer than Dahl's novel. It captures all the original's delicious nastiness, particularly in depicting Matilda's school, Crunchem Hall (motto: "children are maggots"), run by the fearsome Miss Trunchbull, but it also celebrates the solace of books and the transforming powers of the imagination.

The message, that you can control your own story, and rebellion and protest can defeat the bullies, is deeply embedded. Mind you, telekinetic powers help! But even so, when the tots rise up against Trunchbull it is as glorious a moment of rock'n'roll inspired self-determination as you'll ever see in the theatre. Like Matilda herself, the cleverness is evident in Kelly's nifty script, which never shirks the cruelty, or Matilda's feelings of rejection and loneliness, even as it offers children launched into outer space via their pigtails. It's also apparent in Minchin's witty lyrics and playful tunes, in Rob Howell's design with its piles of books and alphabet blocks, and in Matthew Warchus' production keeping things nicely on the boil without ever exhibiting signs of hyperactivity. The production has a razor-sharp tongue-in-cheek edge that cuts in at the slightest hint of sweetness. Yet seldom has the inner rage of the hurt and powerless child been so effectively dramatised.

That everyone is having a good time is apparent in every performance, particularly the children who are terrific. Nowhere is it more apparent than in Bertie Carvel's show-stopping turn as Miss Trunchbull. Imagine a cross-dressing King Herod on steroids with a jutting bosom that is deployed like a weapon of mass destruction to wipe out small children at 100 paces. It's an evening of unadulterated bliss. As Matilda would say: "You could have heard a fly burp."

Bertie Carvel is the son of the Guardian's long-serving former correspondent John Carvel

5 December

Giant Pandas touch down in Edinburgh

SEVERIN CARRELL

With all the trappings of A-list celebrity, giant pandas Tian Tian and Yang Guang touched down at Edinburgh airport on Sunday precisely on schedule, to an eerily auspicious dusting of snow over their new home.

They flew in on a private Boeing 777 airliner complete with customised "Panda Express" livery; a bespoke cuisine of bamboo, apples, carrots and specially prepared "panda cake"; and private suites of Perspex and steel.

As their personalised crates were slowly lowered on to the tarmac by freight ramps, under the gaze of the world's media and the bitterly cold, dour winter skies of Edinburgh, Tian Tian and Yang Guang could be seen slowly ambling around like musicians limbering up for the biggest gig of their careers.

The pandas, whose names mean Sweetie and Sunshine, were then driven to their new home at Edinburgh zoo – to be greeted by scores of flag-waving school children, a massed pipe band, and a welcoming committee of political leaders – with a heavy weight of expectation on their shoulders.

The breeding pair is a symbol of the UK's burgeoning political and economic relationship with China. China's chargé d'affaires in London, Qin Gang, carefully reminded an official press conference that next year will be the 40th anniversary of the UK formally recognising his communist-led government.

The arrival of the pandas would help spread "joy and friendship, and spread understanding and cooperation between the two countries," he added. "We are committed to working with our British and Scottish colleagues to grasp this opportunity and take Chinese-Scottish relations to a new level."

Nicola Sturgeon, the deputy first minister of Scotland, said: "Today is a very, very special day indeed for Scotland." She was standing in for her boss, Alex Salmond, who by careful design had just arrived in China for his third official trade mission, and a week-long cultural and industrial tour taking in Beijing and Hong Kong.

For Edinburgh zoo the pandas are a godsend after the most difficult period in its 102-year history. Last year, the zoo lost £1.5m, saw its visitor numbers slump 15% to just under 550,000, and had to be rescued with a £2m bank loan; while this year it has seen directors suspended for alleged misconduct. One was exonerated and reinstated, one was dismissed and its previous chief executive left.

The idea of bidding for coveted pandas came after a £20m property deal to sell vacant zoo land for housing fell through in 2007, leaving the zoo searching for funds for much-needed renovations and modernisation.

Hugh Roberts, the zoo's interim chief executive, brought in earlier this year to rescue the zoo's fortunes, said the Chinese had kept their cool. "The Chinese remained steady and friendly with us throughout that entire process," he told the Guardian, adding: "It's a big political act. The Chinese aren't going to be derailed by press speculation." Tian Tian and Yang Guang – on loan for $1m (£637,000) a year – are expected to attract hundreds of thousands of extra visitors, boosting ticket receipts by up to 70%, and cementing the Royal Zoological Society of Scotland's credentials for conservation science.

It will be at least two weeks before the public will be allowed to visit the pandas; they are being given a fortnight of solitude to help them settle in and acclimatise.

The scientific focus during their 10-year loan to Edinburgh will be on genetics and cognition research, said Hugh Roberts, but the biggest commercial, ecological and political prize will be if the pair successfully breed, again boosting gate receipts and Edinburgh's global status.

China owns 328 captive giant pandas, which are critically endangered and down to just 1,300 left in the wild. But Jia Jiansheng, of the Chinese state forestry administration, said zoologists now believe up to 400 are needed to ensure a rich and stable genetic stock, to secure their survival and boost successful release into the wild.

Qin Gang, from the Chinese embassy, said both pandas had productive ancestors. Tian Tian has borne and successfully raised twins, and Yang Guang is also already a father. That has particular significance for pandas: the females are only fertile for at most four days a year, and only ready to mate for less than two of those days. Mostly solitary, the pandas will be kept in separate areas of their specially modified enclosures within sight of each other until Tian Tian is ready to mate. "The biggest test will be reproductive," Qin Gang said. "We hope that the cooperation of British and Chinese scientists will help Tian Tian and Yang Guang to become happy parents." And Edinburgh, said Qin Gang, was an "auspicious" location for the pandas, beating Moscow zoo by having the most ideal latitude: pandas prefer cool, damp climates, between 5C and 25C. Edinburgh on Sunday hovered between 2C and 3.5C, and saw its first snowfall of the year.

Edinburgh is the fourth European zoo, after Berlin, Vienna and Madrid, to provide a current home to Chinese giant pandas, and the 13th around the world. It is the fifth time the UK has played host to pandas. The most famous British residents were at London zoo, Chi Chi 50 years ago and then Ching Ching in the 1970s. But none have so far successfully produced young; the last pair, Ming Ming and Bao Bao reputedly fought before they were separated and sent overseas in 1994.

There were no protests by animal rights groups or human rights activists for the new pandas' arrival; the only echo of the civil rights and ethical complaints raised at a distance by Amnesty International, Free Tibet, Born Free and the Captive Animals Conservation Society, came from Rosemary and Stefan Byfield, from New Tang Dynasty Television, a small anti-communist broadcaster.

NTD TV supports the Falun Gong spiritual movement which has been suppressed by Chinese authorities. Rosemary Byfield said the couple had been accredited for the official press conference at the zoo then, when the invitation list was shown to the Chinese embassy, had it abruptly withdrawn.

Henry Nicholls, a science writer and author of The Way of the Panda: the curious history of China's political animal, said it would be wise to ignore the hype.

"It seems like the wrong time to sound a note of caution, but pandas are pretty unpredictable animals about breeding," he said. "Nevertheless, Edinburgh should still consider them incredibly worthwhile as symbolic objects that raise the status of the institution: they are just a pair of bears but, a very special pair of bears."

20 December

After Kim Jong-il's death, what next for the people of North Korea?

TANIA BRANIGAN IN BEIJING AND JUSTIN MCCURRY IN TOKYO

The North Korean dictator died, aged 69 or 70, on 17 December

They howled and whimpered and scrubbed raw eyes with fists. They flailed their arms in grief and marched in their thousands to the capital's landmarks. But no one, outside of North Korea, really knows what North Koreans felt at news of Kim Jong-il's death.

There was shock, of course. Some perhaps wept from sorrow for their Dear Leader, some from sorrow for themselves. Some cried for fear that inadequate public anguish might damn them, and some from anxiety about what lay ahead. Kim veiled his country throughout his life and uncertainty shrouded his death.

State media said he died at 8.30am on Saturday, felled by a heart attack "due to physical and mental overwork", as he travelled by train on one of his innumerable inspection visits. There had been not a whisper of anything unusual in the two days before the announcement.

The official news agency KCNA swiftly hailed his third son, Kim Jong-un, as the "great successor" and "the eminent leader of the military and the party". The young man, thought to be just 28, has been groomed as heir since his father's apparent stroke in 2008.

Autumn

The 69-year-old left his son a nuclear-armed but impoverished country where food is scarce and human rights abuses rife, and his unexpected death sent a chill far beyond the 24 million inhabitants of North Korea. Politicians in Washington, Seoul, Tokyo and beyond weighed the prospects of a third generation of this communist dynasty with the risk of regional instability. Concerns were underscored by South Korean media reports on Monday that the North had fired short-range missiles, although the Yonhap news agency said the tests had been conducted before the death announcement. The defence ministry in Seoul did not comment.

The South's military was already on high alert, while a spokesman for the Japanese prime minister said he had set up a crisis management team.

Officials in the Obama administration, due to hold talks with the North this week and rumoured to be pondering an aid-for-disarmament deal, said it was closely monitoring developments. The UK foreign secretary, William Hague, said in a statement it was a difficult time for the North Korean people, but could prove a turning point. He urged the country to take steps towards the resumption of the stalled six-party denuclearisation talks.

It was left to China, the North's chief ally, to lament Kim's passing. "We feel incomparably anguished, and offer our deepest condolences to the entire North Korean people," the top leaders said in a statement. They described Kim as a great leader and close friend of China, adding that they were sure the Korean people would unify under his son's leadership.

It was a rare encomium. In the wider world Kim was mocked as much as reviled. That is hardly surprising: the claims of his propaganda machine grew ever more extravagant over the years. But those who dismissed him – as a crazed and erratic nuke-toting maverick; as a "pygmy" (George Bush's word); as a pompadoured, platform-shoed buffoon, in the image by Team America perhaps most widely disseminated – underestimated the man.

By turning his failing country into a nuclear state, he reinforced its pariah status, but wielded an influence he could never have otherwise achieved. There was logic in the threats to turn Seoul to ashes, as there was in the shelling and missile launches and nuclear tests. "He left the country with the ultimate deterrent. He ensured it won't be Iraq and won't be Libya," said John Delury, a professor at Yonsei University in South Korea, on Monday.

Behind the oversized, tinted glasses "was a man of some skill", said James Hoare, the former British charge d'affaires in Pyongyang. Foreigners who negotiated with him thought him sharp and knowledgeable, good at mastering briefs, but willing to refer to aides when necessary.

"He was competing in a hostile world and his solution might not be yours or mine, but his country is still there and the elite has survived – which is really what they are concerned with," said Hoare.

The clownish image was still less fair to the people he ruled with an iron grip. Observers have called the country the world's only Stalinist theme park, but there was nothing entertaining about it. Around 200,000 North Koreans are believed to be in prison camps thanks to the system of collective punishment.

Kenneth Roth, executive director of Human Rights Watch, described the country as "a human rights hell on Earth". "Kim Jong-il ruled through fear generated by systematic and pervasive human rights abuses including arbitrary executions, torture, forced labour and strict limits on freedom of speech and association," he said in a statement.

North Korea has long dismissed such criticisms as the jealous and destructive lies of capitalist aggressors. But experts say even its vast propaganda and state security apparatus has struggled to counter increasing domestic cynicism about the regime, which has proved incapable of meeting its people's basic needs. While Kim enjoyed sipping cognac and dining on sushi, his country has struggled with food shortages since the devastating famine of the 1990s, in which hundreds of thousands of people died.

"When the history of North Korea is written I think [his time] is going to be a pretty dark chapter," said Delury. "It was doing well in the 50s; it was starting to have problems in the 1970s, but not totally; it was grinding down in the 80s before the end of the socialist block. Then right after Kim Il-sung dies, it goes into freefall. You go from the paternal rule of Kim Il-sung to famine in the space of a couple of years. "To some extent it was the cards handed him... [But] in the end that's going to be his legacy."

Kim's efforts to transform foreign relations did better. Yet dramatic improvements in dealings with the South, the US and Japan were soon reversed by his own decisions and those of foreign leaders.

In North Korea's media, of course, there was only gratitude and sorrow. "It is the biggest loss for the party... our people and the nation's biggest sadness," a tearful, black-clad anchorwoman told viewers as she announced Kim's death on television. "At this moment of greatest sorrow and grief, people feel as if the sky is falling down. The hearts of all of them are now filled with stronger faith in victory, optimism and solemn pledge," KCNA said.

Footage showed anguished citizens hammering at pavements in Pyongyang; sobbing schoolchildren marshalled into public view; soldiers falling to their knees with undiluted grief. "When I see the videos I certainly don't believe in the first image of a total outpouring of grief. But nor do I believe that it is totally an act and they want to overthrow the government," said Delury.

Associated Press reported that people in the streets of Pyongyang began crying when they learned of Kim's death. Staff at the

Koryo hotel, which usually accommodates foreigners, were in tears. In Beijing, waitresses at a North Korean restaurant wept hysterically and fled the room on learning the news.

Korea specialist Dr Leonid Petrov, of the University of Sydney, said that while many North Koreans would be genuinely distraught, "it will not be as dramatic as it was in 1994 when Kim Il-sung died... political cynicism is growing." He predicted a long and "extremely convenient" state of mourning. Kim's death comes days before the beginning of 2012, which the regime has long heralded as a year of glory. "[Now] they don't need to honour the promise that North Korea will become a strong, powerful and prosperous state... The population will be required to work hard for long hours with very few celebrations of Kim Il-sung's centenary," Petrov added.

Already the transition of power has begun. "The Korean people have suffered the great loss," KCNA said on its website, "but are decisively rising up as they have Kim Jong-un, great successor to the revolutionary cause... prominent leader of the party and the army and people [of North Korea] who is standing in the vanguard of the Korean revolution. He is another great person produced by Korea who is identical to Kim Jong-il."

In the short term, the country is shutting down even further. Foreign delegations will not be accepted during the mourning period. "Come back next year," said staff at the Beijing embassy, when asked if visas were available.

29 December

Country Diary: South Uist

CHRISTINE SMITH

Starting a garden from scratch on a wind-blasted coast is a daunting prospect, and one that demands long-term planning and patience. So this garden, with its established shrubs and small trees to provide cover for birds, was a definite factor in the choice of our new house. And, as we hoped, it does attract a variety of birds that come to feed. Blackbirds, starlings and redwing come and go, but present every day are a couple of muscular greenfinches who have made the bird feeder their own. Any other bird attempting to feed from it is soon chased off by the greenfinches, who appear from nowhere to defend "their" peanuts.

A female chaffinch, another ever-present, manages occasionally to stage a successful raid, as does a dunnock which is more usually to be found, along with a song thrush, scuffling round the base of the shrubs picking up morsels from the leaf litter. A little troop of goldfinches sometimes visit, their bright red faces and buttery yellow wing bars bringing a splash of colour to the greyest of afternoons. One day five redpolls appeared to spend the morning flitting from willow to willow.

But we are not the only ones aware that the garden is frequented by so many birds. When my husband hisses for me to come slowly and quietly to the kitchen window I am not sure what to expect, but there, only a few feet away along the track, is a sparrowhawk. It is fiercely elegant, with long yellow legs ending in curving talons, and it is perched atop a starling it has just brought down. As if buffeted by the wind, the sparrowhawk momentarily loses its equilibrium, but then, regaining its poise, it quickly plucks a single billful of feathers from its prey. The wind snatches away most of the feathers, which drift briefly before falling in a scatter to the wet ground. Warily, alert to possible danger, the bird checks its surroundings and then plucks another billful of feathers.

Suddenly there is an explosion of desperate wing-flapping as the starling, which we had thought dead, struggles valiantly to throw off its attacker's weight. Even as I instinctively raise my hand to bang on the window I realise both the futility and the wrongness of my action. I catch myself in time but the movement alone has been enough to attract the sparrowhawk's attention. We stare at each other, I with contrition at the probable consequences of my reflex response, the bird with the fierce burning intensity of a predator caught between hunger and survival instinct. Suddenly it lifts off, flying low over the field into the fading light, leaving me still feeling the impact of its glare and also leaving behind the starling, for which the intervention had anyway always been too late.

Winter

4 January 2012

The Stephen Lawrence Case: How it changed Britain

HUGH MUIR

Following a six weeks' trial, two men were sentenced to detention at Her Majesty's pleasure, for terms of at least 15 and 14 years, for the murder of the black student Stephen Lawrence in 1993

It was hard to know what to think of Gary Dobson and David Norris as they sat in court 19 of the Old Bailey. Are they the hate-filled loudmouths depicted in the police surveillance film of the 1990s or older, wiser figures brought down by a lamented history? Certainly they seemed bewildered as barristers discussed the science and the new policing techniques that made the trial possible. Over 18 years, as both progressed in a way Stephen never could, the world changed; and today that fact caught up with them. There is irony here. On that dark night in Eltham, their brutal malevolence helped to change it.

Think of Britain before that night in Eltham. More to the point, ask someone black what it was like. You might talk about relations with the police as they then were – a state of ongoing conflict punctuated by occasional outbreaks of warfare. There might be a conversation about discrimination in employment, where the snubs were overt and unapologetic. One might discuss what was a paucity of minority figures in public life and in public administration. But the most profitable conversation would be about attitudes.

Prior to the murder of Stephen Lawrence, and the events thereafter, particularly Sir William Macpherson's public inquiry, we were actors in a farce as enduring and repetitive as The Mousetrap. Black communities would repeatedly complain that we didn't get a fair shake in terms of policing, the criminal justice system, in the jobs market, in the way we were treated by the whole range of public authorities.

And the establishment, both political and social, would say that we were making the whole thing up, or at least exaggerating. Two generations of black people, apparently with chips on their shoulders.

But that unreality couldn't survive the first weeks of the Macpherson inquiry, as the shoddy treatment meted out to one black victim and one black victim's family by the police – that lightning rod for wider society – tumbled into public view. A shock for middle England; catharsis for all whose complaints and warnings had to that point gone unheeded.

The earlier decision of the Daily Mail to label five suspects, including Norris and Dobson, "murderers" had been seismic, but the paper limited its concern to this specific case. It wasn't opposing discrimination. It was raging against criminality on its own terms. It took the inquiry and the doggedness of Stephen's parents to show that the attitudes the Lawrences encountered were those that had bedevilled race relations in Britain for many years. There has never been such a bias against understanding since.

"It was seminal," says Imran Khan, who represented the family at the inquiry. "People forget what it was like living in Britain in 1993.

"There had been three or four racial murders in south-east London. I was working in the anti-racist field and what I was getting constantly was this brick wall from police officers and other agencies saying 'look, this is not about race'. It was almost impossible to get those in authority to accept that race existed as a problem.

"What the Lawrence case did was it made race mainstream. It made it something people had to recognise, acknowledge and accept. Before that, it was something that the left and liberals talked about as a fringe issue. Now suburban England had to accept that race existed."

Khan says the effect of that is felt everywhere. "It pleases me that someone from Big Brother who is said to be a racist causes a furore; that footballers can be admonished in the press and thought of badly because there is a hint of racism. That would never have started in 1993."

Let's not overstate it, he says. "I'm not saying that racism has gone away. There was an expectation, even on my part, that overnight we would get rid of racism. It's changed in the way it is espoused and the way it deals with minority communities. It may be more secret.

"But what we have now is an acceptance within mainstream society that racism is a problem, that people can complain about it and that there is legislation that allows you to do something about it."

John Grieve, a former deputy assistant commissioner at Scotland Yard, ushered in a raft of policing changes as a direct response to the Lawrence case. He headed the racial and violent crimes task force.

Now retired into academia, he too says the case prompted a fundamental rethink. "It influenced the governance of policing, the way police are supervised, the way complaints are investigated. It influenced investigations, family liaison officers, the first hour at a murder scene, the independent advisers. It influenced the leadership of policing; we changed a whole layer of how leadership was trained to think as a direct result of some of the evidence Mr and Mrs Lawrence gave."

The effects, he says, were also international. "A lot of people copied the family liaison system. It also changed the law on racially aggravated offences: hate crime is still a big agenda item – this government is still driving that. It affected double jeopardy – the way people are tried in court.

"You can point to some things and say we haven't gone far enough. There are still issues, not in policing but in other institutions around institutional racism. I have grave doubts about whether the education establishment picked up the recommendations. Stop and search hasn't gone far enough. But I would argue there was a paradigm shift."

And it wasn't happenstance. Dr Richard Stone, who sat beside Macpherson as an inquiry panel member, says the mainstreaming of race relations predated those official hearings. He points to "that time when Mr Mandela was in the country and the parents appeared on TV with him. He made this terrible statement that the lives of black people are treated in the same way as apartheid South Africa.

"That shook a lot of white people in this country. It was a defining moment. It made this case the one that would be the defining one."

Macpherson and the panel spent an initial four months reading documents about Stephen's murder. "We couldn't believe that the police investigated murders in general as they had done with the Stephen Lawrence case. There had to be some other contributing factor.

"Insufficient evidence was presented to us to draw the conclusion that it might have been corruption so we were left with one other possibility, that it had to be racism. When you looked at the mistakes, so many of them were linked to the attitudes of police officers."

Stone sees ebb and flow in terms of societal progress since. There were, he says, obvious improvements in the immediate aftermath of the inquiry as a raft of institutions reacted to Sir

William Macpherson's recommendations. But over time priorities shift, and those resistant to change have asserted themselves. Look at the dearth of senior minority officers in the Met these days, he says. Look at the running sore of stop and search.

"I think both problems are worse. Something went wrong. You were four to five times more likely to be stopped and searched in 1999. Now it is eight to 10 times. When we talk about equalities now, I feel they have dropped off the agenda. In the main three political parties' manifestos in the last election, none of them mentioned the word racism. The momentum has gone and I found that very sad."

And yet, he says, there is a definable shift from the 1990s. "I think the Lawrences educated this country in what institutional racism is all about. People say: 'What is institutional racism?' and I say to them: 'Do you think the police didn't try hard enough?' and they say: 'Yes.'

"Why was that? Because the family are black. That's it. That's what institutional racism is about. The Lawrences taught millions of people that black people had a different experience of policing and a different experience of life in this country. Through their determination and basic decency they told people that racism really matters and I think that is the most important thing that has changed in this country."

Still, they had help. There were those who campaigned alongside. Opened doors. Made representations.

Ros Howells was one of them. She sits in the House of Lords as Lady Howells of St David, but it was as Ros Howells that she brought the Lawrence case to the attention of the government. Jack Straw ordered the inquiry, but the first minister to be involved was a Tory predecessor at the Home Office, Peter Lloyd.

Howells remembers: "I said this is a young black family who are married, they go to church, their children play tennis, they have aspirations for their children, and white boys murdered the eldest boy and the police failed to make an arrest. The more I got to know the family, the more I realised that they were the sort of people who didn't get involved in issues as such. They were a very nice family. The horror of what was happening would never have entered their minds until it came into their home. I was saying this is a family where there are no scandals attached. They are hard-working."

An official wrote her a note afterwards. "He said: 'You didn't leave a dry eye in the room.'" Over time, says Howells, the Lawrence case led many on a quest for self-education. "People were anxious to learn. They didn't like the term that they were racist. It is still an offensive one to people. Therefore people were asking for training; teachers, doctors, magistrates. How do we unlearn this?

"Not everyone. I remember, the day after the report came out, talking to someone involved in recruitment in the civil service. He was very arrogant. He said: 'I have my way of choosing my civil servants and nothing is going to make me change.' But many people who went through training said: 'Yes, I have been racist.' I think a lot of people have moved on. For all that, the fight goes on."

This is, at its core, a tale of contrasts. On one side we see those responsible for Stephen's murder; men who have enjoyed freedom and potential, without knowingly making any positive contribution to society. The lot of the fugitive, their lives consumed by a battle for survival.

On the other side of the ledger there is Stephen, cut down at 18, but whose memory has led others to shape public attitudes and to directly change the lives of third parties. This is true on a macro level. Consider the legislation changes and other national initiatives. But it is also true on a micro level.

At the Stephen Lawrence Centre in Deptford, the trust set up in his name runs programmes to help young people from disadvantaged backgrounds enter the professions. The initial focus was architecture, the career that interested Stephen himself. One hundred bursaries have been handed out; eight recipients have qualified and got jobs.

The centre runs employment programmes and education programmes. And soon it will provide incubator space for young entrepreneurs trying to set up new businesses. Paul Anderson Walsh, the managing director, says each person assisted benefits from an enduring legacy. "We say if you want to improve your life chances, we are here to help you. We call them the 'Stephens'."

4 January

The Iron Lady portrays a very different Margaret Thatcher from the one I knew

MICHAEL WHITE

It would be easy to imagine saying to Meryl Streep, "I knew Margaret Thatcher. You're no Margaret Thatcher," as an American politician once did to a rival who compared himself to President John F Kennedy. Easy, but wrong. Streep's interpretation of Thatcher in three distinct stages of her career, before, during and after her 11-year premiership, is a remarkable and sensitive achievement. Give the woman another Oscar, the pair of them can share it. Hollywood would like that.

The jibe could be levelled against Phyllida Lloyd's film. The Iron Lady certainly contains a selection of Thatcher's greatest handbaggings – which everyone much over 40 will remember with nostalgic glee or a shudder. We all knew her. But it is background. What cinema-goers will remember from this film is its foreground, a brilliant and thus unavoidably cruel portrait of old age, loneliness and decay, the harrowing fall from greatness. It should have been called The Rusty Lady or – Lloyd and Streep's earlier hit – GrandMamma Mia.

As such it is, despite the frenzied flashbacks and bewildering chronology, a fine piece of work, well worth seeing for Streep's performance and several others, including Jim Broadbent's Denis and Olivia Colman as daughter, Carol. They were the nicest members of that dysfunctional family, the ones who usually got the short end of the handbag. But not even Arthur Scargill or the late General Leopoldo Galtieri of Argentina can be so vengeful as to want Thatcher to see herself with dementia, less Iron Lady more Lady Gaga. She won't, the film is right about that. Mercifully, she is too frail.

It was not a description that crossed anyone's mind when I first met her at some reception in the mid-1970s. She had survived the lampooned hats and the milk-snatching as education secretary to see off Ted Heath and his would-be successors to become Tory leader in 1975. In private, the old school, with their country houses and military crosses, were immensely condescending, telling each other not take her wilder utterances too seriously. No 10 would tame her. In Lloyd's film they are seen to whisper a lot. It conveys the flavour of the time.

Thatcher was already famous for passing instant judgments on people she met. I knew I was too young and long-haired, too tentative, too Guardian, to pass muster. On one occasion in the receiving line at No 10 (more formal in those days) she took my hand and yanked me past her with only a perfunctory hullo. Gordon Brown would have done it too, but lacked the nerve.

As the paper's sketchwriter, I came to realise that I did have one advantage during our occasional exchanges. In a small group or at a reception one could make a little joke. Those present would smile or even laugh. Not Mrs T. She didn't do jokes, which put her at a brief disadvantage and caused her to leave a trail of double entendres. "Every prime minister needs a Willie [Whitelaw]" and, during an engineering visit, "I've never seen a tool as big as this."

So Lloyd and the writer, Abi Morgan, have generously credited her with too much humour, mostly in her dealings with her beloved Denis, whom Broadbent portrays as more of a knockabout character (where did that Cockney come from?) than the sub-Duke of Edinburgh type he was. Constantly scolded by the wife ("too much butter, Denis") but still his own gin-drinking man, he was much smarter than Private Eye's "Dear Bill" column could admit, loyal and adoring but also sometimes exasperated.

Thus, when his wife allowed herself to be filmed with a baby calf on a Suffolk farm during the 1979 election campaign, Denis was heard to mutter: "If we're not careful we'll soon have a dead calf on our hands." Sure enough the Mirror rang the farm every day, but Thatcher's luck and discipline held. Far from witnessing a fatal gaffe or calf-killing during the campaign, as Labour prayed, those of us on the campaign plane and bus (only one train, she didn't like them) soon realised she wouldn't put a foot wrong.

It was soft, content-lite Thatcher on display, a succession of photo-ops, telly with the sound turned off – and she won. Only then did the fireworks start and only gradually. Lloyd's Iron Lady takes few serious liberties with narrative facts in a series of set pieces: strikes, the Falklands war and Irish bombs, little on Europe or the cold war, no Westland crisis or Kinnock. Keep it simple for American audiences, and after all most of Thatcher's cabinet will be unknown to younger Brits. This film is only about one person.

As such it exaggerates her resolution and inflexibility, as she did herself. Thatcher could be pragmatic, even indecisive, though we hacks rarely saw it. She could also be kind. We didn't see much of that either. Nor did the miners, faltering cabinet colleagues or Carol whom she makes cry in the film without noticing. I can believe that. The script comes close to caricature, but then so did Thatcher. Streep's skill saves the day.

Is it a leftie assassination job? Or rightwing hagiography? Neither. The odd thing about The Iron Lady is that, for a film about politics, it is not very political. In handling the politics of deeply divided Britain of the 80s it is blandly fair to both perspectives, Thatcher's and her critics.

Why? Because this is a personal, essentially feminist story, about how a shopkeeper's daughter conquered a very patrician world, how she was torn between ambition and family (ambition usually won), how hard it was to become the first woman ruler of Britain since Queen Anne.

Yet here, as in life, Thatcher, housewife and statesman, is not a satisfactory feminist icon. She could have promoted women (only Janet Young served briefly in her cabinet), but didn't. As the film rightly notes, she preferred men and wanted women to win on merit, as she had done, not on gender alone.

Her father, Alfred Roberts (disconcertingly we last saw Iain Glen, who plays him, in Downton Abbey as press magnate Sir Richard Carlisle), is her hero. Lloyd and Morgan get that right. She promoted ideological proteges, all men, but to enhance her isolation we do not see that.

As good sisters Lloyd/Morgan also eschew another aspect of Thatcher's power: her sexual allure and willingness to use it, just as Barbara Castle – Labour's Thatcher – did. Politicians of her generation fancied her ("whisky on her breath tonight") and she always kept some eye candy, a Humphrey Atkins or Cecil

Parkinson, in cabinet. Even Alan Clark, a serious womaniser, once told me how she had squeezed his little finger as they parted. He clearly felt gallant about it – though not even Clark would have tried it on. Ronald Reagan? Perish the thought. Streep's Thatcher having a button sewn on the plunging neckline of her evening dress as she berates the cabinet wets is as close as we get.

In 1966, the year David Cameron was born, Winston Churchill's doctor, Lord Moran, was roundly denounced for publishing The Struggle for Survival, his account of the wartime leader's turbulent health from 1940 to his retirement in 1955. But at least Moran had drawn a veil over his last years and Churchill was dead at the time. In our intrusive, impatient age, they erect statues to the living and film their painful decline as clinically as if it was a decayed pit community.

The Iron Lady is tribute of sorts, but a strange one.

4 JANUARY

Ronald Searle was our greatest cartoonist – and he sent me his pens

MARTIN ROWSON

The artist Ronald Searle died on 30 December, aged 91

About a year ago I received an unsolicited package from France addressed in an oddly familiar, spidery hand. It was from Ronald

Searle, and contained a box of pens he had bought in 1963 and had found at the back of a cupboard.

In the attached note (along with a scrap of file paper on which he'd done some doodles to check the nibs) Searle said he thought I'd like them as he had quite enough pens to see him out. For any British cartoonist this was the equivalent of being given a high-five by God.

Roughly a year earlier Searle had given Steve Bell a box of pens (either before or after he drank Steve under the table) during a visit to Searle's home in France to prepare for a 90th birthday retrospective at the Cartoon Museum, requesting they be passed on to me.

Perhaps it was my effusive letter of thanks that made him think of me again; perhaps he was just clearing out some clutter and, ingrained with the kind of thrift you learn during three years as a Japanese prisoner of war, could never throw away something someone else might want. Either way, I felt like Cruikshank must have done when he was given Gillray's old drawing table.

Searle was, after all, easily the greatest cartoonist of the 20th century. Professional since his teens (though just a townie schoolboy, he got commissioned by Eric Hobsbawm to draw for Granta in Cambridge in the 1930s), in the decade following the war he managed, with St Trinian's and Molesworth, to weave himself into the DNA of the nation.

It is interesting to note how men of Searle's generation – Spike Milligan being another notable example – translated the unimaginable trauma of the war into stuff like St Trinian's or The Goon Show. And how distinctly unsettling it is to when you look at the drawings he produced in secret on the Burma Railway, and then see direct visual quotations of torture and beheadings in his later St Trinian's cartoons.

Even if most Britons will remember him as 'the St Trinian's cartoonist', Searle was much more than that. Without him, it's almost impossible to imagine cartoonists like Scarfe or Steadman or the subsequent generations inspired by them.

In 2005 I presented a BBC4 documentary on Searle in which I did some drawing in his style, trying to capture the peculiar magic of his defining blotchy, beautiful, raggedy, cross-nibbed "line". When I got it almost right I recognised something else: other cartoonists (myself included) can twist a nib just so to snag on the paper and release a spatter of blots that invariably denote blood or shit. But when Searle did it, they were champagne bubbles. With a supply of the master's nibs, maybe one day I'll pull off the same trick.

5 JANUARY

Chewing on some long forgotten gems from the terraces

HARRY PEARSON

On Monday I had a premonition of my death. I was at Brunton Park when it came to me. I saw myself falling to my knees, clutching my throat and turning as pale as Dimitar Berbatov, while all around me men in caps and warm-up coats ignored my final, thrashing moments in favour of howling abuse at the match officials for failing to send off any opposition players.

Later, sitting on the eastbound train surrounded by Sheffield United fans talking in their hand-pulled, cask-conditioned accents (if real ale could talk it would sound like John Shuttleworth), I pictured friends receiving the news and murmuring "...choked to death on a midget gem while stood in the rain at a lower division football ground surrounded by the scent of last night's beer and blokes yelling: 'Away, referee, man. Are your cards wedged up your arse?' Yes, it's sad, but I think it's how he would have wanted to go."

It wasn't the first time I've nearly suffered death by midget gem at a football match. In fact it usually occurs at least twice a season. For those of you unfamiliar with the midget gem I should explain that it is a small sweet of roughly the same size and texture as Sherpa Tensing's toe calluses. It is made from some sort of fruit-inspired gum, but is, intriguingly, much harder than its boastful rival the American hard gum, probably because it is British. The obvious way to cheat my fate is to give up eating the warty little sweets. But to me they are inextricably linked with what Pelé once dubbed "My core business going forward". And what would I chew on during matches instead?

Clearly things have changed in the confectionary industry. These days the retailing of bonbons is no longer the sole preserve of elderly men with Mr Whippy hairdos, fastidiously clean hands and the general air of someone who is one step away from having neighbours describe him as "a quiet man who kept himself to himself" to a huddle of tabloid reporters. As a result there is now a huge range of choice. Or is there?

People constantly assure me that middle-class tossers now overrun football. Yet while there may be grounds in the southeast where the chanting of the faithful is drowned out by people discussing the catchment areas of local secondary schools, and rival firms have prearranged face-offs in the side streets to see who has the most over-qualified eastern European au pair girl, such things have yet to permeate the *banlieu* of the Metropolitan Empire I frequent. So while it may be permissible in north or west London to spend the game nibbling on Piedmontese pralines or sucking Portuguese verbena pastilles, in my goitred neck of the

Winter

woods even the furtive consumption of a Lindor is likely to be regarded with suspicion.

Besides, I grew up watching football in the 70s. Back then, the terraces were no place for Turkish Delight. Or indeed delight of any description. My formative football years were spent in the Bob End at Ayresome Park, surrounded by men brutalised by careers in the chemical plants and fabricating sheds and leisure hours spent watching Dickie Rooks. It was not an environment that encouraged dolly mixtures, or jelly tots.

Most of the men in the Bob End were gnarled combat veterans who favoured masculine sweets such as Payne's Army and Navy Drops, the taste of which evoked fond memories of mustard gas attacks on the western front. Once, aged of eight or nine, on a freezing winter's night in which the surrounding phalanx cackled in bitter glee at the sight of Huddersfield Town's youthful centreforward Frank Worthington, whose long hair they took as a signal of the approach of Armageddon (I believe the Book of Ezekiel also mentions Keith Weller's tights and Peter Marinello's winsome cheekbones as portents of the Apocalypse), I made the signal mistake of taking a sip of hot Oxo while I still had a Victory V lozenge in my mouth. It was the sort of juxtaposition of contrasting flavours that may inspire the radical TV food scientists (which reminds me, I must get that Heston Blumenthal Marmite and cuckoo-spit cheesecake out of the freezer) but even four decades later the recollection still makes me gag.

Shortly afterwards I settled on midget gems as my football pocket sweet of choice. They were colourful and sweet, but had a carbuncle-like recalcitrance that rebuffed any accusations of aesthetic affectation. I have stuck to them, and they have stuck to my teeth, ever since.

I did, I admit, briefly experiment with Haribo Tangtastics, but the damn things are just too edible. I'd get through a large bag in the first half-hour of the match. That's a lot of sugar to absorb, even for a man of my size. By the interval I'd be twitching like Peter Crouch with his finger in a socket. The midget gem, by contrast, is a tough little beast that has to be worked on. Even putting six in your mouth at a time and chewing away as ferociously as Mike Tyson on a stray ear is unlikely to see off more than a couple of dozen per period. They are the football sweet nonpareil as far as I am concerned, and I intend to go on eating them at matches even if it kills me. Which it probably will.

10 JANUARY

Letters

PETE SPENCER AND IAN BURDON

Please could you let me know when you move the obituaries page. For two days I thought nobody had died.
Pete Spencer
Northampton

You print an extract from Gil Scott-Heron's memoir "written before he died" (G2, 10 January). That does tend to be the way of things.
Ian Burdon
Edinburgh

11 JANUARY

Religion for Atheists by Alain de Botton

REVIEW: TERRY EAGLETON

The novels of Graham Greene are full of reluctant Christians, men and women who would like to be rid of God but find themselves stuck with him like some lethal addiction. There are, however, reluctant atheists as well, people who long to dunk themselves in the baptismal font but can't quite bring themselves to believe. George Steiner and Roger Scruton have both been among this company at various stages of their careers. The agnostic philosopher Simon Critchley, who currently has a book in the press entitled The Faith of the Faithless, is one of a whole set of leftist thinkers today (Slavoj Žižek, Alain Badiou, Giorgio Agamben) whose work draws deeply on Christian theology. In this respect, the only thing that distinguishes them from the Pope is that they don't believe in God. It is rather like coming across a banker who doesn't believe in profit.

Such reluctant non-belief goes back a long way. Machiavelli thought religious ideas, however vacuous, were a useful way of terrorising the mob. Voltaire rejected the God of Christianity, but was anxious not to infect his servants with his own scepticism. Atheism was fine for the elite, but might breed dissent among the masses. The 18th-century Irish philosopher John Toland, who was rumoured to be the bastard son of a prostitute and a spoilt priest, clung to a "rational" religion himself, but thought the rabble should stick with their superstitions. There was one God for the rich and another for the poor. Edward Gibbon, one of the most notorious sceptics of all time, held that the religious doctrines he despised could still be socially useful. So does the German philosopher Jürgen Habermas today.

Diderot, a doyen of the French Enlightenment, wrote that the Christian gospel might have been a less gloomy affair if Jesus had fondled the breasts of the bridesmaids at Cana and caressed the buttocks of St John. Yet he, too, believed that religion was essential for social unity. Matthew Arnold feared the spread of godlessness among the Victorian working class. It could be countered, he thought, with a poeticised form of a Christianity in which he himself had long ceased to believe. The 19th-century French philosopher Auguste Comte, an out-and-out materialist, designed an ideal society complete with secular versions of God, priests, sacraments, prayer and feast days.

There is something deeply disingenuous about this whole tradition. "I don't believe myself, but it is politically prudent that you should" is the slogan of thinkers supposedly devoted to the integrity of the intellect. If the Almighty goes out of the window, how are social order and moral self-discipline to be maintained? It took the barefaced audacity of Friedrich Nietzsche to point out that if God was dead, then so was Man – or at least the conception of humanity favoured by the guardians of social order. The problem was not so much that God had inconveniently expired; it was that men and women were cravenly pretending that he was still alive, and thus refusing to revolutionise their idea of themselves.

God may be dead, but Alain de Botton's Religion for Atheists is a sign that the tradition from Voltaire to Arnold lives on. The book assumes that religious beliefs are a lot of nonsense, but that they remain indispensable to civilised existence. One wonders how this impeccably liberal author would react to being told that free speech and civil rights were all bunkum, but that they had their social uses and so shouldn't be knocked. Perhaps he might have the faintest sense of being patronised. De Botton claims that one can be an atheist while still finding religion "sporadically useful, interesting and consoling", which makes it sound rather like knocking up a bookcase when you are feeling a bit low. Since Christianity requires one, if need be, to lay down one's life for a stranger, he must have a strange idea of consolation. Like many an atheist, his theology is rather conservative and old-fashioned.

De Botton does not want people literally to believe, but he remains a latter-day Matthew Arnold, as his high Victorian language makes plain. Religion "teaches us to be polite, to honour one another, to be faithful and sober", as well as instructing us in "the charms of community". It all sounds tediously neat and civilised. This is not quite the gospel of a preacher who was tortured and executed for speaking up for justice, and who warned his comrades that if they followed his example they would meet with the same fate. In De Botton's well-manicured hands, this bloody business becomes a soothing form of spiritual therapy, able to "promote morality (and) engender a spirit of community". It is really a version of the Big Society.

Like Comte, De Botton believes in the need for a host of "consoling, subtle or just charming rituals" to restore a sense of community in a fractured society. He even envisages a new kind of restaurant in which strangers would be forced to sit together and open up their hearts to one another. There would be a Book of Agape on hand, which would instruct diners to speak to each other for prescribed lengths of time on prescribed topics. Quite how this will prevent looting and rioting is not entirely clear.

In Comtist style, De Botton also advocates secular versions of such sacred events as the Jewish Day of Atonement, the Catholic Mass and the Zen Buddhist tea ceremony. It is surprising he does not add Celtic versus Rangers. He is also keen on erecting billboards that carry moral or spiritual rather than commercial messages, perhaps (one speculates) in the style of "Leave Young Ladies Alone" or "Tortoises Have Feelings As Well". It is an oddly Orwellian vision for a self-proclaimed libertarian. Religious faith is reduced to a set of banal moral tags. We are invited to contemplate St Joseph in order to learn "how to face the trials of the workplace with a modest and uncomplaining temper". Not even the Walmart management have thought of that one. As a role model for resplendent virtue, we are offered not St Francis of Assisi but Warren Buffett.

What the book does, in short, is hijack other people's beliefs, empty them of content and redeploy them in the name of moral order, social consensus and aesthetic pleasure. It is an astonishingly impudent enterprise. It is also strikingly unoriginal. Liberal-capitalist societies, being by their nature divided, contentious places, are forever in search of a judicious dose of communitarianism to pin themselves together, and a secularised religion has long been one bogus solution on offer. The late Christopher Hitchens, who some people think is now discovering that his broadside God Is Not Great was slightly off the mark, would have scorned any such project. He did not consider that religion was a convenient fiction. He thought it was disgusting. Now there's something believers can get their teeth into...

Terry Eagleton is Professor of English Literature at Lancaster University.

11 JANUARY

So who is good enough to get into Cambridge?

JEEVAN VASAGAR

It's a life-changing roll call. As the admissions tutor reads out names, the men and women gathered around the table reply crisply to each one: "Yep... yep... yep." Each "yep" is actually a no. It's a rejection of a candidate who has applied for a place at the University of Cambridge.

The weakest of the field have already been sifted out; up to a fifth of applications are declined before the interview stage. Now the tutors are gathered to consider the results of those interviews. Five women and seven men are gathered at a table, in a light-filled, rectangular room at Churchill College to discuss admissions to study natural sciences.

The easy ones go first. These are the candidates whose academic track record is – by Cambridge standards – marginal, and whose performance at interview has been disappointing. As one candidate's name is read out, one of the academics notes that he got an interview score of two, out of a possible 10. "Oh dear," says Richard Partington, the senior admissions tutor, who sits at the head of the table. Next to Partington is a steel trolley with the applicants' files.

Then, they get down to business. After the straightforward rejections, and those they have already decided to offer places to, there is a band of candidates who fall in the middle. They might be teenagers who have done well at interview, but whose academic performance seems patchy. There are some with impeccable credentials on paper – but, in a phrase that is repeatedly used, "failed to shine" at interview.

Cambridge has opened up the admissions process to give a clearer picture of the effort that goes into the assessment of each candidate. Competition is intense: around 16,000 candidates are chasing just under 3,400 undergraduate places. Churchill College has 39 places in natural sciences and more than 170 direct applicants. The academics will make about 45 offers, in letters that arrive on candidates' doormats this week. To help preserve the anonymity of the candidates, most of the academics in the room have asked for their names not to be used.

As the wind shakes the bare branches of trees outside, the academics discuss an interviewee from a sixth-form college. One notes: "He was extremely careful with everything he was doing, but not exactly engaging in the discussion. I think mathematics is something he does quite well, but he doesn't shine."

The boy is an unusual case – he has won a scholarship to study in the UK after going to school overseas. His home country is a poor one, not known for its education system. One of the women says: "I would take him and keep a close eye on his progress. He might need a boost in confidence."

"Let's take him," Partington agrees. "Everyone content?"

Next up is a girl from a leading private school, who was strong on paper but stumbled at interview. "She seemed surprised by quite a lot of the things we were talking about – [she would say] 'Oh right' as if she hadn't seen it before," one of the academics, in a wine-coloured sweater, says.

"Had she not revised?" Partington asks.

"We asked them what they'd done recently, and based the questions on that, so it was starting with something familiar, but seeing it in a different context," the academic replies.

Partington suggests: "One possibility is that she's someone who's learned in a compartmentalised way."

Another tutor says: "The comment I've put down is: 'Needed help with next steps.'"

Partington wonders aloud if tutors can lead a student through an entire degree. "We could," one of the men responds dryly.

Both Oxford and Cambridge are regularly accused of bias against state school applicants – most famously, in the case of Laura Spence, the girl from Tyneside who was refused a place at Magdalen College, Oxford, more than a decade ago. The tutors gathered at this table are aware that Cambridge is committed to admitting between 61% and 63% of its UK students from state-sector schools and colleges. At present, that proportion is 59.3%. The university has also agreed with the Office for Fair Access – an official watchdog set up when the Blair government brought in top-up fees – to increase the share of students from neighbourhoods where few people have gone to university.

Churchill College is a low-rise modernist stack on the edge of the city centre, a series of interlocking brick cubes. It does better on state-school intake than Cambridge as a whole. This is partly because of its reputation for science, which attracts more state school pupils. The split at Churchill is 70/30 in favour of the state sector. That is still out of kilter with the school system as a whole – just 7% of pupils in England attend private schools. But it is a bit closer to the split at sixth form, where private schools account for around 13% of the total number of A-level exam entries.

In its prospectus, the college is described as having a "friendly, unpretentious social atmosphere". It is certainly not as physically daunting as some of the grand and ancient buildings in the city centre. But even here, the surroundings speak of wealth and intimacy with power; the sketches on the walls are by Winston

Churchill, the floor is teak and the room is panelled with another glossy tropical hardwood.

The phrase "a good school" comes up repeatedly in the tutors' discussions. It is used most frequently about private and grammar schools, but also some comprehensive schools, and has a double meaning. "A good school" is a high-performing one. It is a school that knows what Cambridge requires, where the school reference is delivered in the terms the university is looking for – the key phrases are ones that emphasise superlative performance compared with their age group: "He [or she] is best in... he is top of..." But when a candidate comes from "a good school" they are also cut less slack. Of one applicant from "a good school", a bemused tutor says: "The thing that didn't sit with me is, his [predicted] A* is in further maths, but he couldn't do his arithmetic."

The Sutton Trust, the charity that aims to promote social mobility through education, blames the unequal outcomes between state and private candidates at university level on the poor exam performance of some schools. That failure at school level becomes painfully apparent in the case of one of the Churchill candidates. She has had "unimaginable teaching difficulties", the tutors hear. She has taken her A-levels at a school that has had a spectacularly high turnover of teachers.

Peering at his laptop when her name is announced, Nick Cutler, an admissions tutor at Churchill, says there are "multiple flags". The flags are used to indicate factors such as poverty, or a school that performs very poorly at GCSE. There are six categories in all – including whether an applicant has spent time in care. There is evidence that a strong candidate from a bad school is likely to perform well when they come to Cambridge. But the academics are concerned that in this case, the school has been so turbulent that she simply lacks essential knowledge. Her examination and interview marks are low.

The rapid pace of Cambridge would "kill her", one of the academics says. Another agrees: "I would really like to give her a place, but for her own sanity, she's much better going to one of the other redbrick, Russell Group universities, and just taking her time."

Partington says: "If we gave her a chance she would do what everybody else would do, and think: 'I'll probably be all right' and she will probably be wrong."

There is a despairing consensus around the table that the university cannot repair the gaps in this candidate's knowledge. A damning line from the school's reference – which lays bare its inability to teach the candidate – is read aloud by a tutor who raises outstretched hands in exasperation. The candidate's file goes back into the trolley with a clang.

Another candidate from a comprehensive school has four contextual data flags by her name. There is a note too about "teaching difficulties" – a physics teacher who left during the sixth form and a stand-in for chemistry. This is an easier case – her interview scores are high, an eight and a seven out of 10. She has a 92% mark in her chemistry A-level. One of the academics reviews her "flags": "She's got low socio-economic, low-performing GCSE, low Oxbridge – she's nearly got the full set."

Partington says: "Take her."

There is another girl from a comprehensive school who got an eight at interview, but one academic exclaims: "Blooming heck, her GCSE score was terrible."

"The school doesn't know how to write a reference," another comments.

Partington decides to make an offer but to set the hurdle high because of the doubts. "We're going to A* the chemistry," he says firmly.

"I would A* the maths," one of the others suggests. "The other thing I would do is write to her separately, encourage her to do further maths through the Further Maths Network."

The tutors are divided about this – there is a feeling she has already been stretched thin in a "school that's not great". But they decide this will not be an entrance requirement. She just needs a little more fluency in maths to cope at university.

On the table are white china cups of tea and coffee, two barely touched water jugs and a single slightly blackened banana. The academics leaf through coloured spreadsheets with the candidates' names, their exam performance to date, predicted grades, interview scores, contextual flags and ranking – based on exam performance – compared with all of the university's applicants this year.

The pace is swift, despite the meeting lasting five hours. It is occasionally leavened with a touch of humour, or avuncular kindness. One of the academics, looking at a file photo, sighs: "Oh he's young – he looks like one of the Bash Street kids." Another remarks, of a different candidate: "You could conduct a biology study in his hair." Recalling an over-caffeinated and under-dressed teenager, one says: "The T-shirt, oh yes, the T-shirt..."

Although a candidate's ethnicity is generally evident from his or her name and the photograph in their file, there is never any overt discussion of race. This seems surprising when both Oxford and Cambridge have been accused of being racially as well as socially exclusive.

Geoff Parks, director of admissions at Cambridge, says later: "Race doesn't come up in its own right. It's inseparable from socio-economic factors. Cambridge admits a proportion of BME [ethnic minority] students that is above the proportion of the teenage population, [but] with 'low-participation' neighbourhoods we feel we're not meeting a relatively low target. Many people who are first-generation British might also be living in low-participation neighbourhoods."

At times, the procedure seems brusque; a life-changing decision made in a second. In fact, it is the end point of a long, intensive process of evaluating candidates. Most of those who apply are interviewed. And the interviews are designed to probe their knowledge deeply. For natural sciences, the interview has a practical bent, with candidates tackling problems under the gaze of the tutor. Confidence is appreciated. Of one candidate, a boy from an academy school in Norfolk, a tutor says: "He managed to strike a balance between not being fazed by what's going on, and not being cocky either. The sort of person..."

Someone else finishes: "You'd like to teach."

Great emphasis is placed on exam performance, and the academics are keen to drill down into performance in individual modules. One notes approvingly of a candidate who has "done some hard units". There is far less interest than is popularly thought in extra-curricular activity. An academic remarks with bafflement that a candidate has "got his violin grades on there".

It is not just poor teaching – or a lack of teaching – that can wreck a candidate's chances. Their combination of subjects is also crucial. There is consternation about a candidate who is applying to read natural sciences without having either maths or biology; he is taking physics and chemistry but his third A-level is an arts subject. The lack of maths rules him out for the study of physics. The absence of biology means he will struggle to be accepted as a biologist. The school is a "really ropey" one. One of the academics, a man in a grey fleece, comments: "I feel sorry for him, but I don't think we can fix the problem."

The consensus is that they will "stick him in the pool". The "winter pool" is a third option – neither a straightforward offer nor an outright rejection. It means the application is forwarded for consideration by other colleges. Strong candidates who are at risk of being squeezed out because they have applied to an over-subscribed college also get a second chance this way. The pool takes place in early January, around three weeks after the college decision meetings. Admissions tutors from all the Cambridge colleges gather in two rooms at Newnham College, and examine the pooled candidates' folders again.

The main room in which the pool takes place is Clough Hall, an elegant banqueting room with a minstrels' gallery and a ceiling decorated with plaster mouldings of flowers and heraldic beasts. There is very little conversation. Tutors go through bundles of files making lists of candidates they would like to pull out for their college. Anglepoise lamps spill yellow light on to the desks. Outside, it is overcast.

Andy Bell, admissions tutor at Gonville and Caius College, has spotted three potential candidates for places in an arts subject at his college. One of the files that has caught his eye is a boy whose educational background is not that of a "straightforward, standard Cambridge applicant". He is applying from a "perfectly decent" sixth-form college, but before that he had attended a poor comprehensive school. Bell notes: "His GCSE performance is really quite strong, getting a lot of A*s at GCSE. This is someone who's been working far above the level of his cohort from an early age." Outside school, he has displayed an interest in the subject he is applying for – it is such a small course that naming it risks identifying him – through work experience at a university in London, and extensive reading. "This is somebody who's worked really hard for a number of years, who's really serious about making something of his academic ability," Bell says.

Seated at a table by one of the tall, arched windows, James Keeler, the admissions tutor at Selwyn College, has perhaps the most dreaded job – reviewing candidates for medicine, a course so competitive that excellent applicants are routinely turned down.

Keeler opens the folder of a candidate who is applying after taking his A-levels. The school reference describes him as a "strong applicant" and underlines the adjective. This is borne out by his results – he has four A*s.

For medicine, the tutors look for both a strong aptitude for science and the beginnings of a bedside manner. This candidate has divided his interviewers. While the clinicians thought highly of him, there is a question mark over his scientific ability. Keeler seems inclined to attach greater weight to his exam performance than the interview. "The interview is just part of the picture – his four A*s is the summation of many years of work," he says.

He carries on leafing through the folder, looking for evidence of what the candidate is doing now. "Looking at the personal statement for medicine, it's important that they have a range of activities and, particularly, that they have done a serious level of volunteering – handing out teas in a hospice, working with disabled children. Something where they have to take on a caring role and think about why doctors can't cure everybody.

"He's been on a gap year," Keeler notes.

"If he's been sitting on a beach for a year, I'll put him in the bin..."

He turns a page of the folder and reads the candidate's statement: "He's been volunteering with St John Ambulance. And also training to be a special constable – that's something I've never seen before. He's clearly doing something worthwhile. He's currently volunteering at a care home." The admissions tutor smiles. "That's a tick for me."

16 JANUARY

Below the breadline on Liverpool's workless estates

AMELIA GENTLEMAN

Thomas Bebb cranes his head out of his living room window to assess how many of his neighbours are unemployed. He counts the number of flats in this three-storey, brown-and-grey pebble-dash block (12) and pauses to calculate how many contain people in work. There are two: a scaffolder and a nurse. Looking across the courtyard at two other blocks opposite and to the left, he can't think of anyone with a job in either building.

The high numbers of workless households on this estate help explain startling figures produced by the GMB last week revealing that nearly one in three households in Liverpool has no one in work. It is the legacy of historic industrial decline in this area, suddenly worsened by the recent round of public sector redundancies and a new, downturn-related disappearance of retail and manufacturing jobs.

For Bebb, who lost his short-term job as a parks gardener and grounds maintenance worker in November (because of cost-cutting by Liverpool city council, which is in the process of shaving 28% from its budget), the result is that he is living substantially below the poverty line. In practical terms, this means he has only the seven pound coins, plus 30 pence in smaller change, jangling in his tracksuit pocket to last him for the next 10 days, until his benefits are paid again.

He is anxious to find new work and is assiduous about searching for openings. Once a week he has been volunteering with his old employers, because he enjoys his work and wants to be the first back in if there's an opening, obligingly doing his old job for free.

But, with seven unemployed people in Liverpool for every job vacancy, looking for work is a dispiriting process. Local government cuts have led to widespread job losses throughout the city, where almost 30% of all work is public-sector funded. Inconveniently, the cuts have also led to the shrinking of resources available to fund many of the community centres and training courses that might previously have helped him and his neighbours back into work.

Because unemployment is an experience shared by most of his friends, family and neighbours, Bebb, 45, finds nothing remarkable in his situation, and his description of how he gets by is not an appeal for sympathy, just a neutral account of reality.

His two eldest children, who are 21 and 23, haven't found work since they left school at 16, although they are looking. He remembers the years spent on the dole when he left school in a similarly bleak economic period in the early 80s – around the time that Margaret Thatcher was considering abandoning Liverpool to "managed decline", having been warned by her advisers that to try to save it would be like attempting to "pump water uphill".

But Bebb wonders if his children will find things harder. "It's normal for their generation. It's like that for every family around here, very few of their kids have got jobs," he says. More than a third of Liverpool council wards have youth unemployment rates twice the national average, according to council figures.

The nearest shopping parade to his flat on the Tees estate in Kirkdale, north Liverpool, reflects how little money people here have to spend. Two of the local pubs are shut, and of the first six shops on the street, four have recently closed. Along the street, it's not bright signs and awnings that make the facades distinctive, but the range of different materials used to board them up – sheets of wood, corrugated iron, metal shutters.

He sees old school friends in the jobcentre. "It's not a good way to meet them, but it's nice to see them anyway," Bebb says. By contrast with many of them, he thinks he's been lucky to have previously had steady work with the council, and then with a number of private companies that were contracted to take on parks maintenance for the council, for much of his working life.

Losing his full-time grounds maintenance job two years ago was "the end of the world": for a while he found it hard to get out of bed and didn't want to talk to people. His mood lifted when he got a contract job working in the parks, but the work only lasted a few months.

He gets about £67 a week as jobseeker's allowance, but £15 is instantly deducted in child maintenance for the three of his five children who are under 16, none of whom live with him. Another £10 a week is also currently being deducted at source to repay a historic crisis loan that he was given by the jobcentre to tide the family over when he lost his job on another occasion about a decade ago, leaving him with just over £40 pounds. Out of that he is paying back a credit card debt of around £1,000, which he ran up when he first lost his full-time work 18 months ago, and he needed money to tide him over. (He went to his bank to ask for an overdraft facility to help him through that difficult time, and was told he wasn't eligible for one, but was invited to apply for a credit card instead.)

Bebb is paying this off at a rate of £33 a month, which he often finds very challenging. He spends £14 a week on recharging his gas and electricity accounts, so just under £20 is left for food, clothes, bus tickets and everything else. His rent is currently paid by housing benefit.

This is manageable, but only because he has radically changed the way he lives and eats. He goes once a fortnight to one of two local shops that offer heavily discounted food – packets of buy-one-get-one-free frozen burgers for a pound, two-for-£1 ice-cream tubs for his younger children who stay with him at the weekend, a bag of frozen chips, which, if he rations it correctly, he can get four meals out of. When that runs out he eats rice and pasta which he gets for 25p a pack at Tesco. "Sometimes you have to eat crap."

For breakfast now, he has toast rather than Weetabix. If this seems an unremarkable shift, he explains the subtle financial calculations behind the change: a loaf of bread contains, say, 30 slices, and costs around 40 pence, while a packet of Weetabix costs nearer £2 and only has enough for 12 breakfasts, so is less economical. Because he's not eating cereal, he buys less milk, and has switched to getting a litre of longlife so that he can eke it out for as long as possible without it going off. "You've got to think like that when you're shopping."

Bebb can't afford to smoke so he doesn't, and he says beer is an unaffordable luxury: the last time he got drunk was the day he was made redundant from his permanent job two years ago. "I was shocked, I was drowning my sorrows." He hasn't been to a football match since he was a child ("too dear") or to the cinema for years, hasn't bought new clothes since he lost his job. To relax he takes his younger children fishing on the canal, which has the advantage of being free.

The corner shops and chippy survive on the high street, but the discount store Bebb uses is further away and he hasn't bought his children a takeaway meal since he lost his permanent job two years ago (£10 is too much to blow in one go, he explains). "It's a struggle; it gets to you more mentally," he says.

Bebb looks healthy, but admits he sometimes feels wobbly when he does the 45-minute walk to the job centre (a £3.80 day bus pass is usually unaffordable), because he hasn't eaten enough. "Sometimes I've had to stop because I've had the shakes, dizzy."

He is happy to speak frankly and dissect his budget in unembarrassed detail because he thinks people have a distorted idea of how generous benefits are. He has noticed that the new government's tone has become more hostile to claimants, and thinks ignorance may be part of the problem. He doesn't expect empathy from a prime minister whom he describes as a multimillionaire. "If the prime minister can go out and spend £100 a night for his dinner and I don't get that a fortnight, where's the justice in that?"

For the moment, the doors of the Kirkdale Community Centre remain open on the high street, providing a place for local unemployed young people to spend time. At the front desk, Sheena Orton, who helps run the centre, explains that because of funding cuts, they are no longer able to offer courses in IT skills and CV building for the unemployed, the centre has lost 13 members of staff in the past year, and is struggling to stay open. She is still working full-time, but there's only enough money to pay her for 10 hours a week, so she does the rest for free. "It's the 18-24-year-olds who are angry. They want what everyone else has got – they all want a car, they want a phone, they want trainers. Some of them resort to crime and you can see that in the burglary stats," she says.

She is also worried about her own children; three of her four sons, aged between 20 and 38, have recently lost their jobs. "I don't think you could be more motivated than my sons and they can't get anything."

Nick Small, the Labour councillor responsible for employment within Liverpool city council, says the figure of one in three workless households comes as no surprise: "We realise that we have got a very tough situation in Liverpool. In some areas 40% of households are workless. This creates additional barriers to finding work. There's no culture of finding work in the community, no role models. It can be quite disempowering."

Through its Liverpool Into Work scheme, which has a centre on the Tees estate, the council is trying to assist the hardest to reach communities, but Small concedes that "if there aren't the jobs to go into", then helping with CVs and motivation was only part of the solution. "We need to do all we can to stimulate demand," he says.

Kim Griffiths, head of employment with the Liverpool in Work programme, said the combined effect of the downturn and public sector cuts meant that there were fewer jobs available in the care sector, in security, hospitality, tourism and manufacturing. "A lot of the jobs are part-time and funny shifts. There are a lot of people who really want to work. It is really soul destroying to keep getting knocked back. We are not thick scousers who want to sit on our arses all day. That is not the case. We are talented, creative people who really want to work."

Bebb is being helped by the programme: advisers are impressed by his "employability", and hopeful that new work could be found for him. In the meantime, to qualify for benefits payments, he is obliged to apply for at least two jobs a week, to phone at least two employers a week and turn up, speculatively, at the door of two potential employers every week.

Later his six- and eight-year-old sons are dropped off for him to look after for a while. They slide across the floor of his flat on their stomachs, cheerfully eating ice cream and watching television. He is optimistic that things may be easier for them when they leave school, and hopes that they will learn a trade – electrician or gas fitter.

The children have other ideas. The younger boy wants to be a pirate, and the older one says his teacher has told him he is clever enough to go to university. He'd like to be a professor.

After this article was published, some readers got in touch to offer Mr Bebb money. He refused the offers, explaining that the interview hadn't been a plea for help, but just an attempt to educate people. In March he had a heart attack as he walked to the jobcentre to sign on. He thinks it was triggered by the stress of being out of work. He is still recovering, spends two mornings a week at hospital appointments, and has been told by his doctor that for the moment he is too ill to work. He has, however, recently been found fit to work by an Atos medical assessment, which means he has to continue actively searching for work. He does wonder whether employers will be less keen on employing him, because of his heart condition, but he points out that this is a hypothetical consideration because in any case, there are no jobs for anyone. His adult children have not yet found work.

17 JANUARY

Syria: Beyond the wall of fear, a state in slow motion collapse

IAN BLACK

Sipping tea in a smoky Damascus cafe, Adnan and his wife, Rima, look ordinary enough: an unobtrusive, thirty something couple winding down at the end of the working day in one of the tensest cities in the world.

But like much else in the Syrian capital, they are not what they first seem: normally, he is a software engineer and she a lawyer; now, they are underground activists helping organise the uprising against President Bashar al-Assad.

It is dangerous work. Over the past 10 months, thousands of Syrians have been killed as Assad has pursued a ruthless crackdown that shows no sign of ending. But his opponents are equally determined to carry on.

Adnan and Rima are unable to work or contact their families. They have false identities. Adnan changes his appearance regularly. He has just shaved off his beard. It clearly works: a friend at a nearby table fails to recognise him.

Most of their friends are on the run from the mukhabarat secret police. "It used to be scary but we've got used to it," said Adnan. "The revolution destroyed the wall of fear. At school, we were taught to love the president – Hafez – first. And it didn't get any better when Bashar took over. Now, everything has changed. Assad's picture is defaced everywhere and we are certain that at some point we will topple the regime."

Even in the centre, daytime "flash" demonstrations last for a few minutes and disappear before they are pounced on by security forces, the worst of whom are *shabiha* louts in army trousers and leather jackets who loiter at junctions and squares. The demonstrators are ingenious: in one case, volunteer drivers created traffic jams all around the old Hijaz railway station to create a space in which a brief but eye-catching protest could be held.

Creativity and secrecy are crucial. On the first day of Ramadan, loudspeakers concealed in the busy shopping area of Arnous Square blared out the stirring song "Irhal ya Bashar" ("Leave, Bashar"), written by Ibrahim Qashoush, who was murdered in July after performing in Hama. His killers cut his throat and carved out his vocal chords.

"At first, people were frightened," said one Damascus resident who had heard the song. But when it was played for a second time, they relaxed. "By the third time, they were laughing," he said.

The speakers were positioned on a roof and the area around them was smeared with oil to make it harder to silence them.

The tactics are effective but risky: one activist accidentally started playing a tape of the song in a taxi but the driver turned out to be a mukhabarat agent, who handed him in. Jawad, a computer scientist involved in one of these groups, was held for two months and beaten repeatedly to try to make him betray the names of his friends.

Other non-violent acts have been stunningly symbolic: in August blood-red dye was poured into the fountain outside the central bank in Saba'a Bahrat Square, the scene of raucous pro-Assad rallies. Black-ribboned candles have been distributed to commemorate Ghayath Matar, famous for handing out roses to soldiers, who was tortured and killed last September.

Still, some cannot quite believe what they are daring to do. "Look at us," laughed Bassam, a manufacturer in his 20s. "Using false names and driving around to avoid police checkpoints. The first time I went to a demonstration, it was frightening. Now it's exhilarating."

Damascus is surrounded by the army's 4th division, commanded by the president's brother Maher. Government buildings are protected by anti-blast barriers. Roads near the presidential palace and defence ministry are closed. At the state security HQ, in Kafr Sousseh, machine-gun-toting guards look out from sandbagged emplacements.

It was there, two days before a cheerless Christmas, that twin suicide bombings killed 44 people and were blamed (20 minutes after the blasts) on al-Qaida – a reminder of the unrelenting official narrative that Syria faces only "armed terrorist gangs", not the mass popular protests that have become an emblematic event of the Arab spring.

On 6 January, terrorists struck again. In nearby al-Midan, an opposition stronghold, there was what looked, at least at first glance, like another suicide attack, which reportedly killed 26 people. But key details remain confused. Locals spoke of the area being mysteriously cordoned off by police the night before. Many noted the remarkably swift response by the Syrian media and emergency services. And a rapidly assembled crowd of demonstrators, who were not from the neighbourhood, chanted pro-Assad slogans for journalists bussed in by the ministry of information. Suspicions that the event was somehow staged look reasonable, rather than the product of a conspiracy theory.

Abu Muhammad, a chatty Sunni taxi driver, had no doubt about it. "It was pure theatre, all fabricated," he said. "The idea is to frighten people in Damascus." Nader, a shopkeeper, was even blunter: "The government knows Syrians don't believe them. But they count on people being too afraid to break the silence."

The killing of the French TV correspondent Gilles Jacquier by mortar fire during a government-escorted trip to Homs left more troubling questions unanswered. Was it a warning message to the international media? What is extraordinary about all these incidents is the assumption of so many Syrians that the regime would act with such murderous duplicity. "No one has any illusions," said another anti-Assad figure. "People think [the regime] is capable of anything. There are no red lines."

The president's supporters see things very differently. The regime's grand conspiracy narrative, in which the US, the west, Israel and reactionary Arab "agents", led by Qatar, plot against Syria, is pumped out daily by state media. Its most aggressive exponent is Addounia TV, a satellite channel. Above all Addounia loathes the broadcaster al-Jazeera, the Qatari-owned cheerleader for the Arab revolutions, which it has accused of staging fake demonstrations in studio mock-ups of Syrian cities. In his speech the president referred to 60 TV channels as part of this vast "plot". Big lies seem to work. "The emir of Qatar is a Jew, worse than the Jews," an Alawite taxi driver raged. "There are no demonstrations in Syria, or only by people who have been paid, and the terrorist gangs." No wonder so many Syrians berate the few foreign journalists who are allowed into the country and urge them to "tell the truth like it really is".

Regime loyalists who speak to the international media claim to support political reform and dialogue with the peaceful opposition: these are people like the Assad adviser Buthaina Shaaban and Jihad Makdissi, director of information at the foreign ministry, who engages in Twitter debates with supporters of the uprising. Overthrowing the president, warns Makdissi, "will open a Pandora's box". But Syria's powerful security chiefs, who are unavailable for briefings or interviews, emphasise the grave danger posed by Salafi extremists or al-Qaida – the same "foreign fighters" the mukhabarat used to help cross into Iraq to fight the Americans. Stomach-churning pictures showing decapitated bodies or corpses with their eyes gouged out are produced as evidence of the savagery of these terrorists. Opposition supporters do not claim such horrors are faked but insist the regime bears overwhelming responsibility for the current violence.

Sectarianism is also rearing its ugly head, with the opposition blaming the regime for fomenting tensions between Alawites, who dominate the security forces, and the Sunni majority. In the current climate, it is easily done. Mudar, a young Alawite with close establishment links, tells of a soldier cousin who was killed and mutilated, and then clicks on a high-quality video clip of a bushy-bearded man sawing off the head of his screaming victim. In an area near the Umayyad mosque, an Alawite woman visiting a Sunni friend said she dare not take a taxi home because a Sunni driver might kidnap her and sell her on to be killed.

Rumblings of concern are audible. Last spring, a group of influential Alawites urged Assad to apologise for the repression and pursue genuine rather than cosmetic reforms. "Alawites feel their fate is connected to the Assads," warned a veteran opposition leader, "and that is very dangerous."

Pressure is clearly mounting. Alawite businessmen are reported to have been bribing the mukhabarat to avoid releasing their employees to attend pro-regime rallies. Fadwa Suleiman, an Alawite actress, won huge admiration when she came out in support of the uprising, but she was ostracised and denounced on TV by her brother. Christians, traditionally loyalists, are worried, too, especially about the Salafi element of the uprising, and the churches keenly demonstrate public support for Assad. Another sign of Syria's deepening crisis is that the state is no longer functioning properly. It is "collapsing in slow motion", in the words of one expert. Security chiefs are concerned about bribes being demanded to release detainees. Half the weapons acquired by rebels are estimated to have been sold by army personnel while customs agents look the other way as shipments come in from Lebanon. Rumours persist of different branches of the secret police shooting at each other on clandestine operations. And officials are said to have been destroying documents recording off-the-book payments authorised by a phone call from the president's palace.

Syria's economic plight has also deepened in the last few weeks. Power cuts for several hours a day are now routine. Shops in the priciest streets of Damascus depend on generators on the pavement. Petrol is in short supply, in part because of massive use by the security forces, and the prices of heating and cooking oil have risen steeply. The president was ridiculed for praising the quality of the country's olive oil and wheat – an allusion to self-reliance. Yet even if ordinary people grumble and make do, the macroeconomic outlook is bleak. Foreign investment and tourism have collapsed. Hotels are empty. US sanctions block most international financial transactions. The EU has stopped oil purchases. Credit cards can no longer be used. And the value of the Syrian pound has been falling steeply.

The regime understands the dangers but its room for manoeuvre is diminishing: when it banned luxury imports, in November, Sunni businessmen protested. The measure was rescinded a few days later. It is hardly surprising, then, that all this is taking its toll: doctors report an increase in heart attacks, high blood pressure and other stress-related symptoms. Pharmacists are doing a brisk trade in anti-depressants. Two years ago the government introduced a smoking ban, but government offices, cafes and restaurants are still wreathed in clouds of smoke. People are also drinking more." Doctors tell you to go and watch some silly Egyptian films – anything except the news," a friend laughed.

Many now have first-hand experience of the apparatus of state repression, and describe details of underground cells, beatings and torture. It is common knowledge that Iranian security advisers are on hand with their sinister expertise in communications monitoring and riot policing. Damascus feels, and looks, like Tehran in 2009 during protests over the rigging of the presidential election. "The people who are being arrested now don't have Facebook pages," the economist Raja Abdel-Karim said wryly. "They don't care about actors, journalists and writers. The effect of the footage of the demonstrations and the killings is far greater than any quote someone like me can come up with."

Abu Ahmad, a middle-aged man who was sacked from his government job, wept as he described being at a funeral in Midan, scene of the last dubious suicide bombing, with his wife and children when the *shabiha* started shooting. State media reports only on martyrs among security personnel or regime supporters. Bodies are returned to families bearing unmistakable signs of torture. "Perhaps the worst human rights violation committed by the regime against the Syrian people is no time to mourn each martyr, no time to grieve," tweeted the blogger Razan Ghazzawi.

Elements of the anti-Assad opposition are uncomfortable with the "militarisation" of what began as a peaceful uprising inspired by the revolutions in Tunisia, Egypt and Libya. The expectation is that violence will intensify as the Free Syrian Army, composed largely of defectors, continues to grow. "If you shoot at people for months, you shouldn't be surprised when they start shooting back," observed one western diplomat. Overall, Syria's divisions appear to be deepening. "For the last 10 months, millions of people have occupied the middle ground," says Badr, a lecturer. "But Assad is leaving us with no choice."

No one can accurately predict how long the uprising will continue. On the opposition side, optimism of the will is tempered by a realisation that in the short term the balance of forces is not in their favour and is unlikely to change quickly – barring a Libyan-style foreign military intervention, which few want or expect. "Our tomorrow is in our hands," tweeted one supporter of the revolution, "or we will have no tomorrow."

The economist Abdel-Karim takes the long view. "I have no doubt the regime will be toppled. The problem is that the longer it takes, the more powerful the Islamists will become. Those who advocate violence will gain ground. It's a question of time and cost: time is getting shorter but the price is getting higher."

31 January

Occupy London's eviction is a failure for the church not the camp

REV. GILES FRASER

Institutions like St Paul's Cathedral live or die by the myths that surround and define them. In St Paul's case, several narratives remain powerful. Dominant among them is the story of the Blitz. As German bombers pummelled London with thousands of tons of high explosives, the survival of the great dome of St Paul's became a symbol of national defiance. Which is why Winston Churchill repeatedly phoned up the chief fire officer to tell him: "Whatever happens, you must save St Paul's!" I have lost count of the number of cabbies who have proudly boasted that their grandfather was a fire watcher on the roof of the cathedral. Many who have never been inside the place still think of it as their own.

A more recent narrative is that of the wedding of Charles and Diana: the people's princess in the nation's church. This narrative remains especially powerful for Americans and other visitors from overseas. Despite the fact that Westminster Abbey has the official royal connections, St Paul's has a more populist feel. "Robbing Peter to pay Paul" was the original complaint of the abbey (official name, the Collegiate Church of St Peter, Westminster) at the cost of building St Paul's, but the best way to feel the difference between them is to hear the choristers sing. St Paul's: powerful, energetic, Dionysian. Abbey: note-perfect, restrained, Apollonian.

Winter

The war, the wedding and the choristers – these are all engaging narratives, but they are mostly old ones. And they can easily play into the idea that St Paul's is a concert venue run by the National Trust. As the Bishop of London has rightly pointed out for several years now, St Paul's needs to find new stories about itself and what it's for. Which brings me to Occupy.

St Paul's is not the parish church of the City, with its banks and livery companies. It is the cathedral church for the whole of London – for Hackney and Hammersmith and Hounslow. Its constituency includes some of the most deprived inner city estates in the whole of Europe. It does not exist as a gilded dressing-up box for the 1%, nor simply as a place of protest for the 99%, but a place of prayer for the 100%.

And that means there are some huge social divisions for the church to bridge. No doubt this is a tricky business. But the response of St Paul's to the Occupy movement has been a lost opportunity to reach out to a wider demographic and thus to construct a new and compelling narrative for itself. As Occupy faces eviction, St Paul's remains trapped in stories of past glory.

Occupy does not herald the beginnings of a world revolution. But it has given many world leaders a good kick in the pants and made them know, in no uncertain terms, the degree of frustration that exists about an economic system that, among its many other crimes, rewards the rich with huge bonuses and penalises the poor with cuts to welfare.

But to St Paul's, the existence of the camp has been seen too much in terms of a little local difficulty – graffiti, hassle, problems with income and visitor numbers. This is a mistake of perspective that comes about through years of ingrained thinking that the building is the purpose of the cathedral. After a decade-long fundraising campaign to find £42m needed to clean the building, it may be inevitable that the cathedral's whole administrative infrastructure is bent towards this end. Thus it becomes just too easy to worship Christopher Wren and not the God who spoke of the rich having to give up all their possessions. Which is why the forcible eviction of Occupy will be far more a failure for the church than it will be a failure for the camp.

Last week the archbishop of York complained that the Church of England had become too middle class. Nowhere is this tension more evident than on the steps of St Paul's in recent months. For the biggest problem the cathedral has with the camp is that it has not played by the rules expected of middle-class Englishmen. Whereas the cathedral has wanted to address the financial crisis with well-meaning seminars and reports, the camp is all about non-violent direct action. It is angry, it is scruffy and it is loud. Much more like John the Baptist than your average Anglican cleric, who can be too easily conscripted within the bosom of the establishment.

The task of the church is to comfort the afflicted and afflict the comfortable. For far too long the posh bits of the church have comforted the comfortable and allowed those struggling on in poor parishes to comfort the afflicted. The Church of England has never had much stomach for afflicting anyone (except, of course, homosexuals).

With a few tents and shed loads of determination, those who have huddled outside the cathedral in the freezing cold have acted as sentinels for an idea of social justice that can be found on almost every page of the Bible but which the church has too often lost sight of.

Which is why the American author Chris Hedges has posed the challenge thus: "The Occupy movement is the force that will revitalise traditional Christianity or signal its moral, social and political irrelevance."

The Rev. Giles Fraser resigned as a canon of St.Paul's as a result of the cathedral's reaction to the Occupy protest.

7 February

A letter to Charles Dickens on his 200th birthday

CLAIRE TOMALIN

My dear Mr Dickens,

Happy 200th birthday! You yourself were not much given to celebrating anniversaries, but you did go to Stratford-upon-Avon in April 1864, with Robert Browning, Wilkie Collins and John Forster, to celebrate Shakespeare's 300th, "in peace and quiet". And on 30 January 1849, you celebrated the bicentenary of the execution of Charles I with your friend Walter Savage Landor. In so doing, you gave a clear message of how greatly you honoured Shakespeare's writing – "was there ever such a fellow!" – and how heartily you disliked bad government.

Just now, we are all reading and rereading your novels, your journalism, and your story A Christmas Carol, with its pointed message that a decent society depends on the rich learning to be generous and the poor being saved from ignorance and want.

We are talking about your heroes and your villains: Pecksniff, Squeers, Quilp, Murdstone, Headstone; your jokes and your pathos; your silly, pretty little women; your strong women – Betsey Trotwood, Peggotty – and your glorious comic women: Mrs Gamp, Mrs Todgers, Flora Finching.

We note your celebration of the strength and resilience of disabled people: Jenny Wren, whose body is twisted and painful and who makes her career as a dolls' dressmaker; Phil Squod, who can't walk straight and is disfigured, and who is hard-working, loyal and kind; Miss Flite, whose madness sees the truth; crazy Barnaby; hairless Maggie; Sloppy, whose head is too small.

We are enjoying the way you bring London to life before our eyes: streets, river, bridges, shops, dust heaps, markets, prisons. And we are reading your letters – more evidence of your unmatched reporter's eye – with their display of high spirits, enthusiasm, generosity and, it must be said, black temper at bad times.

Novels and letters give us a panoramic view of 19th-century England. But what would you make of the 21st century, the world of 2012?

In London, you would notice at once that the great black bulging dome of St Paul's, as you described it, is no longer black. The fog, the mud and the filthiest slums have gone. The absence of workhouses and the small number of street children would please you, and the lack of blatant prostitution in the Haymarket.

But you would see the same gulf between the rich, at ease enjoying their money and power, and the poor, relying on out-of-date food thrown out by supermarkets and food parcels from charities, and fearing for their jobs. And since you were obsessively interested in prisons all your life, you might be daunted by the huge increase in our prisons and number of prisoners.

A glance at the newspapers would tell you that your crooked financier, Mr Merdle, has many successors, and that Lord Decimus Tite Barnacle and his Etonian friends and relations are still running things.

The biggest human change to strike you must be that Britain is now a multilingual and multicultural society – something you might find hard to understand at first. But you would quickly see what rich material for novels this offers, and that it is being brilliantly worked by a great many writers.

Technological changes, too, you would take note of and investigate. With a sigh, you would learn about easy birth control, which could have allowed you to have no more than the three children you desired. Flying, too, which would have allowed you to travel to Australia, where you would have liked to go – another great subject for your pen.

Radio, television, cinema would all make instant appeal to you. You could be on Start the Week next Monday, on the television news today. Film producers will be calling on your mobile phone – but you will be wary, because you have always had to protect yourself from suppliants and admirers. Could you give up your famous quill pen and ink to toy with a computer? I guess you could.

You would certainly be pleased to see all of your books on sale in bookshops, and online. And to learn that we still have some libraries left, although they are under attack. You always spoke up for them, and we will ask for your support now.

How much we should like to call on you at your Wellington Street office – it's still standing – and take you for a convivial lunch, with good wine and even cigars, in a cheerful restaurant, summoning up some of your friends to join you, as they so often did on your birthday: John Forster, your biographer, the artists Maclise, Clarkson Stanfield and John Leech, the great actor Macready and the comic actor John Pritt Harley, Count D'Orsay, Wilkie Collins, and your loyal manager, George Dolby.

The ladies must come on separate days: Miss Coutts, Mrs Gaskell, invisible Nelly. But we might bring in Leo Tolstoy, who never met you but declared you the greatest novelist of the 19th century, and kept your portrait on his wall.

After which you could slip away (by helicopter?) to Gad's Hill and settle down with another cigar and some punch in the conservatory you built, specially decked out with the scarlet geraniums you liked best.

Mr Dickens, you are still, and always will be, the Inimitable. Many happy returns.

Claire Tomalin is the author of Charles Dickens: A Life.

7 February

Country Diary: When cold strikes the land

PAUL EVANS

Yellow wallflowers stunned by frost. Blackcaps jittery around empty bird feeders, perhaps the first generation of their kind without a memory of migration. Rolled tongues of wild garlic leaves poked stiffly. The ground dry with a strange violet-grey dustiness and a freeze thickened in the mud. The weather forecast was full of predictions for conflict between warm Atlantic air clashing against cold Russian air to bring snow and using the same angst-ridden tones that newsreaders speak of politics and economics in. This ill-humoured petulance pushes us further from our experience of weather.

Out of a puddle-grey sky, the wind bringing the first hint of snow was chill and sweeping in all directions. In the woods, a fall of invisible, hail-like ice crackled like static through bare branches. In the open, the wind roared darkly through pines, soughed in the ash and hissed around limes and oaks. The small birds – blue tits and great tits squeaking in the treetops and wrens plumped up like bobbles – scarpered into the undergrowth. A ratty-winged buzzard trying to get back to safe shelter was intercepted by a raven in a brief ritual skirmish. A gang of jackdaws flung themselves from a lone tree into the wind and back.

Out on the edge, between the woods and the fields, the wind ice came needling, stinging any exposed skin. It took a couple of hours before this turned to snow but it was only a loose swirl of 10p-piece-sized flakes and it softened into white quiet. The following morning the text of another world was written on the snow: trident marks of pheasant, double slots of fallow deer, dabs of rabbit. The slush trickled into drains taking the journal of that night with it. Yellow wallflowers began to recover.

13 FEBRUARY

Whitney Houston: Squandered talent of a singer who had it all

ALEXIS PETRIDIS

The American singer Whitney Houston was found drowned in a bath in a Beverly Hills hotel suite on 11 February

At the outset of her record-breaking career, Whitney Houston did not seem like the kind of artist whose life would end prematurely in a hotel room after years of drink and drug abuse. If she had any problem at all, it was that she was too squeaky clean.

No one ever doubted her talent: descended from a line of great singers, she was blessed with a voice that everyone from Smokey Robinson to Simon Cowell agreed was one of the best in the world. But her critics claimed the records she made with it erred on the safe side, tending towards pop rather than soul, the middle of the road rather than the cutting edge.

But her talent became eclipsed by a troubled personal life: Houston turned out to be far more unpredictable than initial appearances as a consummate professional suggested.

The reactions to Houston's death from her peers and fellow musicians were varied. Some expressed shock at her demise, aged

48. Others spoke of their sadness but seemed less surprised. "We all knew she had issues," said Cowell, referring to a well-publicised struggle with drink and drugs.

The singer's body was found by a member of her entourage in the bathtub of her room at the Beverly Hills Hilton on Saturday afternoon. She had been due to attend a pre-Grammy awards party at the hotel hosted by Clive Davis, the record producer and music industry executive credited with discovering her in a New York nightclub in 1983. Attempts to resuscitate her failed and she was pronounced dead at 3.55pm.

Sources claimed that prescription pill bottles were found in the room, and that Houston had looked dishevelled and disoriented when leaving a Hollywood club after a performance last week. An autopsy will be held in the next two days. "There were no obvious signs of any criminal intent," a Los Angeles police spokesman said.

Houston was born into something approaching soul music royalty. Her mother was Cissy Houston, who as leader of the Sweet Inspirations appeared on records by Wilson Pickett, Aretha Franklin and The Drifters among countless others; Dionne Warwick was her cousin.

She began her singing career in the traditional setting of a gospel church choir, and at 15 sang backing vocals on Chaka Khan's 1978 soul hit I'm Every Woman. However, she made her name dealing not in R&B but in effervescent pop songs such as I Wanna Dance With Somebody (Who Loves Me), How Will I Know and, most famously, big ballads: The Greatest Love of All and her record-breaking 12m-selling version of Dolly Parton's I Will Always Love You.

Her voice was clean and cool, full of melismatic embellishments. It spoke of dazzling virtuosity rather than raw power or emotions dredged from the depths of a troubled soul. Even when her public image spiralled out of control, her music didn't follow suit.

Released after a series of train-wreck appearances and amid lurid rumours about her drug use and the state of her marriage to fellow singer Bobby Brown, 2002's Just Whitney was as glossy and measured as her earlier albums. Its message was business as usual, despite the mounting evidence to the contrary.

Her eponymous 1985 debut album topped the US charts for a record-breaking 14 weeks, sold 25m copies worldwide and spawned three US No 1 singles. It attracted criticism for its mainstream sound at a time when hip-hop was emerging as the gritty, dominant force in black music.

Nominated in four categories at the 1986 Grammy awards, she won not the award for best R&B song or best female R&B vocal performance but best female pop vocal performance. Three years later, when she was nominated for a Soul Train award, the announcement of her name was greeted with jeers by the audience.

Houston nevertheless proved ground-breaking and influential. The single How Will I Know became a success on MTV in an era when other black artists, except for Michael Jackson, struggled to gain exposure on the channel. She was also more steely than her popular image suggested. She had worked as a model, but refused to do business with agencies that had links with apartheid-era South Africa and later became the first major musician to visit the post-apartheid country.

Her second album, 1987's Whitney, contained four US No 1 singles; she again won the best female pop vocal performance Grammy, for I Wanna Dance With Somebody (Who Loves Me) and was again overlooked in the R&B categories.

Her third album, I'm Your Baby Tonight, leaned more towards a contemporary soul sound – she asserted more control over the project than its predecessors and worked with R&B producers

Babyface and LA Reid – but seemed more interested in a career as an all-round entertainer. She focused on acting and did not release another solo album for eight years.

Her first film role, as a singer stalked by a fan in The Bodyguard in 1992, received mixed reviews, as did her contributions to its soundtrack, but they did nothing to impede her commercial success: boosted by I Will Always Love You, the soundtrack became one of the biggest selling albums in history.

Houston made further films, and in 1998 released what may have been her best album, My Love Is Your Love, noticeably tougher and more eclectic than anything she had previously put her name to, touching on reggae and hip-hop.

By then, however, her success was overshadowed by her private life, following her marriage to Brown. He later claimed that at least part of his motivation in marrying Houston in 1992 had been to soften his public image, but in effect, the opposite happened: Houston became embroiled in his drug scandals and legal problems.

In 2000, she failed to appear as scheduled at Davis's induction into the Rock and Roll Hall of Fame and her erratic behaviour led to her being fired by Burt Bacharach from the Oscars show. Her efforts at damage-limitation – including defiant interviews on the Oprah Winfrey show and later appearances in a reality series, Being Bobby Brown – only seemed to compound the perception of her as out of control. "The biggest devil is me. I'm either my best friend or my worst enemy," Houston told ABC's Diane Sawyer in an infamous 2002 interview with Brown by her side.

The couple divorced in 2007, and Houston released an album, I Look To You, two years later. It sold well, but a tour met with a mixed response, with some suggesting her lifestyle had permanently damaged her once-remarkable voice.

13–14 FEBRUARY

Heart of Midlothian

LETTERS

Sorry to hear Heart of Midlothian is having such serious problems ("In praise of...", 8 February). Perhaps a visit from the Queen of the South (Matt 12: v42) would do them good?
Tony Bashford
Carlisle

After your editorial ("In praise of... Heart of Midlothian", 8 February), Hearts lost 0–4 at home to Celtic. Thanks a bundle. As a Hearts supporter, can I ask you to write "In praise of... Hibernian" before next Sunday's Hibs-Celtic match?
Gerry Rubin
Canterbury, Kent

27 FEBRUARY

Leveson witnesses halt tabloid power grab

NICK DAVIES

The phone-hacking scandal never was simply a story about journalists behaving badly: it was and is about power.

On Monday, in an outbreak of peculiarly destructive evidence, Lord Justice Leveson's courtroom became a battlefield for two parts of a defining power struggle.

The first was short term. In the past few weeks, those who lost some of their power last summer, when the facts of the scandal finally erupted, have been trying to reclaim it. In 20 minutes of deftly understated evidence, Deputy Assistant Commissioner Sue Akers sent them packing.

Rupert Murdoch's Sun had led the attempted coup with an outburst of the kind of tabloid fist-waving which has itself been part of the distortion of power. The paper's associate editor, Trevor Kavanagh, reacted to the arrest of 10 of his colleagues by launching a ferocious attack on Scotland Yard. It was full of the rhetorical flourish of great reporting but almost devoid of facts.

Crucially, Kavanagh's claim that the Yard was engaged in a witch-hunt against legitimate journalism was based on a bold assumption that, in the Sun's history of paying sources for stories, "there is nothing disreputable and, as far as we know at this point, nothing illegal". Never pausing to question that assumption, the Daily Mail joined in, reporting the arrests under the headline "Operation Overkill" and running a column by Richard Littlejohn which compared the police to the Stasi engaging in "a sinister assault on a free press".

Lawyers, bloggers and tweeters joined in the attack. Many claimed to know that the police were investigating nothing more than reporters who had paid for a pint for a police officer. Murdoch's Times highlighted claims that the arrested journalists had been acting in the public interest. The Telegraph suggested that police had "overstepped the mark".

Akers took to the Leveson stage and challenged the assumption on which this attack was founded. She was careful to emphasise that she was still dealing in allegation, not proof. She was equally clear that this is not about paying for pints but about the alleged illegal payment by Sun journalists of "regular, frequent and sometimes significant sums of money" to officials in every area of the public life of this country, including the police, military, prisons and health service. "The current assessment of the evidence is that it reveals a network of corrupted officials," she said. And this was not about stories in the public interest, she added, but about "salacious gossip".

The truth about all this remains to be seen. Police inquiries continue – and that, in itself is what is significant. At another time, in another context, the tabloid fist, with the political muscle that lies behind it, might have succeeded in diverting the investigation. But yesterday saw a rare moment, when the power of a cynical press to distort public debate was openly challenged and stopped in its tracks.

Beyond this short-term skirmish, there is a larger and longer-term struggle of power. This is not about the conduct of reporters but about the power of the press in relation to the state, specifically about whether the Murdoch papers had reached a point where the police and the political apparatus had become compliant. Here again, Monday's evidence was peculiarly destructive.

The immediate question is whether to accept Scotland Yard's claim that police failed to expose the truth about crime at the News of the World simply because they had to focus their limited resources on counter-terrorist work where human life was at stake. The evidence disclosed by the former deputy assistant commissioner Brian Paddick and by the former deputy prime minister Lord Prescott keeps alive the alternative theory, that this was an act of favouritism.

If the priority was to protect human life, it is not clear why – as was suggested on Monday – Scotland Yard failed to take any action at all in November 2006 when it found evidence that the News of the World's investigator Glenn Mulcaire had penetrated some of the secrets of the witness protection programme, exposing the new identities of people who were being protected precisely because they were vulnerable to attack.

Equally, it is not clear how Scotland Yard saved resources by writing multiple letters to both Paddick and Prescott, denying that it held any evidence to suggest they had been victims of the hacking, when it could have sent a single letter to each man admitting that both of them were clearly named in Mulcaire's notes – something which, we now know, police had first discovered, in Prescott's case, right back on 8 August 2006, the day they arrested Mulcaire and seized his paperwork.

It is not clear how police saved resources by failing to show prosecutors the now famous "email for Neville", containing the transcripts of 35 voicemail messages, which was the clearest available evidence of Mulcaire's guilt in one of the very few cases which they chose to take to trial, concerning Gordon Taylor of the Professional Footballers Association.

Nor is it clear how they saved resources by telling Mulcaire's trial in January 2007 that he had earned only £12,300 from crime when, according to Monday's evidence, they believed he had earned more than £1m from the News of the World and hacked hundreds of victims.

Nor is there any clear explanation of why the former assistant commissioner John Yates spent two years insisting to press, public and parliament that the scandal had only a small number of victims, all of whom had been contacted by police. Monday's evidence suggested that the original inquiry compiled a "blue book", listing hundreds of victims over 24 pages, almost none of whom was approached by police.

On the question of alleged favouritism, the Leveson inquiry will surely be interested in the evidence disclosed by Paddick that when police in August 2006 went to search the News of the World, they were physically stopped from entering the accounts department and denied access to the computer and safe of the royal reporter Clive Goodman; and that the police responded by drafting a production order and then failing to use it. Paddick said: "It is not usual that a suspect would be permitted to fob the police off in this way."

Now the balance of power has changed. Leveson and Akers have their own power. The FBI may take the inquiry to News Corp headquarters in New York. Murdoch and his allies still control tens of thousands of words of news coverage every day, but they have lost control of events – for now, at least.

3 MARCH

Rage against the Raisins

LUCY MANGAN

"I just can't believe you did it, Dad, that's all," I say, putting down my spoon and shaking my head. "Me neither," says my sister, Emily, pushing her chair back from the Sunday dinner table. "I mean... well, I'm stunned."

"What's happened?" says Mum, returning from her between-courses cleaning of the oven, wiping the floor, rearranging the fridge and sending a batch of instructive memos to insurgent forces in Syria. "Is there something wrong with the pudding?"

"You could say that," I reply, staring hard at my father, into whose purview this dessert falls, as all other desserts have before it.

Emily holds up the dish of apple crumble. "Talk us through it, Dad," she says. "We're listening."

"I took a notion," he says, sadly.

"And what was that notion?" she asks, her voice dangerously kind.

"I thought, I've been making apple crumble for nigh on 30 years now..."

"And...?" I prompt as he pauses, gazing beseechingly at his wife and then – finding no more succour there than he has at any point in the past four decades – anxiously towards the door.

"And... and I thought, I'll put some raisins in it. See how that works out."

"'I'll put some raisins in it,'" I repeat, steepling my fingers and tapping them against my chin. "'See how that works out.'"

"Yes."

"And how did you think it would work out, Dad?" I ask, more in anger than in sorrow. "Did you think that your beloved daughters would greet this unexpected, unwarranted and wholly unasked for innovation with great exultation and a primitive version of the Te Deum played on spoons and Ambrosia Devon Custard tubs? Or did you think they might gaze aghast at the horror lying before them – the grotesque adulteration of the world's greatest foodstuff?"

"Perhaps you think we led lives full enough not to notice?" interjects my sister. "Or were you thinking of your secret second family, which habitually throws open the doors of welcome to any change, eagerly seeking to usher in, with a smile, the opportunity for personal, professional or emotional growth?"

"No," he admits.

"No," she says, with weary despair. "You didn't. You just 'took a notion'."

"It's not as if we ask for much, Dad," I point out. "Just dinner whenever we demand it, assembled to our specifications, cooked in the traditional manner and in quantities sufficient for two sets of leftovers to be boxed up and sent home with us. And for it to be served – hot, steaming, deliciously fragrant – to us while we debate with Mum the finer points of Coronation Street, One Born Every Minute and Call The Midwife until you have missed the start of the football."

"Traditional manner," Em says, nodding sagely. "That's the key."

"We're not expecting raisins, Dad," I say. "Not now, not ever."

"Unless it's a scone. You can put them in scones sometimes," says my sister, generously.

"OK. We'll say no more. Let the wound heal. Biscuits would help."

Dad wordlessly gets up and fetches the biscuits. You see, he's really a very good father. I wouldn't want you to get the wrong idea about that. These are only occasional lapses. He's really very good indeed.

6 March

Putin has six more years to draw level with Brezhnev

LUKE HARDING

Sunday night was Vladimir Putin's Brezhnev moment. It was when he ceased simply being an elected leader and segued towards a lifetime presidency. Having neatly sidestepped the rules by doing a stint as prime minister (no Russian leader can serve more than two consecutive presidential terms) Putin can now go on and on. Brezhnev did 18 years, Stalin 31. Despite the whispers of revolution lapping at the Kremlin's walls, who would bet against Vladimir matching Leonid?

The election – more of a coronation, really – differed from previous Russian polls in one respect. After the public outrage that followed last December's rigged parliamentary poll in Russia, Putin ordered that live web cameras be fitted in each of the country's 91,000 polling stations. Over the past 48 hours, these cameras have reproduced a fascinating slice of Russian provincial life. We have seen cleaners mopping the floors of sports-halls, election officials dozing on the job, even a jolly Saturday evening disco at a polling station in sub-zero Siberia. Chekhov, that great chronicler of the ordinary, would have cheered. But the cameras didn't do what, superficially at least, they were "intended" to do. They didn't stop the fraud. Opposition activists have posted video footage of a host of electoral violations including ballot-box stuffing and paid supporters of Putin being ferried around in an armada of buses to vote in multiple locations. Nor did the cameras catch election officials who fudged totals once polls had closed – the most common form of fraud in December.

For a long time now, "elections" in Russia's ritualised imitation democracy have lacked one crucial element: drama. This was no different. Since he announced last autumn that he was standing for a third time to be president – taking his chair back from Dmitry Medvedev – Putin's victory was a foregone conclusion. It was achieved against a bunch of uninspiring hand-picked opponents, with the invincible advantage of 24-hour pro-Putin state television. There was never any doubt about the result.

But the Putin who returns to the Kremlin in May faces a radically different Russia from the quiescent one he has ruled for the past 12 years. Although he still enjoys support in the provinces, for the protesters who will gather on Monday in their tens of thousands in Moscow's Pushkin Square he has become a figure of loathing and derision. Putin is well aware that the protests now shaking Russia are the most serious since perestroika. They are spearheaded by a sophisticated urban middle class, but they include all kinds of Russians fed up with the falsehoods, feudal condescension and galactic thieving that have characterised his regime. The demonstrators don't agree on who should replace Russia's Duracell leader. But they are united in their desire to get rid of him.

Confronted with the spectre of an Orange Revolution, Putin has two options. He can try to assuage the demonstrators with the vague promise of liberal reforms, or he can use the same lugubriously repressive KGB tactics that have served on previous occasions: black PR against key opposition figures; arrests; and the perennial libel that his enemies are traitorous western stooges and US-backed "fifth columnists". Putin appears inclined towards the second, more thuggish, option. The Kremlin has sent hundreds of riot police and grey army vans to encircle Red Square. It's hard to know if he really believes Hillary Clinton is paying the demonstrators, as he has claimed. Does he really believe the crowds will seize the Kremlin? But in recent months he has slipped further away from reality. Putin's worldview has always been one of anti-Americanism and chippy Soviet xenophobia.

For the west, Putin's return means that Moscow will once again be a tricky and often paranoid partner. Only in the job for a few weeks, the US's new ambassador in Moscow, Michael McFaul, has been on the receiving end of a nasty Kremlin smear campaign. The Kremlin has deployed one of its favoured tricks – creating a fake "McFaul" Twitter account, using an upper-case i as an l. With Putin back on the international stage, the "reset" between Barack Obama's Washington and Medvedev's Moscow will go straight in the dustbin. Relations between Britain and

Russia are also in for a bumpy ride. This autumn, an inquest will be held into the 2006 murder of Alexander Litvinenko. Scotland Yard's evidence will be presented in public for the first time – almost certainly confirming that Litvinenko was the victim of a state-sponsored assassination, sanctioned at the top levels of Russian power. Putin – president again, and inclined to see conspiracy in everything – won't like this much. But, he says, he'll still come to the London Olympics.

At home, Putin has failed to explain why he wants to stay in power for another six years, with the option of another six in 2018. In the absence of any fresh leadership, Russia faces a period of stagnation, frustration and emigration – similar to Brezhnev's Soviet Union. In international relations, it will continue to play a spoiling role, weighing up its own strategic interests against the frisson of annoying the Americans. Many of the best and brightest Russians will leave. Especially if the protests fail to deliver any tangible political change.

For those demonstrating on Monday on Pushkin Square, the difficulty is this: how to bring about the end of the regime? There is no easy answer. Putin has no desire to step down. And given the personalist nature of the system he has created there isn't anybody who can make him. Moreover, Putin understands only too well the logic of the corrupt government model he has created. Any real successor would probably seize his assets, which total billions of dollars, and put him in a jail cell.

Russian politics, then, is entering a period of uncertainty. But we can assume for now that Putin will carry on, as will those who oppose him.

12 March

M25 is UK's newest tourist attraction

PATRICK BARKHAM

Long in tedium, short in dramatic action and inescapably circular, the M25 is not so much The Road to Hell, as Chris Rea once sang, but life itself.

On a bright spring morning, however, Britain's least loved motorway was almost beneficent on Monday when viewed from the seats of the first sell-out coach tour of the 117-mile London orbital. The Middlesex County Asylum, Heathrow Terminal 5, South Mimms services, Badger's Mount; all these landmarks took on a pleasing sheen when subjected to the scrutiny of Nigel Pullen, the guide for the Brighton & Hove Bus and Coach Company's surprise hit day-trip. With his strawberry blond thatch and light-reactive glasses, Pullen looked the tour-guide part and did not disappoint with his deadpan delivery of a stream of trivia that flowed as freely as the traffic. Like estate agents or tabloid journalists, tour guides have their own peculiar argot: toilet stops are "comfort breaks", Thorpe Park's amusements are "thrill rides" while Middlesex Asylum was "now a residential development of outstanding prowess, ie, quite expensive," explained Pullen.

We joined the motorway at Godstone and climbed Reigate Hill to the dizzying heights of 220m, the most elevated spot on the orbital. "Oxygen masks will be dropping from overhead shortly," quipped Pullen. Later we passed a farm where meerkats live 20 yards from the carriageway. "They would be out to sell insurance if we were stuck in a queue," he observed.

After lunch at South Mimms, one of three service areas on the motorway, Pullen was surprised to still have a full coach. Some punters were just surprised to be there.

"I'm speechless and I don't think that's ever happened," said Julie Hayes, 45, taken on the £15 tour as a surprise by her boyfriend, James Smith. "What have I learned?" mused Hayes. "Never to go out with a man from south London." Working as a gas engineer in south London, Smith knew a thing or two about traffic jams and was fascinated by roads. "It's a random thing, it's abstract, it's eccentric. People have different interests. How do you quantify normality?"

And so we learned about the man logging every set of concrete steps on motorway edges around the country and the meaning of those enigmatic blue signs with M25 and a random number on them, which give the distance in kilometres from the Dartford tunnel for the emergency services. Like life, the M25 seduces you with its banality before subjecting you to occasional dystopian extremes. Severe weather on the nation's biggest car park in 2010 caused the Red Cross to provide blankets and tea for motorists stranded in their cars for 17 hours.

Death is also always just around the corner, from the adverts for prostate cancer awareness above the urinals in the services to the coach's own warnings about the risk of deep-vein thrombosis (hence two comfort breaks).

Just as we entered Buckinghamshire – one of six counties the motorway passes – Pullen gave an intake of breath. "This is what we've been waiting for — an incident, folks," he declared as dot-matrix signs ordered us to slow to 50mph.

"Let's see if there are bodies!" cried one passenger.

It was nothing – just a lorry on the hard shoulder.

There were several coach tours of the M25 in the 1980s and perhaps it is no coincidence that the 2012 version has proved so popular. The M25 was opened by Margaret Thatcher in 1986 and will endure as a monument to her era far longer than wars or broken unions. A visible symbol of individualism and the triumph of the car, the motorway was widened by the Blair government, building on the Iron Lady's legacy in every way. All human life was here, including the only Taco Bell restaurant in Britain and the Dartford bridge (designed by a German and opened by the Queen). There was wildlife too: five buzzards, two kestrels, a sparrowhawk and at least 100 plastic bags fluttering in trees. Clacket Lane services is "quite good for rats", pointed out Mark Weston, who works for the RSPB and was assessing whether the coach tour would interest his members.

As we completed our road to nowhere, applause broke out. "Please tell other people," implored Pullen. "Now I've got this far in my research I want to do it every week. Is that all right, Graham?" The driver shuddered. "Find another driver," he growled.

17 MARCH

Printed encyclopedias were once a rare source of knowledge, but no more

IAN JACK

There can be no clearer evidence of the swift and steep decline of the printed reference book than these figures taken from a recent New York Times: in 1990, the Encyclopedia Britannica sold 120,000 sets (each set comprising 32 volumes) in the US. That turned out to be its peak year. Since its last revision in 2010, it has sold only 8,000 sets in the same market. Another 4,000 sets lie in a warehouse. When the last of those goes, the paper-and-ink Britannica will be no more. This week its publisher announced that future editions will appear exclusively online, bringing to a close a printing history that began in Edinburgh in 1768.

The news prompted some retrospection and analysis about what the Britannica had stood for – not so much the meaning of what was inside it as what owning it signified. Aspiration was particularly remembered. Many people who bought Britannica imagined that books containing "the sum of human knowledge" opened the way to a prosperous enlightenment. That at least was the message of the salesman who called, to be treated more reverently than the other men who bent down on the doorstep to open a suitcase and speak warmly of Brasso or Mansion furniture polish. Perhaps he arrived by appointment. Certainly he was honoured as a gentler type and given a seat in the living room, where he sat for what seemed like hours, smiling at any child present and speaking of him or her as an extra special reason for the potential purchaser to part with a couple of months' wages, to be paid in weekly instalments that stretched to the crack of doom. The sacrifice would be worth it. On the tilting deck of the SS Ignorance, so the salesman implied, it was a father's duty to stand back and make sure his children had seats in the lifeboats marked Knowledge and Opportunity.

We were never a Britannica family. The salesman went away with no forms signed, leaving us to get by with what we already had: a mid-Victorian edition of Chambers Encyclopedia, Arthur Mee's Children's Encyclopedia, Pears Cyclopedia, the Vimto Book of Knowledge. All had their drawbacks. The dozen volumes of Chambers had been acquired second-hand before the war and looked splendid in their gilt-lettered spines and marbled

18 NOVEMBER 2011

Occupy London protesters outside St Paul's Cathedral. LINDA NYLIND

12 DECEMBER 2011

Edinburgh Zoo's giant male panda Yang Guang (Sunshine) prepares for his highly anticipated public debut. MURDO MACLEOD

15 JUNE 2012

Supporters of Greece's centre-right New Democracy party come to hear their leader, Antonis Samaras, address them at a final rally in Athens before the election. ANDY HALL.

27 JULY 2012

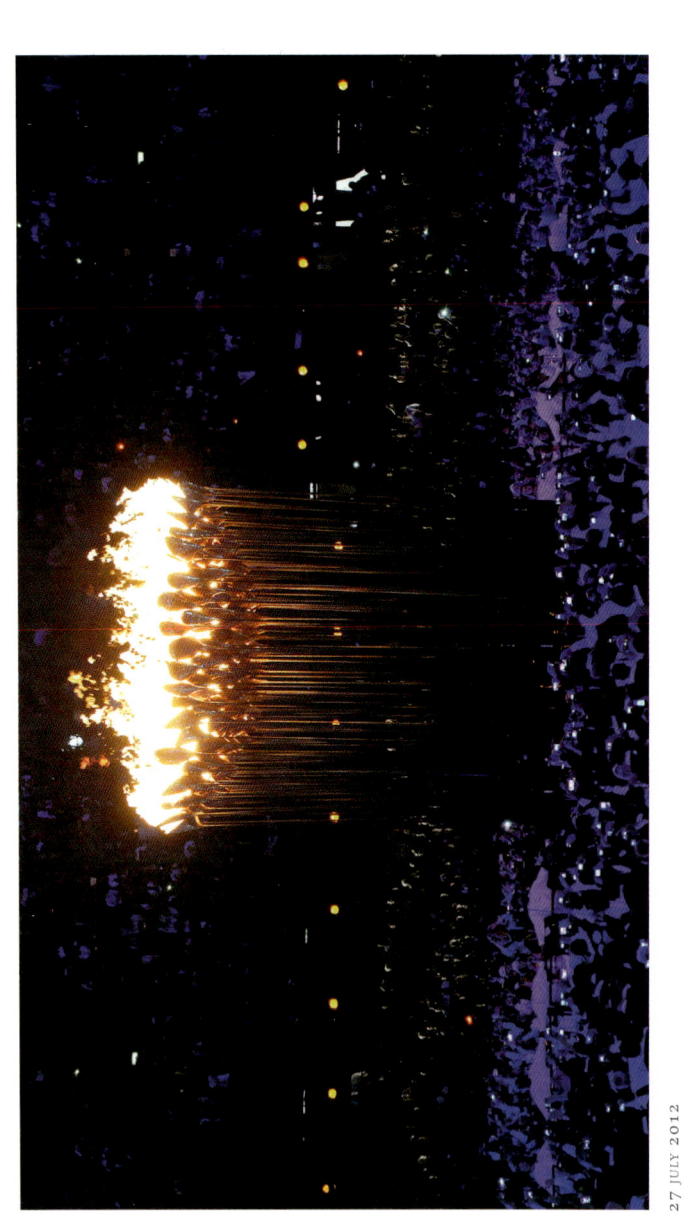

The flame is lit at the opening ceremony of the London 2012 Olympic Games. TOM JENKINS

15 AUGUST 2012

A Free Syrian Army major, Abu Hussien, who was killed by a government sniper in the neighbourhood of Bab al-Hadid in Aleppo. GHAITH ABDUL-AHAD

1 SEPTEMBER 2012

Ellie Simmonds (GB) cries during the national anthem, after receiving her gold medal for the women's S6 400m freestyle final. TOM JENKINS

18 SEPTEMBER 2012

The first flowers at the police cordon in Mottram, Greater Manchester, where two female police officers were fatally shot while responding to a routine 999 call. CHRISTOPHER THOMOND

30 SEPTEMBER 2012

Ed Miliband cufflinks on sale at the Labour party annual conference at Manchester Central. CHRISTOPHER THOMOND

endpapers, but the source of the Nile was only one of many discoveries that came too late to be found in their pages. And while the Children's Encyclopedia undeniably belonged to the 20th century, and had pictures of biplanes to prove it, its sentimentality and capricious arrangement – not so much A to Z as M to C via Y – made it a poor source of information. Pears had a nice frontispiece, Bubbles by Millais, and was good as far as it went (one volume, so not very far). All I can remember about the Vimto book was that it was really just a pamphlet of odd facts and figures, and had a detailed engraving of the Vimto factory, smoking away busily somewhere in Lancashire.

The Britannica would have been a vast improvement, but expense ruled it out. And so we contrived to look down on it – for behaving treasonably and becoming "too American" in ways my father never specified, or for its role as an ornament in houses where, we were sure, nobody ever bothered to disturb its military uprightness on bookshelves that contained no other books. Then one day my father's closest friend came to visit and announced he was about to buy the Britannica, just like that, and not because he wanted his family to do better than he had – he and his wife had no children – or because he imagined the books would enhance his social status. He would buy the Britannica to read it from beginning to end, for no other reason than to be better informed. This mission impressed my father, who himself was no slouch as an autodidact, and from then on we saw the Britannica in a kinder light.

My father's friend, Sandy Paterson, needs a little description, because almost nobody like him is still alive. Like my father, he left school at 14, served a factory apprenticeship and found work as a fitter. They had a mutual enthusiasm for cycling, which was how they met in a small Scottish border town in the 1920s when they were both far from home on a long ride; my father parked his bike against another outside a grocer's shop and went inside to find a young man standing on a biscuit box and declaiming a Burns poem to the shopkeeper. In my father's words, "That was Sandy all over", meaning it was typical of somebody who talked with lively good humour to anyone he came across, who in his 50s could still jump on to the kitchen table from a standing start, who shot rabbits, who made violins as well as played them (purely for the fun of both activities), and who dashed off high-spirited letters that made their recipients laugh.

He and his wife, who'd been crippled with arthritis as a young woman, lived in a small West Lothian village. This was shale-oil country: pink waste heaps rose above fields and woodland, while narrow-gauge railways ran through cuttings to the mines. We would visit as a family by taking a ferry and then the bus, and then climbing the stairs to their flat above the village shop. There was no electricity; not even gas. When it got dark, Sandy would pump up the Tilley lamp, which then hissed in the background all evening as the adults' conversation moved from the personal and present to the general and historic, from (say) the alleged misrule of the local landlord, the Marquess of Linlithgow, via Kant to the reign of the pharaohs. Sandy did most of the talking, but nobody minded – he was so amusing and vivid. He sucked at cigarettes and threw their ends impatiently into the fire.

I realise I'm in danger here of creating a kitsch version of a painting by Joseph Wright of Derby, but it really was as I describe. When Sandy consulted the Encyclopedia Britannica and read aloud a passage from one of its entries, the decoration on the binding would glisten in the light of the Tilley lamp. How much of it he managed to read eventually I have no idea, but he wasn't a man to give up lightly on a self-improving ambition.

Information – "the sum of human knowledge" – had a different shape then, and for 40 years after. Rather than an invisible omnipresence that can be tapped into wherever a laptop or a phone can find a signal, it lived like miser's gold in hard, little piles that were distributed unevenly throughout the country. The Britannica gave Sandy one such pile. To find another in his vicinity might have been difficult. You might have needed to take the bus all the way into Edinburgh, where the piles turned into towers in libraries, bookshops and museums. To the city, in fact, where 244 years ago a baker's son and a wigmaker's son got together to publish the first instalment of the work they called an encyclopedia, printing summaries of knowledge alphabetically in the belief that people liked to find out.

26 MARCH

Imagine if you can Richard Littlejohn's worst nightmare

STEPHEN MOSS

The Guardian held an open weekend for readers at its Kings Place offices in March

"Curiosity and conviviality, the two Cs, were our watchwords," explained Madeleine Bunting, director of the Guardian's Open Weekend. There was, in fact, a third C – compote – which Felicity Cloake was making for breakfast in front of an audience of 100 or so as I arrived. Food for thought.

It was Richard Littlejohn's worst nightmare. Not just Cloake's fruit compote and Scotch pancake – he is surely a bacon roll kind of guy – but 5,000 Guardianistas gathered under one roof at Kings

Place in London at the weekend for a festival of reasonableness. The weather was perfect, proving that God, whatever the Bible might suggest, is a centrist. Not even the Heathen's Manifesto, being concocted by philosopher Julian Baggini at the same time as the compote, made Him veil the sun or send a plague of frogs, interesting though that might have been for Paul Evans's country ramble round King's Cross.

The programme had been artfully devised to make you feel guilty. Each hour there were around 10 events. Cloake's compote was up against not just the Heathen's Manifesto but the Role of Women in the Arab Spring, Zac Goldsmith being brutally honest about the limitations of Tory environmentalism, and a talk on terrorism in Kashmir.

When it came to a choice between What is the Future of Capitalism? and The Art of the Cryptic Crossword, there could only be one winner. John Halpern, aka crossword-setter Paul, was generating waves of love among the cryptologists gathered in the Scott Room. Except for one woman, who said she found his puzzles too hard. "I see your name on a crossword and give up immediately," she said. "What is the secret of solving them? Can you give me a clue?" "Perseverance," said Halpern sternly and uncryptically.

Another woman had a more practical suggestion. "Work backwards. Look at the answers the following day, and try to get inside Paul's head." It took Halpern 10 years to become a full-time setter, and in his early days he had to do other jobs to make ends meet, including transporting urine samples from a hospital to a lab for testing. "I was the official piss-taker," he said. In a way, he still is. His crosswords aren't just puzzles; they're offbeat views of the world. He aims to subvert and satirise, and also likes to smuggle in smut. Mistakes are a catastrophe. When he placed Settle in Cumbria rather than North Yorkshire, the Guardian switchboard was jammed for days. As an act of reparation, he had to compose

Winter

a puzzle in which settle featured in every clue. "I had to settle up and settle down," he said.

The weekend was challenging to report. There were an awful lot of wannabe journalists, including James Carroll, a student doing English at Oxford, who pointed out that my scribble was not proper shorthand. "We're told you have to have shorthand now to get hired," he said. He had come as an antidote to reading Chaucer for his imminent finals. How did the weekend compare? "Faster paced, but just as difficult to understand," he said pithily. He will go far, damn him.

I also talked to the editorial team from the Boar, Warwick University's student newspaper. They were £17,000 in debt, but were pinning their hopes on a digital future, rejected the idea of a paywall and hoped to break even through advertising. "If we had a paywall we would just be talking to ourselves," said editor Natasha Clark. Perhaps they could consider a festival. There was a farmers' market next to the canal with olives, crepes and a juice bar, as well as a cheese boat where you could taste Welsh cheeses. The queues at the stalls were long; the cheese disappearing rapidly. I bumped into Alan Rusbridger, editor-in-chief of the Guardian, who was on his way to a debate about phone hacking, and told him I'd found a new business model for the media.

Forget all this digital stuff and concentrate on pancakes, smoothies, mature cheddar laced with whisky, and of course crosswords. He gave me a slightly quizzical look.

Grayson Perry, in conversation with Decca Aitkenhead, was a great hit.

"It's one of my deep fears that I might become fashionable," said Perry, a natural aphorist. "All that means is that you are on the verge of being unfashionable." Most of the questions were posed online by readers. The first came from Perry's wife. "What's for dinner?" It was Perry's birthday and at the end of the session he was presented with a cake. "Very unusual," he said. "It looks like spam and avocado."

Guardian Society editor and committed apiarist Alison Benjamin presented a talk on keeping bees in cities. "How did it go?" I asked her afterwards. "Buzzing," she said.

Because I was late I wasn't allowed into the How to Be Happy session, which made me furious. But I was cheered up by Simon Hoggart's one-man show, which was wise as well as witty. "Why have you stayed at the Guardian for 45 years?" he was asked. "Because they let you write what you want." As for parliamentary sketchwriting, it was better than working, he said. Though he admitted Welsh questions on a wet Tuesday was tough.

Steve Bell also did a brilliant turn, running through the past 30 years of British history as seen through his cartoons. Very occasionally his scabrous humour had been too much even for the Guardian's liberal editors, and he showed one cartoon from the Falklands war which had never seen the light of day. "But on the whole I've been very lucky," he said, "though I suppose I have to say that because I'm here in the editorial conference room."

Sunday morning was tough. "Did no one planning this realise we were losing an hour?" complained one frazzled woman as she bought her latte. Ed Balls, on early in the main hall, was undeterred, telling interviewer Katharine Viner he was in training to run the London marathon. Probably wise, as Labour's road back to power could be long and arduous.

The foyer at Kings Place had a stage with musicians and dancers performing energetically throughout the weekend, and there was a wall on which cartoonist Martin Rowson and illustrators Scriberia (motto "Visualise your thinking") were mapping the day's events. I noticed that when they went home on Saturday evening, a sign was pinned to it – "Please Do Not Draw On This Wall". Crowdsourcing and mutualisation evidently have their limits.

Winter

I liked the middle-aged group who spent a large part of Saturday sitting in the foyer reading the Guardian. It felt like a piece of situationist art. Everywhere you looked there were live-bloggers, tweeters and vox poppers. I vox-popped a trendy young woman reading Sartre's Iron in the Soul and asked her what she thought of the weekend. It transpired she was at Kings Place for an ultra-cool jazz concert that had nothing to do with the Guardian. "I'm probably not the best person to ask," she said with what I thought was unnecessary condescension.

I did steel myself to go to some of the more serious events. Andrew Adonis and Simon Hughes debated Britain's "progressive dilemma". I'd expected Hughes to be torn apart by the audience, but he was treated relatively gently. "You never fend people off by not coming and having the debate," he told me afterwards. "Some people think we have betrayed them, but in coalitions you can't deliver everything you want." Come the next election, he said the Lib Dems would present themselves as "a progressive party willing to do a deal with a progressive Labour party". The question of whether that other C would form part of this potential progressive alliance was left hanging.

David Miliband was less forthcoming when I buttonholed him after his session, which posed the question "Are we facing a crisis of democracy?" "Are you writing a puff piece for the Guardian?" he said. No, a hard-hitting piece of investigative reporting, I insisted.

The philosophical starting point for the weekend was: where does the Guardian go from here? How do we carry on in a world where newspapers are dying and social media are becoming ever more central? Here made manifest was the community which might eventually replace the traditional us-and-them relationship.

Clay Shirky, the pope of openness, was interviewed by Rusbridger on Sunday morning, and even a dinosaur like me who thinks this piece should be 5,000 words long and written in dactylic hexameters found him persuasive. "Every time a technology comes along that allows citizens to communicate more freely the legacy industries flip out," he said. He recalled that TV companies had likened the video recorder to the Boston Strangler when it was launched. Shirky argued that in the modern media world, loyalty was everything. Should media organisations offer a product, a service, or strive to build a different sort of organisation – a group of like-minded people who thought "God forbid that the Guardian should ever go out of business?" It was clear what shape the 300-strong audience thought the Guardian of the future should take. These, after all, were the loyalest of the loyal, people who had given up their lost-hour Sunday to ponder existential media questions and eat a lot of free cheese.

The weekend was principally about those readers, and meeting Cathy Robertson, who had come down from Liverpool with her Guardian-agnostic husband, summed up its purpose. "It's a fantastic opportunity to get closer to the paper I've read for years," she said. "After this I'll be reading it with new insight. I'll feel closer to it; feel it's even more my paper and that it reflects my values. It's been a wonderful experience."

And, with apologies to Miliband, it had. Hardly any children fell in the canal; I managed to miss Tim Dowling's banjo session; and very few people mentioned "the digital journey".

Rusbridger told me the festival would definitely be staged again next year, though that this overview would probably be compiled by multiple interactive curators and presented as a videographic.

Truly a revolution. Yet the Guardian likes to stress continuity too, and in 84-year-old Alec Gilmore, who was here with his wife Enid for the whole weekend, I found a man who embodied it. He had been reading the paper religiously (he is a Baptist minister) since he was 18.

More than that, as a boy his printer father had given him a tour of the Guardian's office and printworks in Manchester.

That was in 1938, and here he was in 2012 visiting the new digitalised, mutualised, Shirkyised Guardian. Did he recognise the Guardian across those 70-odd years? "The grammar's not what it used to be," he said, "but the spirit of the thing hasn't changed."

28 MARCH

Borat's hymn to Kazakhstan not the only anthem to stir emotions

FRANK KEATING

We are about to overdose on national anthems. And with the surfeit of brand new nations there'll be many a slip 'twixt cup and lip. At last week's shooting championships in Kuwait, the Kazakhstan gold medallist Maria Dmitrienko stood down from the podium understandably demanding an apology when the organisers not only played the wrong tune but very much the wrong words, which they had taken from the anthem parody of Sacha Baron Cohen's 2006 movie Borat which satirically hymns praise for Kazakhstan's potassium mining "and having the cleanest prostitutes in the region".

Not a one-off. At the last Euro football championship, the Swiss national broadcaster fined itself after playing, before Austria's match with Germany, the latter's national anthem containing martial lyrics last officially used during Hitler's Third Reich. Same cock-up at the 2003 Davis Cup final against Australia in Melbourne, when the Spanish players refused to begin until the band had played their modern anthem and not the 1930s triumphant serenade to General Franco's grandeur while their sports minister, Juan Antonio Gómez Angulo, flamencoed round the court in a furious stomp demanding an immediate cessation of diplomatic relations.

Most assuredly over the next few months the British are in for a record-breaking basinful of their own particular dirge to mark the Queen's jubilee. A host of other nations will vie for their own reedy, discordant wheezes to have a hearing, so between next week's world cycling championships, the football Euros and the Olympics the summer of 2012 promises a deafening jumble of jarring jingoism. All bands to the pomp.

Anthem is as anthem does. The French have the best – "*Aux armes, citoyens*" – while the Welsh choral in excelis – "*Gwlad, gwlad*" – shares the silver medal with *Nkosi Sikelel' iAfrika*, the incomparably haunting South African refrain. And with those three, you can be pretty sure each one of their sportsmen or women knows every word when called upon to sing. When that Daily Mail reporter the other day challenged the American-born so-called "plastic Brit" Tiffany Porter to recite the first verse of God Save The Queen, she should have simply replied: "Sure I will – if you begin the game by reciting, word perfect, the second verse?" Who can? So game, set and match to Tiffany.

There's nothing like the first time and I happily confess to being soulfully stirred on my initial experience of seeing the flag run up and hearing the national anthem played those four memorable times at the Tokyo Olympics in 1964 when the honours rang out successively for Lynn Davies, Mary Rand, Ken Matthews and Ann Packer. Tears for souvenirs. Four years later in Mexico City, an anthem was embedded imperishably in sporting and political legend when the American 200m medallists Tommie Smith and John Carlos listened to the Star Spangled Banner with bowed heads and raised gloved fists in pointed Black Power salute. (The Daily Mail, by the way, next day described that as "Olympic sacrilege and disgrace".)

For the Moscow Games, Mrs Thatcher banned the British team from flying its flag or playing the national anthem – something about someone invading poor little Afghanistan? By happy fluke, Britain's first gold medal was the swimmer Duncan Goodhew's. Typically, one-off Duncan had premeditated victory and, elated, clambered out of the pool – at once, gloriously, to wrap himself into a homemade red-white-and-blue Union Jack dressing-gown. Who needed flags or anthems then?

Nor, to be sure, a few days later at the athletics stadium when tough-of-the-track Steve Ovett beat hot favourite Seb Coe in the 800m final. On the podium, no flag to salute, but national drama enough when Seb, blank-eyed and shattered, leaned up to accept reluctantly a handshake from winner Steve – and the following Sunday, Clive James in the Observer gorgeously described the look on Coe's face "as if he'd just been handed a turd".

Nice Mr Lancaster's "new" fresh-faced England rugby union team of the last couple of months seemed more collectively and determinedly choral at anthem time than any recent predecessors, literally all singing from the same hymn sheet. Their roof-raising coincided with the former England hooker Brian Moore admitting on Radio 4 the other day his fond memory, for all his vauntedly proud republicanism, of singing the pre-match anthem at Twickenham with "a frisson of passion and thrill down his spine every time" – and equal, apparently, to his first hearing the Queen of the Night aria from the Magic Flute.

Balladeer Tom Jones watched a few of Wales's matches this year and each time I was touchingly reminded of that mighty fine little one-time Neath fly-half of the 1980s, Dai Parker, who unluckily missed out on a deserved Welsh cap because, in his prime, the No10 factory was still on full production. Dai was enchanted, however, late in his career, before Neath played a club game in Dublin, when he heard the announcer order both teams to line up for the national anthems. Hooray, Dai whooped to himself, at last he would experience the legendary orgasmic sensation: "I stood proudly to attention in front of the band, the tears welled, and I could feel the hairs stiffen at the nape of my neck as they began to blow" when, oh dear, out of the loudspeakers blared ruddy Tom Jones's ruddy Green, Green Grass of Home.

28 MARCH

Third time lucky: Galloway shakes up Labour relations as Bradford goes to polls

HELEN PIDD

George Galloway caused an electoral upset by winning the previously safely Labour constituency of Bradford West in a byelection on 29 March by 10,140 votes

"Check this out," said Mohammed Ali, delving into his jeans pocket. The Bradford taxi driver, 34, fished out his wallet and opened it up to reveal a Labour party membership card. "I'm terminating my direct debit and voting for George. I'm hardcore, me."

If the scenes on Bradford University campus last week were anything to go by, Labour should be a little bit worried about the byelection in Bradford West on Thursday. Their man is going up against a candidate viewed as a superstar by many of the Muslims who make up 38% of the constituency: George Galloway, a master orator and political prizefighter who has become one of the most divisive figures in British politics since his expulsion from the Labour party in 2003. No wonder Labour has sent up the big guns to shore up support: Ed Miliband visited on the weekend, following heavyweights such as Dennis Skinner, Yvette Cooper and Ed Balls.

To New Labour, Galloway is the bogeyman. But to young Asians such as Yasser Hussein, a Bradford student who had been a fan since watching a YouTube clip of Galloway savaging the US senate in 2005 over the Iraq war, he is simply a "legend" and "the only politician who tells the truth". In the student union, one woman squeals when she has her picture taken with him. Cherifa Baazis, the university's Muslim faith adviser, tells him he appeared to her in a dream: an omen. Yes, she said, he had her vote.

Labour may have held Bradford West since 1974 – with the well-liked incumbent, Marsha Singh, even managing to increase his majority to 5,763 at the 2010 election – but with Singh standing down due to ill health and Bradford in the doldrums with mass unemployment, poor schools and a city centre marred by a big black hole where a shopping centre was meant to be built, Galloway has sniffed an opportunity to return to parliament.

Since relinquishing his Bethnal Green and Bow seat and failing to win another east London constituency in 2010, Galloway has been searching for a way back into mainstream politics with his anti-war Respect party. Having failed last year to persuade Glaswegians to make him an MSP, could it be third time lucky for Gorgeous George? The bookies reckon he will finish second – it's 10/1 against him winning the seat – but Galloway said he would bet his house on doing at least that well – he insists he is "in it to win it".

Walking around Bradford West last week, it was clear many of those planning to vote for Galloway were jumping ship from Labour. No wonder the Conservative candidate – a local businesswoman, Jackie Whiteley – told the Guardian she was happy Galloway was in the race. She hopes he will take Labour votes. He's already nabbed their staff. One of Galloway's campaign managers, Naweed Hussain, switched sides 10 days ago, despite having done the same job for Singh over three general elections. He was fed up, he said, with Labour "bypassing democracy".

Singh is Sikh, having won over all colours and creeds in the multicultural constituency. But to succeed in the Bradford Labour party these days, said Hussein, you needed roots tracing back to Mirpur, a poor area of Kashmir, where around 70% of Bradford Pakistanis hail from. "Bradree" is a word you hear whispered a lot in Bradford at the moment. Loosely meaning "family", this Urdu word denotes a hierarchical system of clan politics where leaders are chosen on their connections, rather than their talents.

As Galloway sees it, Bradree has resulted in "second- and third-rate politicians particularly but not exclusively from the Labour party being elected to the city council on the basis not of ability, not of ideas, not on records of experience but on whether their father came from the same village as someone else's father 50 or 60 years ago". He gained a big cheer at one hustings when he said Bradree "has led to a situation where this city is slowly sinking and where mediocrities are running around the corridors of power and scratching each others backs and feeding each other doughnuts".

The new Labour candidate in Bradford West, criminal defence barrister Imran Hussain, 34, was born in the city to a family from Mirpur and viewed as a shoo-in for the Labour candidacy after serving as deputy council leader. Out canvassing in the Allerton ward, Hussain dismissed all talk of Bradreeism. "The concept that this election is stitched up is not true," he said. "My values are based around equality, justice and fairness, not where I am from."

He rejected claims made on the doorstep by one young constituent, 23-year-old Mahmoona Begum, who said she was voting Respect because "Labour in Bradford look after their own. I want someone who can sort out this city's schools – we're 145th out of 155 in the league tables – rather than someone who will spend his time sorting out restaurant and taxi licences for his friends."

Hussain also insisted he would not attend any public hustings alongside the other candidates because he thought knocking on doors was a better way of drumming up support – he is not scared of Galloway, he said, and his absence is not a sign of complacence.

Talking to voters on the doorstep, it is clear there is a large contingent of entrenched Labour supporters for whom the candidate is irrelevant. They are going to vote Labour, they always do. A retired couple, Alice and George Greenwood, tell Hussain he has their vote – even though they despair of the state Bradford West is in after almost 30 years of uninterrupted Labour rule. Asked what they wanted, George said simply: "We want Bradford back." Like many locals, they wanted a few concrete things: for the Westfield shopping centre to be built in the centre so they don't have to go "all the way to Keighley for decent shops"; for the Odeon cinema to be restored.

"We need someone who understands the city, someone who has really looked under the skin of Bradford rather than taking a superficial view," said Jane Vincent, a Bradford businesswoman who was so fed up with Bradford being rubbished in the media that she set up an initiative called Positive Bradford. "Whoever becomes the next Bradford West MP needs to be a strong voice for the city – not just themselves."

Vincent doesn't name names. But the most common criticism you hear about Galloway in Bradford is that he cares far more about his own profile, than Bradford. Nonsense, he said. He isn't seeking the limelight. He doesn't court the media: the media courts him. "It's you who asked to interview me. I didn't ask you. It's your cameraman who is currently shooting me through his lens."

He maintains that the murkier claims from his past never come up in Bradford – particularly the suggestion he was a friend of Saddam Hussein, and the Charity Commission ruling in 2007 which found that Galloway's appeal for Iraqi children found that at least £230,000 in the fund hailed from "improper donations" linked to Hussein's oil-for-food programme. Nor is he asked about his infamous feline impression on the 2006 edition of Celebrity Big Brother. "Big Brother has not come up once. Never. That's the kind of thing that preoccupies people in Guardian newsrooms, it's not what preoccupies the people of [Bradford West ward] Manningham."

Spring

13 April

Anders Behring Breivik: The father's story

JON HENLEY

The trial of Breivik, charged with killing 77 people in terrorist attacks in July 2011 started in Oslo on 16 April. He was found sane and sentenced to 21 years' imprisonment for terrorism and premeditated murder in August 2012 and is unlikely ever to be released.

It is an unassuming bungalow in a nondescript village on the edge of a small town in southern France. An unmade driveway runs from the road between similarly recent modest villas to the bars of a large electric gate.

The house beyond is spare but comfortable; three plump cats roam the terraced gardens, by some margin the house's most attractive feature. The floors are tiled, the sofas shiny, the television new but not flashy. That's where he saw the news.

"We had a call from Norway," he recalls. "They said, something's happening in Oslo, in the government district. We turned on the TV; we have BBC and Sky here, no Norwegian channels. We sat and watched. Glued, of course."

All that afternoon and evening, 22 July, nobody could say who it was. Eight people had died in the bombing and a far larger number – it would ultimately be 69, mostly teenagers attending a Labour party youth camp – in the subsequent mass shooting on Utøya island.

"They did not know who was responsible," he says. "They were guessing. An Islamist? Then they started to say, a typical

Norwegian. Tall, blond. They did not know who. We went to bed. It was late; we were upset. This was our home country."

It wasn't until the next morning that he turned on his computer and saw that the man who had carried out the bloodiest massacre in modern peacetime Europe had been captured, and that his name was Anders Behring Breivik, his son.

He is not a large man, Jens Breivik. Cautious. Precise. White hair, steel-rimmed specs, sober jumper; ask casting for a 76-year-old retired Norwegian diplomat and you surely wouldn't get better. Visibly ill at ease, for at least the first hour.

"I was so... shocked, I did not know what to do," he says. "I couldn't... I was unable to do anything. I sat with my head in my hands. It was a terrible moment. I just could not face it. The media got here that evening and I hid. My wife told them I was in Spain."

Several months later, with his son in the dock – first judged criminally insane, now declared sane enough to face trial and jail – he still feels "terrible. Such pain. Constantly, I am reminded who I am. In the first few weeks, I thought seriously of taking my own life. I've lost the retirement I always imagined; that's gone. I will forever be asking how a man could possibly develop such thoughts. And could I have done something?"

It may not, of course, have made the slightest difference. But could he?

Others, to Breivik's distress, have not been slow to suggest that he could. Assorted commentators have called him "selfish", "narcissistic", "a terrible father". Katharine Birbalsingh, who describes herself as "Britain's most outspoken and controversial teacher", told the Telegraph she was certain his failings had sown the seeds of his son's madness.

It is, to be fair, not a very straightforward story. Nor, maybe, for those who wish to judge such things, a very admirable one. For

Spring

Jens Breivik, sitting stiffly at his dining-room table confronting roads travelled and turnings taken, it is certainly not easy to tell.

He and Wenche Behring had been together for two years when Anders was born on 13 February 1979. Both had been married before: Jens, then economic affairs counsellor at the Norwegian embassy in Lancaster Gate (his second tour in London), had three children from his first marriage, which had lasted nearly 13 years; Behring, a nurse, had a young daughter, Elisabeth, with her previous husband, who was Swedish.

The couple separated within a year of Anders's birth. "I don't think," says Breivik, cautiously, "she was really interested in marriage. She was an... unusual person. I think what she wanted to be was a single mother. She just left, anyway, went to Oslo with Anders and her daughter. Didn't want me to see my son. You get help in Norway, as a single mother."

(Behring, who later would marry a Norwegian army captain, has never given her side of this story, consistently refusing all media interviews. In a conversation with the psychiatrists who evaluated Anders, leaked to the Norwegian press, she has said only that she first noticed signs of her son's "paranoid delusions" in 2006.)

Breivik senior, meanwhile, stayed in London. Behring reluctantly brought the infant Anders from Oslo to see him, staying at one stage for several months even though the marriage was beyond repair. Then in 1983, Breivik got married, for a third time – to Tove, a colleague – and was posted to the OECD in Paris, subsequently transferring to the Norwegian embassy there.

Anders liked Tove, his new stepmother, and in fact stayed in touch with her until just before the attacks. But soon after the couple arrived in France, Breivik says, it became clear that Anders, now four, was not faring well in Oslo.

"There was a formal report, in 1983, from the Norwegian childcare authorities," he says. "They recommended he should be moved. They said his relationship with his mother, her emotional incapacity to care for him, made it harmful for him to stay. But it was very difficult; Wenche would not admit to any problems. She wouldn't talk to me."

Breivik and his wife applied through the Norwegian courts for custody, hoping the report would work in their favour. It didn't. "This I do not understand, and nor do many people in Norway," Breivik says. "There was an official report saying my son was being harmed by living with his mother. But in Norway, the presumption is always with the mother."

Despite that ruling, father and son appear to have got on fairly well when Anders was still a young child. "In Paris, he visited quite often," Breivik says. "He travelled as an unaccompanied minor; I'd meet him at the airport." Anders stayed at Breivik's embassy apartment, on rue Spontini in the 16th arrondissement; there were summer holidays at a cottage in the Normandy countryside, 10 minutes from the sea at Cabourg.

Anders describes this period in his 1,500-page online "manifesto", remarking that he had "a good relationship with [his father] and his new wife at the time, until I was 15." His upbringing was "privileged", he wrote, in "a typical Norwegian middle class family", with "responsible and intelligent people around me… and no negative experiences" (although he now regretted a "lack of discipline".)

In 1990, Breivik returned to Oslo. "We had what I think anyone would call a normal relationship between a divorced father and his son," he confirms. "He came to my house several times a week, and at weekends. I had a small chalet in southern Norway; he stayed there often, too." There was a trip to the Tivoli amusement park, in Copenhagen, when Anders was 13.

How does he remember his son at that time? Breivik considers. "An ordinary boy. Maybe… not quite ordinary. He was never

Spring

very communicative; quite withdrawn. He wouldn't talk about his mother, home, school. He came to my place to relax, have a good meal, then – when he was a bit older – to go out afterwards into the city centre to meet his friends."

But by this time Breivik's marriage to Tove was breaking up, too. He is, understandably, reluctant to talk about this; three failed marriages reflect well on no one. This one finally collapsed, he says, when he asked her to contact Alcoholics Anonymous.

Then in 1992 he met Wanda, his fourth and current wife; they married three years later. Wanda "saved my life. Really. I was in a bad way when I met her. Three marriages, three divorces. Wanda's strong. She's helped put me back together. She's helping me through this, too. Though I'm not sure, frankly, that either of us will ever truly get through it."

With his marriage to Wanda, however, the children from Breivik's first marriage decided they wanted nothing further to do with their father. "They're angry with me," he says, flatly. "They think I have made too many... mistakes. Done too many stupid things."

Anders, too, cut loose around the same time, in 1995. Over the previous two or three years, things had become increasingly difficult. In his manifesto, the killer blames his father for the estrangement, saying Breivik "isolated himself when I was 15. He was not happy with my 'graffiti' phase from 13 to 16. He has four children, but has cut off contact with all of them. So I think it is pretty clear who is at fault."

Breivik disputes this. "It's true I was angry," he says. "Several times the police called me to say he had sprayed buildings, trains, buses. He was also shoplifting. But I was always willing to see him, and he knew that. It was Anders who cut it off. His decision, not mine. He was 16, building his own life. He had his hip-hop, too."

Wanda says that the couple saw Anders "regularly" before he finally disappeared. "We invited him to supper, once a fortnight," she says. "I tried with Anders; I really tried. I knew about teenage boys, I knew what interests them. He was always: don't know. Don't care."

Whoever took the initiative, father and son met for the last time in 1995. "He borrowed a jacket from me for his confirmation," says Breivik. "He told me he aimed to study in the States, on an exchange. When I heard no more from him, I thought that was what he had done." Breivik kept sending money, some £200 a month, to Anders's mother.

The two were in contact, briefly, just once more. In 2005, Breivik had a phone call out of the blue. "He told me he was doing well," Breivik says. "He had his own company, data processing, two employees. He didn't want anything; he was just anxious to tell me he was doing well and was happy. I had health problems; I said I was pleased to hear from him, and we should stay in touch. We never did."

In his manifesto, Anders claimed the business was the first step in a nine-year plan leading to the 22 July attacks; a front "for the purpose of financing resistance/liberation-related military operations". Subsequent police inquiries have shown much of this to be delusional – fabulation or wild exaggeration.

This trial will, perhaps, shed some light on what so warped Anders Behring Breivik's perceptions that he was prepared to slaughter 77 of his fellow countrymen in order to "save Norway and western Europe from cultural Marxism and a Muslim takeover".

But in his modest bungalow in France, Jens Breivik lives haunted by the part he may have played in the creation of a monster. Last month Norwegian police, assisted by French officers, spent nearly 13 hours interviewing him in Carcassonne.

Spring

The psychiatric report on his son makes clear, he stresses, "that I could have done nothing to prevent what happened." Moreover, he's convinced "I really did all I could when he was small." Maybe, it's true, he could have tried harder to stay in touch later, after 1995.

"But I honestly thought he was okay. Quiet, awkward, but not... abnormal. If he didn't want to see me, there wasn't really much I could do. I had no leverage. And anyway, after that he seemed successful, with his own business, employees. That was good, wasn't it?"

Yet however much he protests, however much he tried or didn't try, Breivik's regrets, one senses, run deeper. He knows his choices have not always been the wisest. Of his relationship with Wenche Behring, he now says: "I was stupid not to see I was being used." His third marriage, to Tove, embarked upon while the wreckage of the second was still smouldering, was also "not perhaps the right step".

In a phrase in his manifesto that, for once, might just come somewhere close to the truth, Anders sums his father up as "just not very good with people". While the photographer is busy with Breivik outside, Wanda seeks to explain.

Her husband is not someone who talks easily, she says. "I ask him to try, to let his feelings out; he really can't. He's trying to write them down. Sometimes, it's true, he has just... followed his feelings. And sometimes he has done things that are not in his own best interests, not at all, so as not to hurt or upset people. But he is a good man."

Both Breivik and Wanda are sure he will never be able to return to Norway. "Some people do feel I am guilty," he says. "I do have feelings of shame, disgrace. Damnation. Maybe... maybe I am to blame."

He has not kept any photographs of Anders, not even as a small boy, for a long time. He moved around a great deal with his job, of course. "But also," he says, "sometimes, when you have made a very serious mistake, you just want to forget it. Not be reminded."

18 April

François Hollande: From marshmallow man to Sarkozy's nemesis

ANGELIQUE CHRISAFIS

In a gymnasium in a poor mixed suburb in the north of Paris, the crowd chanted "François president! François president!" A small, bespectacled figure took to the stage with outstretched arms. "I don't want ghettos in the republic, not ghettos for the poor, not ghettos for the rich!" hammered the Socialist François Hollande, his voice hoarse from a bruising schedule of campaign rallies fuelled by honey throat-lozenges.

Shaking fists in front of his chest, waving his right arm and leaning on his lectern, he performed his trademark mimicry of the gestures of the last Socialist president, François Mitterrand, as if through body language, he could channel the legacy of the 1980s and win this Sunday's French presidential election for the left for the first time since 1988.

This rural MP, fiscal policy wonk and self-styled Mr Normal remains the pollsters' favourite to become the next president. In terms of personality, he is the ultimate anti-Sarkozy. If the pres-

Spring

idential race is a battle to elect a republican monarch from an array of flamboyant ego-driven personas, the plodding, managerial Hollande is its antithesis. He reasons that after five years of the testosterone-fuelled, frenetic, rightwing Nicolas Sarkozy, and with an economic crisis threatening France, this is the moment for a Mr Ordinary.

A former Socialist party leader, he is a jovial, wise-cracking believer in consensus politics, who aides say never loses his rag and who so hates fights that he was once nicknamed "the marshmallow" within his own party, or "Flanby", after a wobbly caramel pudding. When, at the start of the year, Hollande still zipped around Paris on his sensible, three-wheeler scooter, one MP in his party warned he looked "more like a pizza delivery man" than the next president.

Hollande's placidity and refusal to stray from his tranquil path on the campaign trail despite Sarkozy's verbal attacks, has sometimes frustrated even his own supporters. "I wish he would just let go and savage Sarko," said one suburban Hollande voter. In private and with journalists, Hollande still cracks his quick-fire gags, but some fear that his deadly serious attempt to "presidentialise" himself by toning down his sense of humour has appeared to drain him of charisma.

"His is calming, the opposite of Sarkozy, that's key," insisted Bernard Cazeneuve, the Socialist mayor of Cherbourg and one of his campaign team.

At lunch with correspondents, Hollande slips off his modest wrist-watch and taps it on the table as if checking it still works. Deliberate or not, it's a canny contrast with Sarkozy, the "president of bling", who at an open-air rally in Paris this week was seen tucking his £45,000 watch into his pocket for safe-keeping.

Asked about fears that he was too bland to be president, Hollande said: "Everyone says François Mitterrand had huge charisma. But before he was president they used to call him badly dressed, old, archaic and say he knew nothing about the economy... until the day he was elected. It's called universal suffrage. When you're elected, you become the person that embodies France. That changes everything."

Hollande's rise has been tortoise-like, and to his opponents, unexpected. For more than 30 years, he has held some of the most thankless jobs in French leftwing politics. For more than a decade, he was leader of the fractious Socialist party, where he once reportedly likened the constant task of calming of ego spats and political rows to clearing up dog turds.

For years, he fought an uphill battle to establish a provincial base in the enemy territory of Corrèze in south-west France, then the rural fiefdom of rightwing Jacques Chirac. After a marathon of hand-shaking at village markets and local politicking, Hollande was elected MP in Corrèze, then mayor of Tulle, a rural town famous for accordions and arms-making, and finally leader of Corrèze's general council, inheriting the poisoned chalice of the most indebted department in France. He would regularly make the 600mile round trip from his Paris home by car.

Leather briefcase in hand and portly frame bursting out of ill-fitting suits, he smoothed cracks behind the scenes in a party so volatile he was once nicknamed "Meccano-builder" for all the bridges he mended. In 2007, he watched the mother of his four children, Ségolène Royal, run for the presidency in his place while their relationship broke down in what one member of his party called a "Shakespearian drama".

Only three years ago, Hollande was in the political wilderness. He had quit the party leadership and was seen as such a rank outsider that his name barely featured in the polls.

Then last May, the then head of the International Monetary Fund, Dominique Strauss-Kahn, seen as obvious Socialist presidential candidate, was arrested in New York over an alleged attempted rape of a hotel maid and saw his political hopes collapse.

Hollande had already begun a campaign to run as an "ordinary guy" against Strauss-Kahn. He had astounded friends by losing 12kg (26lb) in the most famous crash diet in French politics and invested in his first made-to-measure suits.

With Strauss-Kahn out of the contest, Hollande won the Socialist primary race. His supporters argued that as a moderate from the centre ground of the Socialist party, he was the only one who could beat Sarkozy. He promised to tackle the inequalities in society, give some hope back to youths battered by failing schools and high unemployment, and raise taxes on the rich.

Stéphane Le Foll, the Socialist MEP who has been one of Hollande's closest aides for 17 years, and is co-directing his campaign, said Hollande had quietly planned his presidential bid for 10 years. "He has always been underestimated. He's affable, nice, close to ordinary people and very urbane. Some say he's too nice, but behind that nice side, there's a redoubtable political animal. He's coherent: in 17 years, I've never seen him change his view on the fundamentals." He said Hollande used jokes to seduce those around him.

Within the Socialist party, Hollande has always had a moderate, social-democrat brand of politics. He is not seen as an ideologue or a tub-thumping visionary but a managerial politician, an economic policy nerd. He was once a state auditor and taught economics, and believes France, which is facing a spiralling debt crisis, must balance its books. His manifesto contains none of the high-spending promises of French Socialists gone by, and no raising of the minimum wage. Conscious of the public anger at banking, he declared his enemy was the faceless world of finance, and has promised a 75% tax on income over €1m.

The man who, on entering a room insists on painstakingly pressing everyone's palms, recently declared, "I like people," saying others, namely Sarkozy, preferred money.

In French presidential myth-making, a candidate's childhood is key. Sarkozy has stressed the trauma of his parents' divorce, and his absent father. Hollande hates psychobabble. But his relationship with his authoritarian father, who once ran for election for the extreme-right, is seen as key.

Born in Normandy, Hollande grew up in a smart suburb of Rouen. His father was a doctor who dabbled in property and ran for local election on a far-right ticket in 1959. Hollande's surname is believed to come from Calvinist ancestors who escaped the Netherlands in the 16th century and took the name of their old country. He was brought up a Catholic but quietly rebelled against the strict religious brothers chosen by his father to educate him.

In 1968, when Hollande was 13, his father abruptly moved the family to Neuilly, the moneyed suburb west of Paris, with no warning, binning the contents of Hollande's bedroom, including his prized Dinky cars collection. His elder brother who rebelled was sent to a tough Catholic boarding school as a lesson.

Hollande's jokes and joviality are a way of dodging conflict, his biographer Serge Raffy believes. "His relationship with authority is linked to the way he constantly had to duck and dive against the impetuous, authoritarian character of his father. It was his only way to survive." At a vast campaign rally in January, Hollande made a rare reference to his father: "The left wasn't my heritage, I chose it."

Hollande's mother, by contrast, was a cheery presence and Mitterrand fan who voted left. She once told French TV that Hollande had said as a child he wanted to be president but that no one had believed him. A senior French journalist who went to

Spring

school with Hollande remembers a smiley, rotund teenager with glasses and a big group of friends.

Hollande is a career politician who, from his first teenage candidacy as classroom rep and then student union leader, was interested in elections and how to win them. Unlike Sarkozy, he studied at the Ecole Nationale d'Administration (ENA), France's graduate school for civil servants, known as the "factory of the elite".

Dominique Villemot, a lawyer friend from student days, said Hollande didn't fit the typical ENA image of Parisian technocrat "cut off from reality" but was more shaped by his venture into rural politics. Aged 27, Hollande took an advisory post at the Elysée when Mitterrand became president. He was never a Mitterrand protege, but took a pearl of wisdom from him: to reach the top in French politics, you need a rural base.

When the young Hollande first ran against the mighty Jacques Chirac in Corrèze, Chirac dismissed him as "less known than Mitterrand's labrador". Hollande turned it into his own gag at a rally and succeeded in getting his name in the papers.

Villemot, who now advises Hollande, said: "His flat was always pretty sparse, the furniture simple. He didn't have a car, he had a scooter. In Corrèze, he slept in a little room above his office. He never wore smart suits, even at ENA. That's part of his personality."

Hollande met Royal at ENA. As MPs in the 1980s and 90s, they became the first power-couple of the French parliament, resolutely opposed to the bourgeois institution of marriage but inviting the cameras into their home to photograph them having breakfast with their four children.

Then everything imploded at the last presidential election in 2007. Hollande had met someone else, the political journalist Valérie Trierweiler, who covered the Socialist party for Paris Match. Royal ran as the Socialists' first woman presidential candidate, trampling his ambitions. The couple's secret break-up and personal rivalry at the heart of the party machine was in part blamed for losing the election. Now Trierweiler, Hollande's partner, has an office in his campaign headquarters and he is often seen arm in arm with her.

Sarkozy, who entered parliament as an MP on the same day as Hollande in 1988, once likened him to a sugar cube, arguing he "dissolves in water". He has attacked Hollande for being afraid to say no, unable to make a decision. One senior Socialist, who in the past opposed Hollande within the party, said he was intelligent and demanding, though never grandiose or cruel.

Hollande once told a magazine he preferred being nice "because in the films, the bad guys always lose". A recent poll showed a majority of French people saw him as nice, but less than half saw him as presidential. He quipped that presidential stature came when you were elected, but becoming nice was less certain.

24 APRIL

The hell of Russian bureaucracy

MIRIAM ELDER

A few weeks ago, I got to a dinner party, promptly hid myself in the host's bedroom for 15 minutes and collapsed into a cascade of tears. The cause? Dry cleaning.

On the face of it, Moscow has most of the trappings of modern, European life. There are cafes, even non-smoking ones, where you can order a flat white. There are websites that will deliver your weekly supplies of hummus, fresh apricots and rich French

Spring

cheeses. And there are dry cleaners which, in theory, will whisk your clothes away to some unseen locale and steam them spotless in the blink of an eye.

They key phrase here is, of course, "in theory". In practice, daily life in Russia is an endless battle against shopkeepers and waiters steeped in the best traditions of Soviet-era manners (walk into a shop and the first thing you'll hear is: "Girl! What do you want?"); those fresh fruits will probably be black by the time they make it through the city's gridlocked, muddy streets. And dry cleaning – that's a whole other experience altogether.

It goes something like this. You get to the dry cleaner. There's a woman, let's call her Oksana Alexandrovna, sitting behind a low counter, row upon row of clothes in plastic wrap behind her. She's dealing with a customer. This gives you time to reflect. "Russia is amazing," you think. "The changes this place has seen – 25 years ago, would I even be standing in a shop like this? The lady in front of me certainly wouldn't have been handing in a MaxMara dress to clean. A true middle-class experience. In Russia. I'm living it."

By now, about 12 minutes have passed. Oksana Alexandrovna is caressing the woman's clothes. Much paperwork is exchanged. A stamp machine is placed on the counter. You wonder what is happening – but soon enough you will know.

Finally, it is your turn. You put six items of clothing on the counter. Oksana Alexandrovna lets out a sigh. This would be the point where you would normally get your receipt and go. But this is Russia. It's time to get to work. A huge stack of forms emerges. Oksana Alexandrovna takes a cursory glance at your clothes. Then the examination – and the detailed documentation – begins. This black H&M sweater is not a black H&M sweater. It is, in her detailed notes on a paper titled "Receipt-Contract Series KA for the Services of Dry and Wet Cleaning", "a black women's sweater with quarter sleeves made by H&M in Cambodia". Next, there are 20 boxes that could be ticked. Is this sweater soiled? Is it mildly soiled? Very soiled? Perhaps it is corroded? Yellowed? Marred by catches in the thread? All this, and more, is possible. The appropriate boxes are ticked. But that is not all – a further line leaves room for "Other Defects and Notes". By now, you have spent less time wearing the sweater than Oksana Alexandrovna has spent examining it. This process is repeated five more times. Except with that white cardigan that has 11 buttons. Why do you know it has 11 buttons? Because Oksana Alexandrovna has counted each and every button. Twice.

The process is almost over. Oksana Alexandrovna asks you to sign your name. Five times. She firmly stamps each page (for your detailed receipt has now run to two). You clutch the document, hand over 1,500 roubles (£32), say goodbye to that 40 minutes of your life, and go on with your day.

If only that were the end of this tale. Some time wasted, nothing more. But five days later, you must pick up said clothes. And that's where the real problems can emerge. In between the dropping-off and the picking-up of the clothes, Russia had a presidential election. Riot police, troops and military trucks poured through Moscow. Protesters took to the streets crying foul, dismayed at the prospect of living another six years under Vladimir Putin. And I lost my dry-cleaning receipt.

This is the horror of horrors. Oksana Alexandrovna was not pleased. This meant more paperwork, more signatures, more stamps. The first thing demanded – my passport. "What does my passport have to do with my dry cleaning?"

"Passport!"

I handed it over. She wrote down every bit of information, making sure to note my registration (every resident of and visitor to Russia must make police aware of their residence, a Soviet holdover that shows no sign of disappearing). Next, I was to write down descriptions of each item of clothing I had handed in. "Five black sweaters and one white one." "Not good enough!" "The white sweater had 11 buttons?" "Please take this more seriously!" More signatures. More stamps. "You've stolen more than an hour of my life!" I yelled. Another passport check. "Give me my clothes!" Forty minutes later, I had them in hand. My nerves were somewhere else entirely.

The frustration stems not just from the loss of time but from the knowledge that despite Russians' love of documents, stamps, identification procedures and painstaking handwritten notetaking, it all means nothing. The country's endless bureaucracy spreads its tentacles everywhere. No good concerts in Moscow? "Just try filling out the forms to get equipment into the country," one promoter told me (not to mention the bribery needed to get things through customs). Want to order a taxi by telephone? You will be asked a series of questions that appear to have nothing to do with the order. And 20 minutes later, you will be called and asked them again. Need to use an ATM? Get ready to press a half-dozen buttons (Which language would you like to speak? Which account would you like to use? Roubles or dollars? What size notes do you need? You want to take out more than $100? Then repeat the process again because every ATM inexplicably has a cap).

What it comes down to is the bureaucracy doesn't work. Let's say I stole some other woman's clothes. Despite the forms and the stamps, the (double) passport check and notes, the woman would have no recourse. Court system? Busted. Police? Corrupt. I spent nearly two hours of my life filling out forms – in order, need I remind you, to freshen up some cheap sweaters – because that's simply what has always been done.

Take the students at Moscow State University, Russia's most prestigious institution of higher learning. Founded in 1755, it was home to Anton Chekhov and Mikhail Gorbachev, nearly a dozen Nobel laureates and an untold number of scientists. Last week, the university let it be known that any student fees paid through MI-Bank were lost, as the bank had filed for bankruptcy. One can imagine the endless paperwork (and stamp stamping!) required to make such payments. But all trace of the payments has been lost. The school's solution? The students must pay again.

This is what has turned many people in Moscow against Putin. It's not just him, but the system – one that began corroding in Soviet times, before a flicker of hope emerged with the fall of the Soviet Union, only to settle back into a non-functioning corrupt bureaucratic nightmare that now has the added bonus of wheedling itself into the private sector. So much has changed – and so much has not.

25 APRIL

Etan Patz: The tragedy that still haunts me

HADLEY FREEMAN

Last Thursday, the pickaxes arrived. On Prince Street in the SoHo area of downtown Manhattan, 40 investigators turned up, armed with equipment to dig up a basement beneath what is now a jeans store. To New York's shock, sadness and relief, it was possible that, less than a block from where his parents lived, Etan Patz had been found.

Almost 30 years before Madeleine McCann disappeared from a hotel bed in Praia da Luz, a six-year-old boy named Etan Patz

Spring

(pronounced Ay-tahn Pay-ts) walked out of his parents' home in SoHo, wearing his beloved pilot's cap and a corduroy jacket. It was the first time he had been allowed to go to school on his own and his parents, Stanley and Julie, had only relented, reluctantly, after much pleading from their son. It was not until the end of the day that they learned he had never made it to school. He never even boarded the school bus. On 25 May 1979, Etan Patz disappeared and his case sparked as much national attention and ensuing hysteria as Madeleine McCann's would decades later.

The Patz parents have never moved house or changed their phone number, in the hope that, one day, Etan would find his way home. They watched from their window last week as the investigators removed concrete and bricks from the basement of the nearby building which had, according to the New York Post, been used as a play area for local children when Etan was little. They had to listen to the noises of investigators searching for their son's remains while they stayed behind a locked door, still waiting for Etan.

Although Etan himself disappeared, his shadow was long and dark, and all children, including me, who grew up in New York in the late 70s and early 80s lived under it. Stanley Patz was a photographer and pictures of his son – tender, unforgettable and, suddenly, ubiquitous – filled the city. Everyone knew what Etan looked like, but no one would see him again. Even if your parents protected you from the specifics of Etan's disappearance, you felt its ramifications, either through your parents being more vigilant – "His vanishing ushered in the modern era of permanently heightened alert about the dangers of letting children walk the streets alone," as the New York Times put it – or through the new focus on missing children in general.

Putting photos of missing children on the backs of milk cartons was just one of the developments to come out of Etan's disappearance – another was the establishment of National Missing Children's Day on 25 May, the day he vanished – and he, of course, was one of the first children to feature.

As soon as I was old enough to read, I studied the milk carton notices carefully as I ate my breakfast. I would always check to see whether the missing child lived in New York, like I did, whether they had a sister, like I did. The more different they were from me, I'd tell myself, the safer I was.

I remember learning about Etan very well, over my Cheerios. He was from New York. He had a sister. He was Jewish, too. He was born six years before me, but it felt close enough. If the kidnapping of Etan Patz woke up New York parents to the dangers of the street, it taught me that mothers and fathers could not always protect their children, children just like me.

While Stan and Julie Patz have done much to try to prevent other parents from going through what they have suffered, their pursuit for justice for their own son has consisted of nothing but more pain and disappointment. To help him get through the first three years of his son's disappearance, Stan tried to convince himself that Etan had been taken by "a deranged but well-intentioned motherly type [who] was loving Etan somewhere," Lisa R Cohen writes in her 2009 book on the case, After Etan: The Missing Child Case that Held America Captive. This self-sustaining myth soon collapsed and he, along with many others, strongly suspected José Ramos, a drifter who had known one of Etan's babysitters. Ramos admitted in 1982 he had tried to molest the little boy the day he disappeared but insisted he hadn't killed him. Ramos has been in prison since 1987 for other abuses but no one could connect him to Etan's murder, and there was no body in any case. But every year, on Etan's birthday and on the anniversary of his disappearance, Stan sends Ramos a lost child poster of Etan and writes on the back: "What did you do to my little boy?"

Spring

Last week, a police dog showed signs of smelling human remains in the basement and another suspect, a local handyman who had known Etan, emerged when he blurted out: "What if the body was moved?" But by Tuesday, there was disappointment, again. Nothing had been found in the basement. The investigators went home. Stan and Julie stayed inside.

According to the US Department of Justice, 2,185 children are reported missing in America every single day. In a fairer world, all would get the attention that Etan did. In a fair world, none would vanish at all. For whatever reason, one case occasionally emerges that haunts a generation. While the other children of their era grow up, become adults and have children of their own, those lost few are frozen forever in the photographs their desperate parents release to the media, their toothy childish smiles the only replies to unanswered questions.

1 MAY

A Month in Ambridge

NANCY BANKS-SMITH

After April, you might reasonably expect the Am to burst its banks and flood Ambridge with endangered native crayfish. Not a bit of it. The thwack of leather on willow is heard at the Jack Woolley pavilion and they are dancing round the maypole on the village green. No wonder this blessed plot, this earth, this Ambridge, is so attractive to outsiders.

Two of them turned up last week, stole everything not nailed down and left Adam for dead. He was unconscious for days and there was an unspoken dread that he might be a vegetable. Which is, sadly, rather appropriate.

Radio listeners are in Adam's position. We cannot see but we are abnormally sensitive to the fluid light and shade in any voice. Listening to Jill Archer, for instance (played by Patricia Greene for 55 years), is like hearing a hidden songbird. Four generations of Archer women now gathered around Adam like a murmuration of starlings, and chattered to him for four days. Until he finally groaned and regained consciousness like a grumpy man roused by the dawn chorus. Sometimes, as Dorothy Parker mentioned, it is just simpler to live.

Ambridge maidens are historically dazzled by bounders from the bright lights of Borchester. Bounders always have names like Leon or Jude and really annoying jobs, while Ambridge men are called Bill or Ben and have a leg at each corner. Carl – "He works for IT in car components" – qualifies on all counts. This month, he slithered in and seduced the vicar's guileless daughter Amy. I never liked the man. Carl, it turns out, already has a wife, described as "a hotshot lawyer". At this point, you give a low admiring whistle. A snake, agreed, but a snake with nerves of steel.

Good news. Or perhaps not. Alice, who has the brains of a guinea fowl, has graduated as an aeronautical engineer. Those exams are really getting too easy.

Spring

5–10 MAY

Les regles du subjonctif

LETTERS

Si François Hollande est élu président, moi, je pars en France (Report, 3 May).
Phil Jones
Eastington, Gloucestershire

If Phil Jones were to move to France (Letters, 5 May), he'd need to brush up on his subjunctives.
Margaret O'Hare
St Albans, Hertfordshire

On 5 May you printed a letter from Phil Jones in perfectly correct French. Two days later, you printed one from Margaret O'Hare (Letters, 7 May) suggesting Mr Jones should have used the subjunctive. In neither French nor English does the sentence "If François Hollande is elected president, I'm leaving for France" require a subjunctive. Que la bonne grammaire soit respectée! (that's a subjunctive).
Michael Bulley
Chalon-sur-Saône, France

I'm afraid that Margaret O'Hare has got her conjunctives and subjunctives in a bit of a twist. If the outcome of the French presidential election were uncertain, one would use the imperfect followed by the conditional.

Having followed the election campaign from January, for me

the outcome was a foregone conclusion, so the present followed by the present (in French used in place of the future in such patterns) is an accepted construction. "Je pars dans dix jours, mais je continuerai à lire ce grand journal."

Phil Jones
Eastington, Gloucestershire

"An assumption introduced by si is in the indicative; introduced by que replacing si it is in the subjunctive" (A Grammar of Present Day French, JE Mansion). So Phil Jones's letter is correct. I hope he goes on to have a great time living in la France socialiste, where he'll have no problem communicating. In past decades the use of the tricky French subjunctive tense has been dwindling, especially in informal and spoken language, and trying to show off that you can use it outside the few set phrases that are commonly used could result in funny looks, especially if you try to use it after si.

Jenny Moir
Chelmsford, Essex

Si Margaret O'Hare allait en France, elle pourrait apprendre les règles du subjonctif.

Joe Hehir
Ayr

Much as it may be wished otherwise, the word féminisme is masculine ("Vive la femme?", G2, 8 May). Moreover, Jenny Moir (Letters, 8 May), the subjunctive, tricky or not, is not a tense but a mood.

Maurice Zeegen
Watford, Hertfordshire

After more than 60 years, I still remember our French teacher's pronouncement: "There's only one thing you need to know about the subjunctive – and that's how to avoid having to use it."
David Jeffers
Haslemere, Surrey

8 MAY

Maurice Sendak: The fight in him was an expression of life

EMMA BROCKES

The American author and illustrator Maurice Sendak died on 8 May aged 83

I was genuinely frightened when I went to interview Maurice Sendak at his home in Connecticut last October. I had read the cuttings and most interviews with him seemed to descend quite quickly into a series of gruff clampdowns of what he saw to be stupid or condescending questions from the journalist. And he looked terrifying: fierce eyes, wild hair. I was prepared to be unnerved.

And I was, although in a completely unexpected direction. Sendak, promoting Bumble-Ardy, a story about a pig who loses his parents to the slicing machine on the first page, was furious with everything, appalled by modern life, his own publishers, charmless children, Gwyneth Paltrow, anything that came up, but with such energy and wit, the effect was one of joyous abandon. Memorably – and, I should add, not without affection – he referred to Salman Rushdie as that "flaccid fuckhead", an insult to which Rushdie magnanimously responded, with equal affection, on Twitter.

Sendak was playing, but the roots of his play went to very dark places. He spoke in the language of his books, at a kind of mythical level that contained the terrors of life by naming them, which allowed for the possibility of love in the most difficult landscapes. As a colleague just pointed out to me, the thump in the chest one got this morning on news of his death has to do with his voice in one's head – those words we were all read 3,000 times sound to many of us like the "cadences of childhood".

There was something else from that interview that stayed in my mind for the singular way he expressed it. It sounded like a translation from the Yiddish, which it probably was. Sendak was talking about the day of his bar mitzvah, when his father got word, "that he had, no longer, a family. Everyone was gone." The murder of his parents' entire families by the Nazis and the deranging effect this had on his childhood, drove Sendak's art. He still felt searingly guilty about how insensitive he was to his father that day. "I made him suffer more than he had to." Sendak spat it out in disgust: "This 13-year-old ersatz man." He was as tough on himself as on everyone else.

After the interview, we went out into the garden and Tim the photographer took photos. Sendak posed with his dog, Herman, and made some lively suggestions about the proximity of Tim's groin to his face.

He was fantastically, ebulliently alive. Which was always his point, I suppose. The fight in him was an expression of life, will, engagement with the world; an expression of wonder, ultimately. There were so many dark elements in his work, but it came down to love in the end. "If it's true," he said, "then you can't care about the vicious and the painful. You can only be astonished."

Spring

10 MAY

Queen opens Parliament with a festival of bling

SIMON HOGGART

The last session of parliament was the longest for 100 years. At the previous state opening, the Queen had been on the throne for a mere 58 years. She looks a little more elderly these days, a little more stooped, and she walked with that slight caution that you would have if you were carrying the weight of a large bag of potatoes on your head. Or a crown as we call it.

You could hardly call it an austerity opening, though looking round the House of Lords I could see only about a dozen tiaras. The place still looked like a festival of bling, a convention of white rappers all desperate to show how minted they were. The event was designed hundreds of years ago to convince continental ambassadors that this wet, windswept country off the west coast of Europe was immensely wealthy. That might well be part of the intention today.

Samantha Cameron was in the gallery, wearing a simple black jacket and no hat – a stylish move when you contemplated the riot of scarlet, gold and ermine below. It might possibly be the last occasion these peers can get together with all their finery if, though it seems highly unlikely, parliament gets round to getting rid of the whole lot of them before the next state opening.

We could follow events outside on the TV screens. A black coach arrived and out came a crown. Yes, the crown has a coach to itself! No one can say that public transport is in a mess when even our crowns travel on time, in luxury.

Having been helped out of the coach, the crown was carried by the Lord Great Chamberlain, the Marquess of Cholmondeley, or Dave Rocksavage as he is known to his pals in the film business, in which he works.

He bore it like an aged waiter in the Tour d'Argent, terrified of dropping it, but knowing that a scrumptious pressed duck would be revealed when he lifted it up.

The Lord Speaker, Lady D'Souza, appeared in her formal clothing, all black and gold, a long train held up by a train bearer.

You'd imagine that Lord Speakers have been dressed like that since medieval times but, in fact, the office was only invented in 2006. So not only do we have ancient flummery, we can do brand new, off-the-shelf 21st-century flummery, too! No other nation can make this claim.

Ken Clarke, whose day job is justice secretary, but who also moonlights as the Lord High Chancellor of England, appeared looking grumpy. He isn't a grumpy person; it's just his default expression. He was carrying what looked like the cushion cover your aunt spent months embroidering. It contained the speech.

Then suddenly, at 11.17, silence fell on the chamber, broken only by the traditional squeak of the mobile phone that one of the peers had forgotten to switch off.

The Queen and Prince Philip arrived. She was covered in diamonds. It looked as if she had been rolled in jewellery like a chicken nugget in breadcrumbs. The TV lights seared down. Every time she made the slightest movement, her entire ensemble flashed like a disco ball.

Black Rod went off to fetch the Commons, who arrived noisily. Sam Cam looked down on her husband and gave him the sweetest, tenderest smile.

The speech was the usual clanging, clanking collection of boilerplate ambitions cloaked in the language of cliche. "Promote enterprise and fair markets... my government will strive to improve the lives of children and family... diversity..."

The speech is always heard in silence, as if it were the Queen's own words. For the first time I can remember, she fluffed a couple of words and twice talked about the "intelligent agencies" instead of intelligence; you too would find your epiglottis freeze if obliged to recite this stuff.

Back in the Commons, after lunch, Ed Miliband continued his improvement. He quoted Boris Johnson, now officially the only popular Tory in the country, who told his supporters in private that his campaign had survived wind, rain, the BBC, the budget and "even an endorsement from David Cameron".

In what might have been an echo of Vince Cable's "Stalin to Mr Bean" gag aimed at Gordon Brown, Miliband said that, in two years, the prime minister had gone from "David Cameron to David Brent".

Cameron was less aggressive than he has been lately, possibly because he did want to plug the Queen's speech. But he said that Labour's response to "too much borrowing, too much spending and too much debt" was more borrowing, more spending and more debt.

I saw that the bald patch on the back of the prime minister's head is now larger than a goujon; it has grown to the size of a small plaice.

11 MAY

Manchester City fans dare to hope

SIMON HATTENSTONE

A strange thing has happened to Manchester City fans this season. They have taken to quoting Brian Stimpson, the headteacher played by John Cleese in the film Clockwise. "I can cope with the despair – it's the hope that's killing me."

On Sunday, one way or another, they will be put out of their misery. The English football season reaches its climax and if City beat Queens Park Rangers (barring Manchester United winning by eight more goals than City do) Manchester's perennial underdogs, the club that was relegated to the third tier 14 years ago, the club that invariably snatched defeat from the jaws of triumph, and whose former manager Joe Royle coined the phrase Cityitis to describe just that phenomenon, will be crowned champions – and the Clockwise quote will be consigned to oblivion.

Ellis Steinberg was trying on a smart green dotted jacket in the City store in the centre of Manchester. The only thing that made the jacket a City product was the club logo on the breast. It's a sign of how far City have come in the world of merchandising – City babywear, City stationery, City rubber ducks are all on sale here. Steinberg is a 63-year-old socialist, with a touch of the Woody Allen about him. "I'm very excited. Very nervous." He's worried about Cityitis? "Yeah." He gulped. I know what he means. I've been a City fan for 40 years.

Four years ago City were taken over by the Abu Dhabi United Group (a worrying name if there ever was one), which was almost

Spring

the same as being taken over by Abu Dhabi. Overnight the club went from the verge of bankruptcy to being the richest in the world. Last season City won the FA Cup, their first trophy in 35 years. Since its inception in 1992, United have dominated the Premier League, winning it 12 times.

Did Steinberg think there had been a power shift in Manchester? "Yes, definitely. It's all oil money." How did he reconcile this with his socialism? "Having had years of misery, I've got to say I'm fine. Anyway, when United fans have a go at me, I remind them they paid the highest fee ever for a teenager in Wayne Rooney, and Rio Ferdinand was the most expensive defender in the world."

For decades City fans have been singing surreal songs of denial. The most famous is "We are not, we're not really here, just like the fans of the invisible man we're not really here." They used to sing it because they could not believe how bad things had got. Recently, it's been sung with a new kind of disbelief.

This is not simply a story of one local club toppling another. More important for the city is that whatever happens on Sunday Manchester will have the Premier League's two most successful teams this season – and many people expect it to stay this way for a long time.

Amid the gothic grandeur of the town hall, the council leader, Sir Richard Leese, was sitting at his desk. "In terms of international marketing, economic development and so on, it is unquestionably the case that Manchester United until recently made a much more significant contribution." But not now, he said.

What does that mean for Manchester? "Having two massive clubs means the hotels are full every weekend rather than every other weekend." But, he said, it's far more significant than that. "We can go from Manchester to almost any place in the world and there will be recognition of Manchester the place because of the association with the football. If you're trying to build economic links of any sort, it opens the door, it gets you to first base."

The recent derby between City and United drew the biggest worldwide audience for a Premier League match – an estimated 650 million. Leese said there were any number of people trying to calculate how Manchester's footballing success can be monetised, from industry to tourism.

Not least at Eastlands, City's home, where the statistics were coming thick and fast – 34% more registered members since the beginning of the season, 216% more international registrations in the same period; a 50% increase in international website visits since last season; commercial revenues up by 182% since 2008; the fastest growing club on Facebook with 2.5 million fans, and a 200% rise in global broadcast coverage since 2009. Make no mistake, this is big business.

At the town hall, the council leader said he had something to show me, and whipped out a blue-and-white scarf from his desk drawer. Leese, who hails from Mansfield, has had a season ticket for 13 years. What difference does footballing success make to daily life? "Not much, except I think the Blues are a bit less miserable."

As he led me through the Victorian corridors of power, he talked about the arrangements for whichever Manchester team wins the title. "We've got contingency plans for two different victory parades... but we're only planning for one."

At City's stadium all was sky blue – the concrete, the stalls, the seats. A group of French pupils were touring the ground and said they had no time to visit United's stadium at Old Trafford. Another sign of the times.

At the reception, hydrangeas nuzzled up to lilies in a tall vase – City blue and white. The former goalkeeper and local hero Alex Williams, who runs the club's community programme, passed by.

Spring

He talked about how City used to be regarded as a comedy club and how that has changed. "We're getting to a stage where other teams, including our local neighbours, believe we are now the real deal." Did he call them neighbours because he could not bear to use the U word? "No... not necessarily."

When City joined the nouveaux riches, some fans displayed an unappealing hubris. They had money to boast about back then, but not success. So they taunted opposition teams with the chant: "We'll buy your club, we'll burn it down." These days the fans are more dignified about the wealth, and the songs are more ironic than triumphalist.

A few years ago when United fans suffered a bad result, they sang: "This is how it feels to be City/This is how it feels to be small" to the tune of the Inspiral Carpets song. Now City fans sing their own version, with a mocking reference to the fact that it is the Blues rather than the Reds who can buy the top players. "This is how it feels to be City/This is how it feels to be small/You sign Phil Jones/We sign Kun Agüero."

In the City shop, two skinheads were discussing what to buy. Darren Statham pulled off his top to try on a City shirt before deciding it was not quite him.

How long had he been following City? "Thirty-five years." How old was he? "35." Yes, he said, of course they had bought success – that was the only way. "I'm going to buy one of the old retro shirts and I'm going to put on it 'Champions 2012', and on the back I'm going to put 'We bought it, and what?'"

Andrew Mather did not have a ticket for Sunday, but he will be watching on a big screen outside the ground with an estimated 10,000 supporters. And what would happen if...? He didn't let me finish the sentence. "I'm not saying it. No, you can't just say it."

"You just can't." Statham echoed. "Cos it's going to happen. They're going to win... Aren't they?"

A Norwegian film crew, recording a programme about City's rise, was hunting for the first division championship trophy City won in 1968. In the late 1960s and early 1970s, before the drought, the club won every domestic competition. But it was nowhere to be found. Journalist Jonas Bergh-Johnsen said: "We went to the stadium, the dressing room, the directors' boxes, everywhere. But nobody seems to know where it is." The one thing the club forgot to build when it moved into the City of Manchester Stadium in 2003 was a trophy room. Back then it wasn't a priority.

Across the road at the Maine Road Chippy, Lynn Warburton, a United fan, believes City's success has been good for her estate. "The club is investing around here; it's great for the community. There's a new swimming baths coming soon," she said.

Sal Pardkh, who owns the chippy, handed Lynn her curry and chips. "D'you want to know how confident I am of City winning?" He goes to the back of his shop and returns with a big smile on his face and a keyring in his hand. It says Manchester City Premier League Champions 2012. "That's how confident. They cost 50p each. I've had 200 made for my most loyal customers."

City won the Premiership that weekend: their first league title for 44 years

23 MAY

Christine Lagarde: Can the head of the IMF save the Euro?

DECCA AITKENHEAD

When Christine Lagarde became the first female finance minister of a major global economy, it's a measure of how much happier

Spring

the world was back then that media interest focused chiefly on her talent for synchronised swimming. She was the foxy Frenchwoman who'd won medals in the national team in her teens, then worked her way up to chair an American law firm in Chicago, before being invited back to Paris in 2005 as trade minister and promoted two years later to the Treasury. Journalists had lots of fun picturing her upside down in a pool, wearing waterproof lipstick and a nose clip – and Lagarde played along with the joke, crediting the sport with teaching her a useful political skill: "To grit your teeth and smile."

No one is writing about synchronised swimming any more. On the day we met last week, the papers were agog with economic Armageddon, as the new French president flew off to Berlin to face a German chancellor whose austerity creed appeared to be on a collision course with France's new mission for growth. Athens was unravelling into chaos, unable to form a government and forced into fresh elections, plunging the markets into freefall as Europe's leaders abandoned any pretence that a Greek exit from the euro might not be imminent. The future of the euro itself was, one headline declared, "a chronicle of a death foretold". When François Hollande's plane was struck by lightning, the heavens themselves seemed to be trying to tell us just how much trouble we are in.

Coming face to face with Lagarde, however, you could be forgiven for thinking you must have imagined the whole crisis. We meet at the Paris office of the International Monetary Fund (IMF), a concrete grey modernist building so unassuming as to lack even a sign advertising its existence. Inside, the decor is plain and functional, the atmosphere eerily hushed. An empty lift glides up to a floor of deserted offices, where I wait by myself for a while until a tall, strikingly self-possessed woman appears and greets me with the elegant serenity of a Parisian hostess receiving a dinner party guest. "Let us sit here," she suggests, ushering me to a window seat beside a vase of flowers. "You can look at my orchids."

The managing director of the IMF may look like one of those statuesque silvery models who appear in Weekend's All Ages fashion pages, but she is one of the world's most powerful women, in the eye of the world's worst storm in living memory. In the years leading up to the 2008 crash, the IMF had been starting to look, if not quite redundant, then not massively important; most of the world's economies appeared to be ticking along quite happily without it. But the crash changed everything, so I'm curious to know when she first thought of running for the job. Actually, she says, it wasn't her idea, but George Osborne's.

"We were travelling together and we were sort of thinking about the political scene, and he said you know [Dominique] Strauss-Kahn is bound to be a candidate for the French presidential elections. What's going to happen with the IMF? Have you thought about it? That's how it started. That's when I started to play with the idea."

But events moved faster than expected last May – "Yes, faster than we ever thought!" – when the incumbent, Strauss-Kahn, was accused of the attempted rape of a New York hotel maid and forced to resign. On top of the sex scandal there was a ding-dong over whether the post should go, as it always has, to another European – another French one, at that – when the global economy today bears no resemblance to the one for which the job was originally designed in 1945. A French candidate would have to be extraordinarily impressive – and Lagarde is certainly that, lauded by everyone from Alistair Darling to Timothy Geithner, who praised her "lightning-quick wit, genuine warmth and ability to bridge divides". But, 67 years after its creation, I'm not sure everyone even really understands exactly what the head of the IMF is meant to do, so I ask Lagarde to explain in words an 11-year-old would understand.

"Well, I look under the skin of countries' economies and I help them make better decisions and be stronger, to prosper and create employment." You could think of the IMF as a global payday loan company for countries who have got into trouble and can't meet their financial commitments – the difference being that instead of charging sky-high interest rates, it demands radical economic reforms. And if they say they don't like the sound of that? "If I'm confident that the sound of it is accurate, I say, well, I'm terribly sorry but this is the sound we are making."

Voters in Greece and France have decided they don't like the sound of it at all and so, as the crisis accelerates, Lagarde's job is looking increasingly indivisible from a mission to save the euro. Some critics have suggested that the appointment of a Europhile former French finance minister was akin to putting a drunk behind the bar; a former IMF chief economist has warned she is essentially in denial about the fundamental flaws of the euro and likely to "throw loans" at its problems, while Ed Balls has argued, "The IMF's job is to support individual countries with solvency crises, not to support a whole monetary union which cannot agree the necessary steps to maintain itself." So I ask if she would be trying just as hard to save the single currency if she were, say, Mexican.

"Yeah yeah yeah yeah yeah. There is an emotional side of me that is pro-European," she acknowledges. "But I try to not be French, not be European, when I do my job. And I know that resolving the Euro area crisis matters also to the Mexican, the Australian, the Brazilian."

She has travelled the world asking countries to contribute to a firewall fund, but several have asked – not unreasonably –

why they should have to pay for Europe's mistakes, when Europe is still richer than most of the world. Does the eurozone crisis matter more to their own interests than they realise? "Oh, I think they realise it," Lagarde says quickly, sounding deadly serious. "There has not been a capital I have visited in the last 10 months where the first question has not been: what is the situation in Europe? Are the Europeans sorting it out?"

Nevertheless, while this might come as a surprise to Greeks suffering under extreme austerity, some say Lagarde's approach to the eurozone is less draconian than the IMF's traditional policy towards developing world economies. Is it easier to impose harsh demands upon small economies, but much harder to tell difficult truths to the big ones – particularly fellow Europeans? "No," she says firmly. "No, it's not harder. No. Because it's the mission of the fund, and it's my job to say the truth, whoever it is across the table. And I tell you something: it's sometimes harder to tell the government of low-income countries, where people live on $3,000, $4,000 or $5,000 per capita per year, to actually strengthen the budget and reduce the deficit. Because I know what it means in terms of welfare programmes and support for the poor. It has much bigger ramifications."

So when she studies the Greek balance sheet and demands measures she knows may mean women won't have access to a midwife when they give birth, and patients won't get life-saving drugs, and the elderly will die alone for lack of care – does she block all of that out and just look at the sums?

"No, I think more of the little kids from a school in a little village in Niger who get teaching two hours a day, sharing one chair for three of them, and who are very keen to get an education. I have them in my mind all the time. Because I think they need even more help than the people in Athens." She breaks off for a pointedly meaningful pause, before leaning forward.

Spring

"Do you know what? As far as Athens is concerned, I also think about all those people who are trying to escape tax all the time. All these people in Greece who are trying to escape tax."

Even more than she thinks about all those now struggling to survive without jobs or public services? "I think of them equally. And I think they should also help themselves collectively." How? "By all paying their tax. Yeah."

It sounds as if she's essentially saying to the Greeks and others in Europe, you've had a nice time and now it's payback time.

"That's right." She nods calmly. "Yeah."

And what about their children, who can't conceivably be held responsible? "Well, hey, parents are responsible, right? So parents have to pay their tax."

Lagarde is a beguiling mixture of steel and silk, for she can switch seamlessly from this sort of hardball talk to nimble diplomacy. Asked if she expects to be the last European to run the IMF, she replies, "Well, I hope I'm not the last woman." But the last European? "I don't know." She smiles, adding playfully, "I might last for a long time."

I begin a question about British Eurosceptics – "Lots of people where I come from" – but she can see what's coming and interjects warmly, "A *beautiful* island." When I ask if she enjoyed dealing with Gordon Brown, she offers, "Erm... I don't think he was ever finance minister when I was." That's a rather graceful way of avoiding the question, I say, smiling. Lagarde affects a blank expression of innocence, and starts to laugh.

Everybody talks about Lagarde's phenomenal charm and it doesn't take long in her company to see why. She goes, "Pouff!" when I say so, batting the compliment away with a flick of the wrist, but she is neither an economist, nor even really a politician – she spent just six years of her career as a minister in France – so I wonder if charm is actually the key qualification for the job.

"Well, I think when you drill down and ask what it takes to be managing director of the IMF, then the ability to listen, the ability to understand the perspective of your entire membership, the respect and tolerance for the political diversity, the cultural diversity, I think that's very important actually. I mean, it's often underestimated because many people will say you need to be a very strong economist. Well, maybe so. But I wouldn't qualify for the job. I'm not the top-notch economist; I can understand what people talk about, I have enough common sense for that, and I've studied a bit of economics, but I'm not a super-duper economist. But, yes, that appreciation for the interests pursued by the other side at a negotiation table, a sense of the collective interest and how that can transcend the vested individual interests of the members, that matters."

She doesn't claim these as feminine virtues, but acknowledges, "I've criticised enough women who are fighting so hard to look like a man that it destroys half of their own sanity and humanity." How often does she feel judged as a woman at the IMF? "Oh, quite often. That wouldn't surprise you! Come on." When she had the temerity last autumn to point out the obvious truth that Europe's banks were under-capitalised, "that's an occasion where I think some observations were related to me being a woman." She drops her voice to mimic the catty whispers: "'She doesn't know what she's talking about, silly woman, she must have been poorly advised.'"

So what does she do about it? "I think you can choose one of two options. Either you become bitter, and you complain constantly about it, and argue that people will criticise you or undermine you because you are a woman. Or you decide to take advantage of it. Not overplaying the feminine side of things; not being on the seducing side, not playing the attractive woman in high heels – I've never done that and I think my mother would be *horrified* if I did, and I don't want that to happen because I loved her very much. But..." She falls silent. But what? "Men will not insult you or will not easily say no when you tell them you need more money to secure the institution and make sure it can do its work." Does she mean it's easier for her to ask for money as a woman? "Yes," she flashes back. "Yes. Yes. Absolutely." Because masculinity responds to a woman saying I need more money? "Yes," she agrees, smiling. "People have said that to me. 'How can I say no to you?'"

For all Lagarde's charm, it's hard not to feel a sense of Alice In Wonderland bewilderment about the IMF's work. The Americans are recovering with a stimulus programme more familiar to Europe than Washington, while a Frenchwoman is trying to save the eurozone with austerity measures that would please the Tea Party. The whole point of the European project was to prevent the sort of conflict that once engulfed the continent, and yet the IMF's life support strategy has seen neo-Nazis elected in Athens, and now risks destabilising the marriage between Germany and France on which the European dream depends. When democratic elections produce politicians unwilling to play by the IMF's rules, they have been replaced by unelected technocrats – Mario Monti in Italy, Lucas Papademos in Greece – gifting Eurosceptics evidence for their charge that the EU is fundamentally anti-democratic.

Were voters in Greece and France basically wrong to elect anti-austerity politicians? "You are never wrong when you have voted because you've acted in accordance with your conscience and your beliefs, and you've exercised your democratic right, which is, you know, perfectly legitimate in our democracies."

But Germans elected Hitler in 1933, and we don't think they were right, do we?

"Well, somebody once said if people are not happy with their government, you change the people." She laughs, deftly sidestepping the question. "What's really interesting," she says more seriously, "is that wherever you see a change of government, for instance in Spain, do you see major changes from the economic and financial policies that were conducted by their predecessors? No." She suspects we will see a similar pattern now in France. "I'm very much a believer that it's action that matters much more so than, you know, the flurry of political promises and statements and slogans that are used during political campaigns. So let's see."

Is she saying there's no need to panic about a rift between Paris and Berlin? "I should think so," she agrees quietly, with a knowing smile. "I think it's largely overstated."

Lagarde's unflappable calm seems to come quite naturally. She was born in Paris in 1956, the eldest daughter of a university lecturer and a teacher; her father suffered from motor neurone disease and died when she was just 17. After failing twice to get into the prestigious Ecole Nationale d'Administration, the elite incubator for French civil servants, she joined the American law firm Baker & McKenzie and rose to become its first female chairman. In her early 30s she had two sons with her first husband, but after that the details get a little hazy; she married again while in Chicago, to a British businessman, but now lives with a Corsican she first met in her 20s at law school. In the French tradition, that's about as much as we know of her private life, apart from the fact that she is teetotal, vegetarian and a fanatical swimmer who will stay only in hotels that have pools. "She radiates," an acquaintance once said of her. "I think that's because she swims so much."

She certainly radiates assurance, but of course part of being reassuring means not saying anything very bold. I ask how she squares austerity with growth, but she thinks the furious debate between the two is generating more heat than light.

Spring

"What we say is it cannot be either or; it's not either austerity or growth, that's just a false debate. Nobody could argue against growth. And no one could argue against having to repay your debts. The question and the difficulty is how do you reconcile the two, and in which order do you take them? I would argue that you do it on a country by country case; it's not going to be a one size fits all."

In the UK's case, Lagarde thinks we are broadly on the right lines; public spending cuts, quantitative easing and low interest rates all meet with her approval. I tell her it doesn't feel that way to a lot of people here, and ask for an exit narrative – the story of how we'll get out of this mess – that could cheer people up.

"There will be an exit," she says firmly. "No question about it." Yes, but what is it? "Well, we're going to invent it. To give you a couple of positive messages, firstly, protectionism is not reappearing. The second reason for optimism is, there's a lovely sentence by Robert Musil, which says, 'Man is capable of anything – including the best.' And when you see how a situation can be turned around by one individual – get Mr Berlusconi out, you bring Mr Monti in, he's dedicated, he couldn't care less about his political future because he's not interested. And he does the job. And he changes the perception, and restores confidence. That's also a sign of hope."

That may be true, but it's not an exit strategy narrative. "Ah," she says briskly, laughing. "You'll have to come back for that." Could she at least say where we are on the curve; is this as bad as things can be, or will they get worse? "I'm not in the business of reading tea leaves. I don't have a crystal ball. Some of the major issues are being resolved – but it's not over now. Let's face it, it's not over yet."

And for Greece – is the euro over? Lagarde won't say. I ask if I'll be packing euros if I go on holiday to Greece next year and she just smiles. "A holiday in Greece, it's a good investment for the country!"

She will put her name to just one firm prediction: she's going to be at the synchronised swimming at the Olympics this summer. "Osborne promised me that I would be invited, so, yes, I will try to do that. I'm desperate to."

I try once more. When history books are written about the financial crisis, they will say it began in 2008. What date will they give for its end? "Hmm, after the hyphen? After 2008? Two thousand," she says firmly. How odd, I think – her English is perfect, but she must have misunderstood the question. I ask again, but she is laughing. There was no misunderstanding.

"Well, I'm sure about the first two digits: 20. But I'm not sure about the last two digits."

23 MAY

A message to Damien Hirst: Stop now, you have become a disgrace to your generation

REVIEW: JONATHAN JONES

The last time I saw paintings as deluded as Damien Hirst's latest works, the artist's name was Saif al-Islam Gaddafi. A decade ago the son of Libya's then still very much alive dictator showed sentimental paintings of desert scenes in an exhibition sponsored by fawning business allies. Searching for some kind of parallel to the arrogance and stupidity of Hirst's still life paintings, I find myself remembering that strange, sad spectacle.

Spring

There is a pathos about Two Weeks One Summer, in which Hirst shows paintings of parrots and lemons, shark's jaws and foetuses in jars in a vast space in White Cube Bermondsey. It is the same kind of pathos that clings to dictators' art. This is the kind of kitsch that is foisted on helpless peoples by Neros and Hitlers and such tyrants so beyond normal restraint or criticism they believe they are artists. I am not saying this to be cruel. There is a real analogy: Hirst like an absolute ruler must be utterly surrounded by a court of yes-people, all down the line from his painting shed to the gallery, if there is no one to tell him he is rowing himself to artistic damnation with these trivial and pompous slabs of hack work.

This is the third exhibition by Damien Hirst to open in London this spring, and it retroactively mocks the others. His retrospective at Tate Modern is brilliantly edited. It includes all the best vitrines, and none of the rotten "proper" paintings that he now makes at home in Devon. To paraphrase the epitaph on Albrecht Dürer's tomb, whatever is immortal (or at least memorable) of Damien Hirst is in that exhibition. But here is the other side of the story: an artist so wealthy and powerful that he can kid himself he is an Old Master and have the art world go along with the fantasy. The most recent paintings here were finished this year, so the fantasy is still very much alive. So is the courtiers' chorus of support.

The exquisitely produced catalogue has an essay by a senior curator at the Prado in Madrid, who draws comparisons with Caravaggio and Velázquez. Yikes. It would be impressive stuff if we did not have the paltry reality of Hirst's paintings before our eyes. At White Cube, I pass from picture to picture, trying not to crack up laughing or actually swear out loud. The exercise feels like a parody of being an art critic, for these are humourless parodies of paintings. Like the Prado expert I can spot the analogies – lemons, how Zurbarán – but they work only to destroy and humiliate Hirst's daubs.

Seriously – Mr Hirst – I am talking to you. It seems you have no one around you to say this: stop, now. Shut up the shed. I say this as a long-time admirer, not an enemy. No encounter with a contemporary work of art has ever thrilled me like the day I walked into the Saatchi Gallery in 1992 and saw a tiger shark's maw lurch towards me. But these paintings are abominations unto the lord of Art. They dismantle themselves. Each of these paintings – from the parrot in a cage to the blossoms and butterflies – takes on the difficulties of representational painting and visibly fails to come close, not merely to mastery, but to basic competence.

At least it can be said for Hirst that he shuns the cheap tricks of other contemporary painters. If he used the glib formulae so common in painting today, such as whimsical abstraction and projected outline images, he might get away, as others do, with a total lack of true painterly knowledge. Instead, in a bizarre act of historical arrogance, he seems to think that if he tries to paint like Manet, he is suddenly Manet. Hey – how rich was Manet? Not very, right? Well then… So he takes on the Great Tradition with none of the training and patience that made those guys what they were.

If Hirst did not try to paint an orange accurately, no one would know he can't do it. But he has tried, at least I think it's an orange, and the poor sphere seems to float in mid air because of the clumsy circle of shadow below it. For a moment I thought this was intentional, then I realised it was a competence issue. Such issues abound. You look at a branch and it is obvious he has worked at it: equally obvious the work was wasted. At their very best these paintings lack the skill of thousands of amateur artists who paint at weekends all over Britain – and yet he can hire fools to compare him with Caravaggio.

This exhibition is a warning to young artists. At 18, you may long to be Damien Hirst when he was 30. But in his 40s, Hirst apparently wishes he was the artist that, who knows, he might have been, had he spent his youth drawing day after day after day. He has left it too late. Instead he looks like a tyrant lost in a world of mirrors, like the world's most over praised child, like a disgrace to his, my, generation. Are we this bankrupt?

1 JUNE

No good options for an economy that flew too close to the sun

LARRY ELLIOTT

The soup kitchen opens at noon but long before then the queues start to form in the hot Athens sun. A couple of streets away from where sardines, red mullet and squid are piled high in the fish market, those down on their luck line up. While elsewhere life goes on seemingly as normal, students, jobless people, single parents and pensioners swallow their pride and wait patiently. They get two meals a day, at midday and 5pm. This is what a depression looks like.

At first blush, Greece seems no different from any other developed country. People sit in the city centre cafes sipping their iced coffees; yellow taxis cruise the streets; the shops are open for business. But different it is, and it is not hard to spot the signs that this is an economy that has contracted by 20% since the downturn began three years ago and that it is still falling.

You don't need to know that spending in the shops is down by a sixth over the past year; it is obvious from the empty cabs and those shops open but with no customers. You don't need to know that the official unemployment rate is well above 20% and youth unemployment is nudging 50%: it's obvious from the young men idling on street corners and openly dealing drugs.

Greece is broke and close to being broken. It is a country where children are fainting in school because they are hungry, where 20,000 Athenians are scavenging through waste tips for food, and where the lifeblood of a modern economy – credit – is fast drying up.

It is a country where the fascists and the anarchists battle for control of the streets, where immigrants fear to go out at night and where a woman whispers "it's like the Weimar republic" as a motorcycle cavalcade from the Golden Dawn party, devotees of Adolf Hitler, cruises past the parliament building. Graffiti says: "Foreigners get out of Greece. Greece is for the Greeks. I will vote for Golden Dawn to remove the filth from the country."

As ever, it is economic collapse that is pushing politics to the extremes. Businesses that have not already gone bust are clinging on by their fingertips hoping the country's second election in two months will be a turning point. Not the moment when the economy starts to recover, because Greeks have seen enough and suffered enough to know that the slump will grind on through 2012 and 2013; instead, they are banking on the rest of Europe cutting Greece some slack for fear that a nation accounting for less than 3% of the eurozone's output could be the catalyst for a terminal crisis that will destroy the single currency.

"Things are getting worse," said John Milios, economics professor at the National Technical University in Athens, and a candidate for the leftwing coalition, Syriza, in the election. "The economy is in a devastating state mainly due to the austerity programme. Practically all the banks are bankrupt and there has been a very large redistribution of wealth in favour of the rich."

Spring

It is too late now to say that Greece should never have been admitted as a founder member of the euro, although there are those in Brussels, Frankfurt and Berlin who rue the day when European solidarity was deemed more important than economic common sense.

There are many cultural reference points for what has happened to the birthplace of democracy over the past decade: some call it a Greek tragedy, others say the austerity programme is akin to the torture of Sisyphus, the king condemned to push a giant stone to the top of the Hades hill only to find it slipping and rolling to the bottom each time he neared the summit.

But the best metaphor is Icarus, the boy who flew too close to the sun. The government in Athens used the cheap interest rates that came with euro membership to spend too much and borrow too much, all the time oblivious to the fact that the country was becoming less and less competitive in comparison with the rich countries of north Europe.

Crony capitalism, economic incompetence, and downright corruption left Greece vulnerable when the crash came. At the end of 2009 it emerged that the government had been telling lies about the size of Greece's budget deficit, and the financial markets no longer considered Greek debt to be all but the same as German debt. Athens got its first bailout in May 2010, a second in February this year. But on both occasions strings were attached: cut wages, cut pensions, cut public spending, privatise the economy, embark on structural reforms.

Austerity has been a failure, for Greece and for the rest of the single currency. The idea was to end the recession quickly and prevent the contagion spreading to the other 16 members of the club. Neither has happened.

"There is precisely zero chance of austerity working," said Yanis Varoufakis, once a speechwriter for the former socialist prime minister George Papandreou, now an economics professor in the US. "It is the same as thinking you can escape from gravity by waving your arms up and down."

Varoufakis is scathing about how the crisis has been handled. "Europe's made a mess of Greece for the past three years. Those responsible will go down as the biggest idiots in the history of economics."

There have been domestic and political ramifications of the failure to tackle Greece's problems effectively. Internally, there has been a loss of support for the mainstream parties thought responsible for the economic collapse. Externally, the belief that Greece will be merely the first eurozone domino to fall has led to pressure on Ireland, Portugal and, recently, Spain.

The strength of support for Syriza's anti-austerity message in the inconclusive election held shocked the Greek and the European political establishments. Despite attempts to portray Syriza as the party that will propel Greece towards an exit from the eurozone – something 80% of the population oppose – polls suggest that support for the charismatic Alexis Tsipras, leader of Syriza, has held up.

"After the elections of 6 May we can see that a large fraction of the population has hope for the first time," Milios said.

Tsipras is adamant that he doesn't want to return to the drachma. He wants instead to renegotiate the terms of Greece's bailout, with the country's creditors agreeing to lower interest rates on debt repayments, more time to hit deficit reduction targets and money from Europe's structural funds to back growth. In the game of political chicken being played between Athens and Berlin, Tsipras believes Angela Merkel, for all her tough talk, will blink first.

Alex Jacovides, chairman of Genesis Pharma, a company that imports drugs for the Greek healthcare market, said: "We need a

Spring

compromise for the benefit of Europe, an extension of the memorandum [the bailout agreement] because people are feeling the pressure and cohesion is at stake.

"People are not all like the Germans. There is a limit to what Mediterranean people can accommodate. Greece was living beyond its means for a number of years – this has to stop. But it can't happen overnight. It has to be a step by step approach. Who's going to invest in Greece when it's going down so rapidly?"

The company has been hit by a triple whammy: a 50% drop in demand from a contracting economy, a 14-month delay in being paid by the government, and the €170m loss it took on the bonds that it accepted as payment from the state but which were subject to a 70% write down as part of February's bail-out. "We can survive a few more months," said Jacovides, "but not much more than that."

He added, however, that he wanted the next government to be pro-Europe and pro-euro, but insisted that this was not just a crisis for Greece. "This is an inflexion point for Europe. We have to decide whether we take the federal road or go back to single nations. We need time, support and the realisation that if Greece fails it will be the end of Europe as we know it."

Thus far, there has been precious little sign that Germany's chancellor is prepared to soften her line. And sympathy from other quarters has been in limited supply too.

Christine Lagarde, the managing director of the International Monetary Fund, provoked fury when she said in a Guardian interview that she had more sympathy for poor children deprived of a proper education in Niger than she had for those guilty of not paying their taxes in Greece.

No one in Greece would deny that tax-dodging is a serious problem. What they objected to was the failure of Lagarde to make a distinction between those who pay their full whack – the less well-off wage earners – and the middle class, self-employed, professionals and super rich who can find ways, legal and illegal, to minimise their tax liabilities. There are those, too, who think that the austerity imposed by the troika — the IMF, European Central Bank and the EU — has made matters in Greece worse, not better.

"The government and the troika took a Greek recession and turned it into a Greek depression," said Thanasis Maniatisan, an economics professor at Athens University. "It is a great humanitarian crisis, similar to that suffered in advanced economies during the 1930s. There is no light at the end of the tunnel."

Not everybody agrees with this bleak assessment. One senior banker, speaking anonymously, said that the restoration of political stability could lead to the return of the €80bn removed from bank deposits since the start of the crisis. Some of the money has fled overseas, some has been used by the newly impoverished to maintain living standards, some is being kept under the mattress in case the banks go bust.

A return of even a fraction of this capital would provide the banks with scope to lend more money and so finance a slow recovery, the banker said.

Dimitris Tsigos, founding president of the Hellenic Start-up Association and founder of a software company, says that Greece has plenty of things going for it: a well-educated workforce, plenty of sun that attracts tourists and can be a source of solar power, and a thriving biotechnology sector. But he believes the country needs a clean break with its bad old ways.

For many years, Tsigos said, graduates aspired to working in a public sector that was expanded to cater for them. "This vision has collapsed with the crisis and now people have to make up their minds what they will do. Emigrating is one option. To stay here and fight is another. Doing that in a zero liquidity environment is challenging but that's what we are trying to do."

Spring

The crisis, he says, has hit the poor, the wage earners and parts of the middle class but not Greece's oligarchs, ship owners and bankers who control the media and have had close links with the parties of the centre-right and centre-left that have dominated Greek politics since the mid-1970s. "Greece is a country governed by a group of gangsters. Either the Greek people will kick the gangsters out or they will have the fate they deserve."

Defence spending, where corruption has been endemic, said Tsigos, has so far escaped the swingeing spending cuts imposed on health and education. "Corruption is everywhere. You must think of a Latin American or African model to understand Greece."

This, then, is Greece as it faces its second recent election: a country with dysfunctional politics, a crippled economy and creditors rapidly running out of patience. There are no good options, only bad ones.

One posited solution is to leave the euro and return to the drachma. This would intensify the slump in the short term. The National Bank of Greece, a commercial bank, estimates that output could fall by a fifth and unemployment could rise to 34% of the workforce. But there are those who believe that there is a chance that a cheaper currency and a debt default would, as was the case with Argentina a decade ago, offer the chance of recovery.

Leonidas Vatikiotis, a leftwing academic, says leaving the euro is a prerequisite for recovery. It would, he said, have to be accompanied by nationalisation of the banks, capital controls and debt default. "There is meltdown in the economy. Nobody pays anything. Businesses don't pay their suppliers. Suppliers don't pay their taxes. The solution is the overthrow of austerity policies. Greece has been an ideal laboratory for the most brutal neo-liberalism."

This, though, is still a minority position. Stefanos Manos, leader of the small Action party, says Greece must remain in the euro and favours even more radical structural reform than proposed by the troika. "In terms of shrinking the state, the memorandum is very timid. I would do more."

Varoufakis says the comparison with Argentina does not stack up, because Argentina had retained its own currency while pegged to the US dollar, and there was strong global demand for its commodities after it devalued the peso. He says Greece should default within the euro.

As the debates rage over whether Greece should be in or out and whether it should stick to its austerity plan or not, one thing is clear: the country is perilously close to the edge of economic and social catastrophe.

Sofia Argyropoulou owns a printing house that has specialised in upmarket books since it was founded by her father in 1956. There have been bad times before, she says, especially the period of the military dictatorship in the late sixties and early 1970s when her father ran the printing machines without paper "just to hear them".

"What I want is work," she said. "I don't care whether we have the drachma or the euro. What matters is to have work." Like many other Greeks she knew that the boom years were just too good to be true. "But I couldn't believe we were going to be in this position. People are sitting on their money because they are afraid."

Argyropoulou cut her workforce from 14 to seven and moved into smaller premises, but she said she was still losing money. "We can survive for another six months. After that I will use my savings to close. I will give everybody what I have to give and say goodbye."

Spring

1 June

All Hail Her Majesty

MARINA HYDE

Wherever you stand on Her Majesty Queen Elizabeth II, although actually standing on her is obviously treasonous, she is the last silent celebrity. In an age where the drive has been toward ever more extreme and frequent acts of self-disclosure, she has always grasped that silence is the most intriguing statement of all. We know more about someone who has been a contestant on a reality show for one week than we do the woman who has been on the throne for six decades.

Public figures who do not grant interviews make hen's teeth look like spam emails. Kate Moss was briefly one, staring mutely out from photoshoots and paparazzi shots, and all the more fascinatingly mysterious for it. But I remember stumbling on a documentary in which she was shown arriving at Glastonbury and, for the first time in my experience, opening her mouth. "You've no idea what a facking nightmare we've had getting here," she squawked at some backstage greeter. It was akin to the needle being scraped across a record. It wasn't that Mossy was being unpleasant – she wasn't – it was just that the spell was broken. Since then she's given all sorts of interviews, and the compelling unknowability has vanished.

Of course, we've heard the Queen speak (if not say the word "facking"). But since she's never given an interview, the assessment of Where She's At Right Now is limited to analysing scarcely perceptible eyebrow movements during the so-called Queen's speech, or decoding her studiedly code-free Christmas messages.

You can't even liken her to stars like Greta Garbo, who withdrew from the public gaze, because she never has. She is an emotional recluse on public parade – perhaps the only emotional recluse in modern public life, where you can't win an election or even read the news without affecting a full range of sensibilities.

Rather than running the gamut of emotion from A to B, as Dorothy Parker remarked of Katharine Hepburn, Her Majesty declines even to admit to A. She just keeps buggering on, inscrutably. It's remarkable how much of what we think we know about her is fiction, a composite born of Alan Bennett and Helen Mirren, which people choose to find more convincing than the supposedly real-life sovereign stylings of Paul Burrell. (My favourite "recollection" of Princess Di's butler, who you'll recall had half her dresses in his attic for safekeeping, will remain the several hours he spent alone with the Queen shortly after Di's death. "Be careful, Paul," she apparently implored the future I'm A Celebrity contestant. "There are powers at work in this country of which we have no knowledge.")

The only time the emotionless strategy appeared to have failed Her Maj was in the bizarre period after Princess Di's death, when she was bombarded by all those mawkishly hectoring tabloid headlines claiming "your people need you, ma'am". Who knows what the Queen's private verdict on such naked buck-passing truly was, but perhaps she thought that what her people actually needed was to pull themselves together.

And oddly, that was certainly the opinion to which plenty of those who briefly lost their heads to the emotionalism eventually came, somewhat sheepishly. What an irony that the thing the Queen was judged to have got most wrong was perhaps the thing she was most right about, the ultimate instance of being able to retain perspective when all around are losing theirs. Meanwhile, Tony Blair, amusingly lauded for his general response to Diana's

Spring

death and his scenery-chewing reading of Corinthians at her funeral, is now the name most frequently cited by those warning republicans to be careful what they wish for. President Blair, they screech (annoyingly missing the obvious point that presidents are only presidents for the period of time the people elect them to be so).

It must be said that Her Majesty hasn't managed to transmit the power of silence to her children, though that famous picture of her merely shaking the hand of the three or four year-old Prince Charles after months away might suggest she has tried. For a couple of decades back there, the clan became our version of The Simpsons, the most high profile dysfunctional family in the land. The Windsors lacked the warmth and charm of their Springfield counterparts, of course, but were a similarly nuclear family, in a Chernobyl kinda way. They certainly never let you down with an episode, lurching from The Grand Knockout Tournament through Charles's tampon fantasy to a few soap operatic divorces. Since the Burrell trial and its hilarious fallout, though, they've been disappointingly quiet on the unplanned entertainment front.

That may well change, given that those upon whom it will fall to be operational – Prince William but most pressingly Charles – appear not to have identified that inscrutability has been the keystone of the Queen's mythmaking. Pettish, peremptory, idiotically conservative, lacking in self-awareness, and perhaps a hundredth as clever as he thinks he is – if only we didn't know quite so much about Charles and his views on everything. There are less scrutable Big Brother contestants. *Après mama le déluge*? Well, perhaps it's not the weekend for issuing flood warnings.

2 June

The Queen's Jubilee: Diamond is not forever

GUARDIAN LEADER

Royal diamond jubilees do not come round often. That of Queen Elizabeth II this weekend is the first since the end of the 19th century. It seems likely, given the ages of the Queen's prospective successors, that this will be the first and last diamond jubilee which any British person alive today will witness. Because of this rarity, it is tempting to invest the event with more significance than it merits. Yet this is to misunderstand the difference between a historically remarkable event and a historically important one.

This jubilee is undoubtedly remarkable, as that of Queen Victoria also was, and charged with enough meaning to keep commentators and academics profitably engaged for the week to come. It will be marked by great national happiness – and hopefully by good weather. But it is surely not an event of great historic significance, any more than Victoria's turned out to be. In 2012, for one thing, just as in 1897, national self-confidence is too fragile for that – and for some of the same reasons: a distant and divisive war, a deteriorating situation in Europe, uncertainty about the future unity of the kingdom and the shadow of recession.

Any monarch who occupies the throne for 60 years becomes a symbol of continuity and of stability. It happened to Victoria. Today it has happened to Elizabeth II. For most of us, she is the only British monarch we have ever known. Both queens have become symbols partly through the sheer passage of time and partly through an institutional adeptness for adapting. The monarchy's watchword, as Robert Hardman's recent biography stresses, has been to keep doing the same thing differently. Across the course of 60 years, that strategy has been very successful. As her best biographer, the late Ben Pimlott, wrote, while it is hard to point to major achievements, it is also hard to think of mistakes. The Guardian/ICM poll last week found the monarchy enjoying record support. The Queen herself enjoys personal ratings that our despised politicians would die for. The political parties could learn from her ability to build a majority.

Fifteen years ago, such a situation could not be predicted with total confidence. But the difficult 1990s, the years of the marital separations, indiscretions and the Windsor fire, now seem distant and unrepresentative. In the hysterical aftermath of the death of Princess Diana, courtiers feared the Queen might be booed. The golden jubilee of 2002 tapped into a very different mood on which 2012 has built. The national mood today is of periodic public identification with the Queen combined with healthy indifference the rest of the time. This weekend there are few fears of booing. She will surely be cheered wherever she goes.

It is nevertheless a mistake to suppose nothing has changed. Those who remember the silver jubilee, never mind the coronation, will need no reminding that those events occurred in a very different Britain. In both 1953 and 1977, there were more flags, more parties and larger crowds than are likely this weekend. That's not to belittle this year's flags, parties and crowds. But those earlier events were attempts to persuade Britain that national and imperial decline had not really occurred or did not matter. That is neither the purpose nor the mood today.

Yet it is still important to ask the question which Jeremy Bentham posed about any law, custom or institution: "What is the use of it?" The jubilee is an opportunity to have a party amid hard times, but it should also be an opportunity to debate the institution more thoughtfully – because it defines this country and it will have to change after Elizabeth II's reign is over. Yet it would be churlish not to acknowledge that the principal public feeling this weekend is respect for a woman who has done her strange, anachronistic and undemocratic job with tact and judgment for far longer than most of the rest of us could ever contemplate doing ours.

It rained. There were large crowds. And no debate about the institution.

9 JUNE

Back to the workhouse

JOHN HARRIS

If the diamond jubilee celebrations were meant to somehow reflect 21st-century Britain, it was only fitting that two unshakable features of modern life would find their way into all the pomp and silliness. First came yet another example of the screaming hostility that rises up whenever the BBC does anything even slightly untoward, then an outbreak of angst about the growing numbers of people who are expected to work for nothing.

A brief recap, then. On the night of Saturday 2 June, a security firm called Close Protection UK bussed around 80 people from Bristol, Bath and Plymouth to London, where they were to work as stewards in and around the jubilee river pageant. Fifty were classed as apprentices and rewarded to the tune of £2.80 an hour. Another 30 were "customers" of the government's work programme, given training placements with Close Protection

Spring

UK and promised temporary paid work at the Olympics – but for their travails at the jubilee celebrations, they were paid nothing. Having arrived in the capital on Sunday morning, all of them were told to sleep under London Bridge from 3am to 5.30am. After long hours working in the cold and wet, they then made their way to a campsite in Essex, where they bedded down in conditions described by some of them as "swampy".

The Guardian's Shiv Malik broke the story 24 hours later, and in the following days, everything needed for a national shoutfest fell into place. There was the obligatory phone-in on the Jeremy Vine show, items on Today and Newsnight, and a tour of the studios from an angry John Prescott. Downing Street claimed the incident was a "one-off". In all the debate, though, one big fact was overlooked: that the 30 stewards on the work programme were one small part of a national army of unpaid labour, which seems to be growing bigger every month.

Much of this can be traced back to innovations by the last government, which decisively embraced what some people call workfare – though the coalition has expanded such practices to mind-boggling proportions. Sometimes this is a matter of people being forced to work for nothing under pain of having their benefits stopped. Slightly higher up the employment hierarchy, it might be a matter of a jobcentre or work programme adviser telling them a spell of unpaid work will brighten up their CV, or lead to a proper job with the same employer. Politicians praise all these things as a means of getting people into work and thereby attacking unemployment; what nobody mentions is that expanding unpaid labour ensures there is even less proper work in the economy.

On Friday, I spoke to one of the 30 unpaid people at the heart of the controversy. This young woman had been made redundant early last year. Eventually, she was referred by her jobcentre adviser to Tomorrow's People, a charity administering the work programme, and persuaded to train for a qualification in security work. As part of her training, she had already worked for nothing, but only once: at a football match, "observing the crowd and making sure there were no issues", with six other people on the same scheme. When she and others were informed about the jubilee weekend, she said, they were at first told they would be paid around £400, "but at the last minute, they said, 'You're not getting anything – it's work experience'."

Sleeping under London bridge, she said, had been impossible: "It was too cold, it was raining, and there were way too many people." She thus started work at 9.30am, having had no sleep for upwards of 20 hours. She put on her work clothes "in public, in the cold". Breakfast – "piddly", she said – had not arrived until 9.15am. The first chance she had to use a toilet, she claimed, was at 2pm. She was supposed to stop work 12 hours after she started, "but me and some other people gave up, cos we were that cold and wet, at six o'clock." She was then told to take the tube to the end of the Central line, whereupon she called her mother and stepfather almost 150 miles away and asked them to come and get her. "I was that distraught. I had five layers on, and I was soaked through. I was having trouble breathing. After standing up for nine hours, I had a back spasm; I could barely walk. I'd just had enough."

"I'm signing on tomorrow," she said, "and I'm asking to be withdrawn from Tomorrow's People. I can't trust them. I don't want to be treated like dirt, working long hours for nothing.

"There's work experience, and there's slave labour. I wouldn't mind work experience for free if it was in good conditions and I was treated properly... not being asked to change in public and having no access to a toilet." (By way of a response, Tomorrow's People supplied the Guardian with a list of contact numbers for other work programme participants who had been taken to

Spring

London on an unpaid basis; they proved to be either unavailable, or unwilling to talk).

The companies that either are, or have been, involved in welfare-to-work schemes extend into the distance. As well as charities and social enterprises such as Tomorrow's People, there are the specialist companies that deliver such projects as the work programme (G4S, Serco, the now-notorious A4e), some of which benefit from work experience by giving unemployed people placements in their own offices. Further along the chain are the high-street businesses that take on unemployed people as temporary unpaid workers.

Government schemes that stipulate unpaid work has to be of "community benefit" also involve an array of organisations specialising in supposed voluntary work, which often use unemployed people to staff their offices and shops; there is a lot of noise on activists' websites about the British Heart Foundation, which has 700 such outlets. Its policy director Betty McBride told me that: "As things stand, in every one of our shops, we have work programme placements – some mandatory, some voluntary." The public sector is also involved: last month it emerged that Sandwell and West Birmingham hospitals trust was planning to use unpaid unemployed people on hospital wards, performing such tasks as "general tidying" and "assisting with feeding patients".

What all this means for wider society and the economy is highlighted by the 20 minutes I spent talking to a 22-year-old work programme "customer" from East Anglia (as with just about everyone I've ever contacted about welfare to work, he insisted his identity was kept secret). His last job before nine months of unemployment was with a mobile phone repair company; late last year, he was put on the work programme with the welfare-to-work company Seetec. Seetec recommended that while he continued to claim jobseekers' allowance of £56.25 a week, he should do a four-week work experience placement at a city-centre branch of Argos, which began last month.

"I said I'd only do work experience if there were vacancies at the end," he said. "But at every point Seetec were like, 'They employ people all the time.' And as soon as I went into Argos, the people there said: 'There are no jobs at the end of this.'" He said he tried to leave the placement, but was told that if he did, his benefit would be stopped.

In his first week, he worked for 30 hours ("10 hours more than anyone who was getting paid to work there"), before contacting Seetec and discovering he was only meant to put in 16. "I was doing the bit where you get the item from the warehouse and put it on the shelf, for [the customer] to collect it," he said. When he arrived, he was one of four people on jobseekers' allowance doing supposed work experience; three weeks later, there were six such people, working a variety of shifts, out of a workforce of between 15 and 20.

One man sent to Argos by Jobcentre Plus, he said, had been working unpaid for 30 hours a week in a six-week placement. "No one who was paid was getting overtime any more," he said. "Everyone was being cut down to four-hour shifts. A guy who worked there told me that. The staff were very demoralised that we were taking up so much potential shift work."

Training, he said, was flimsy. Health and safety instruction – "How to walk up a ladder and lift up boxes" – lasted for half an hour, an explanation of the basics of the job and a formal induction took 90 minutes, and that was that. He finished the placement last Saturday, and is now being put on a retail training course: "I said to my adviser, 'I don't know what that entails, but I might as well do it, because it's proper training, not work experience.'"

In response to his story, Seetec said it could not comment on individual cases, but was "investigating the allegation". An Argos spokesperson said the company "understands there are concerns about our involvement in the government work experience programme", but its stores "have clear principles for helping

Spring

young people into the world of work". She claimed that its policy on placements is to "only use Jobcentre Plus as a partner" and offered to "investigate where another supplier has been used". The six-week placements organised with jobcentres, she said, are offered "only where there is the prospect of a permanent job" and there is always "a training plan that helps the individual go on to secure a job, either within the business or elsewhere". Argos, she said, is committed to ensuring that unpaid unemployed people "work alongside, not replace, paid colleagues".

One particular pressure group has made the running on the issue of unpaid work: Boycott Workfare, one of those nimble, non-hierarchical, online-focused organisations that regularly crash-land in the news. When I spoke to a member of the group called Joanna Long, she said that at any given time hundreds of thousands of people could be working for nothing, undercutting paid workers' terms and conditions, and providing a vast subsidy for the private sector. She also said the group was looking forward to 26 and 27 June, when two judicial review cases against the Department of Work and Pensions will come to the High Court in London. One is being brought by Cait Reilly, the geology graduate who was forced to give up volunteering in a museum and work unpaid in a Birmingham branch of Poundland.

"We're talking about tens of millions of pounds being handed to companies in unpaid work," she said, before suggesting that the issue undermines the fashionable idea that most Britons want to throw people on welfare to the lions. "People know it's their jobs and overtime that are being attacked. So it's not good for them, and they know it's not good for unemployed people either."

Like some of the companies involved, the government is sensitive about all this. Back in February there was a spectacular burst of protest focused on the government's key work experience programme for young people, whereby the unemployed under

25 are encouraged to put in up to eight weeks of work experience – and, as things stood then, risked losing benefit if they left any placement once the first week was up. Zeroing in on this element of the scheme, protesters targeted an array of big retail chains – Tesco, chiefly – and after many companies vowed to pull out, the government pledged to make participation voluntary, while also decrying those who took issue with such schemes as "job snobs". Pressure groups such as Boycott Workfare claim people are still effectively being forced into taking part – and in any case, whether it's voluntary or compulsory, the practice of employing people for nothing is expanding at speed.

Last month, the government vowed to double the numbers of unemployed people forced to work for their benefit – for four weeks at a time, up to 30 hours a week – under what officialspeak calls mandatory work activity, which could mean an increase to around 80,000 placements a year. The coalition is also aiming to create 250,000 work experience places for young people before 2015. The official blurb says the latter are a matter of "voluntary work experience", though when George Osborne announced the scheme last year, he said: "Young people who do not engage with this offer will be considered for mandatory work activity, and those who drop out without good reason will lose their benefits."

Then there is the work programme, launched in June 2011, focused on people unemployed for a year or more, and built around the private companies and charities that are paid according to how many people they get into work. At the last count, around 565,000 people had been referred to the scheme over the six months to January 2012. Unpaid work experience is an inbuilt element of what the work programme offers to its participants. How long placements can last is by no means clear: the government says its so-called "black box" approach means that it is down to the discretion of A4e, Serco et al, and Freedom of Information requests have revealed that at least one work programme provider, the multinational firm Ingeus (owned by the city giant Deloitte), can put "customers" in unpaid work for up to six months.

And so the array of schemes and projects goes on. Some 300,000 people, either suffering from a long-term illness or disabled, are included in what the government calls the work-related activity group, and there have been proposals to introduce many of them to the wonders of mandatory work experience. There is also a pilot scheme called the community action programme (up to 30 hours of unpaid work a week, for as long as six months), and sector-based work academies (combinations of training and unpaid work lasting up to six weeks). All of this points up one of the most sobering things about modern Britain: there may be a paucity of proper work, but there seems to be no shortage of the unpaid variety.

When it comes to young graduates, meanwhile, rules long since imported from the US mean that unpaid work experience is an increasingly obligatory step on the road to professional employment. The thinktank IPPR reckons that at any given time around half of the 250,000 internships in the UK are paid below the minimum wage and 18% – around 45,000 – are wholly unpaid. Note also the government's plans to double the number of people doing full-time paid work in prison, much of it for private companies. Most working inmates are paid very low wages: news emerged this week of the contract for prison work handed to the food packaging company Calpac, which pays an "office manager" £40 for a 40-hour week, and puts a "manual packing operative" on 55p an hour.

To finish, back to our hardworking and comfortably off monarch. Just as the jubilee celebrations got going, the Queen paid tribute to "the continuity of our national story and the virtues of resilience, ingenuity and tolerance that created it". She had a point

– but there is also a very British tradition of grim exploitation, embodied by such inventions as the workhouse and the sweatshop. And at this rate, it may be about to return, in spades.

In August the High Court ruled that the Government's back to work schemes were lawful.

21 JUNE

Sound the trumpets: Today's the day for the Cultural Olympiad

CHARLOTTE HIGGINS

In the Community Campus of Raploch, a housing estate on the outskirts of Stirling, 120 children aged between six and 13 are rehearsing the Rondeau from Purcell's Abdelazer – familiar to most as the imposing opening theme of Britten's The Young Person's Guide to the Orchestra. This is the Big Noise Orchestra; but before the music can begin, this rustling, restless, excited gaggle of children must be calm.

"Let's have some Big Noise silence now," says the conductor, Francis Cummings, a former violinist with the Chamber Orchestra of Europe.

"We are going to sit in silence until you listen. What we need to do is start from silence."

Eventually, through squeaks and shuffles, through parps from the brass and bashes from the timpani, through the grunts from the basses and jitters from the violins, peace comes. And then the music starts.

Spring

In another part of the building, beyond the gym and the hairdressers, a second orchestra is preparing to rehearse in the sports hall. The musicians of Venezuela's Simón Bolívar Symphony Orchestra, most of whom are in their 20s and early 30s, are making as much noise as 200 people with musical instruments can. There's a clatter of chat and tuning; lads in jeans and baseball caps are swapping violins, trying each other's instruments by turning musical tricks of insouciant virtuosity.

Then Gustavo Dudamel, their 31-year-old conductor, comes to the podium and sits down on his high stool. He looks up, and slightly raises both arms. At this simple gesture, all sound falls instantly away.

The two orchestras are rehearsing for the same event: a concert to be held in Raploch. It will open the London 2012 festival, the summer of cultural events ushering in the Olympic Games: an open-air concert for 8,000, to be broadcast live on BBC4. After that, the Venezuelans travel to London, for concerts at the Southbank Centre.

Although the two orchestras appear so different – the Venezuelans with their grown-up professionalism and absolute concentration; the Scottish children still fresh to their instruments – they are related. Later Dudamel, who is also the much-fêted chief conductor of the Los Angeles Philharmonic, calls the Scots "our little sons and daughters".

The children are the young members of Sistema Scotland, a radical social-intervention programme based on the model that produced these Venezuelan musicians. Like its Latin American exemplar, Sistema Scotland is hoping to change the lives of the children of an underprivileged community through immersion in classical music.

The Venezuelan El Sistema was founded by José Antonio Abreu, who began teaching music to 11 students in a Caracas garage. Thirty-seven years on, two million people – including, most famously, Dudamel and the players of the Simón Bolívar Orchestra – have passed through the programme.

Since that orchestra's sensational UK debut in Edinburgh and the Proms in 2007, it has exploded many British people's ideas about what classical music can be: these players perform with a fiery passion and joyous exuberance that counters the reputation of classical music as a polite pastime for the middle-aged middle classes.

The man behind the Scottish version of El Sistema is Richard Holloway, the author and former bishop of Edinburgh. Tipped off by the Guardian in 2005 about how El Sistema was trying to tackle social inequality in Venezuela, he travelled to Caracas, and was impressed.

"I felt in my bones it was what was needed. It was incremental, it was organic. It wasn't quick. To create a great orchestra is by definition slow. It's like growing hard, hard wood... Scotland, like other parts of Britain, has a problem with deprived communities that nothing seems to shift... I've been interested to see if there's not something in the world that would turn that around."

At the same time as Holloway was discovering the Venezuelan Sistema, Stirling council was trying to tackle the problems of one of its most deprived areas: Raploch. In 2004, it began a regeneration project in an area where, at the time, the average income was £6,240; a fifth of the residents were on incapacity benefit, and half of them had no formal educational qualifications.

"All the things that happen in deprived communities were happening here: underachieving children, unhealthy adults, a drug problem, kids fed into the criminal justice system," said Holloway. "But it also had a lot of feisty eager people who loved their children and wanted the best for them."

Holloway approached Stirling council and "they were as mad as we were". In 2008, Sistema Scotland began its work in Raploch,

Spring

and now 450 children from the area (whose population is a little over 3,000) are learning how to play musical instruments. The scheme costs £750,000 a year – just 14% of which comes from the public purse.

But can classical music really be the instrument of social change? The truth is that the effects of Sistema Scotland will only really become clear when the children who started in its 2008 cohort grow up: will they escape the poverty trap and what Holloway calls the "revolving doors" of the youth criminal-justice system?

Even now, walking round the streets of Raploch – whose idyllic position on the banks of the Forth, beneath the benign gaze of Stirling Castle, stands in stark contrast to its history of social deprivation – it is impossible to find anyone with a bad word to say about Big Noise.

It is a tight-knit community where everyone knows everyone, which means everyone knows a young musician. Taf Magoche, whose daughter Chantelle plays violin, says: "It's a thing that brings the community together, and in the long run it's sowing a lot more benefits because when the kids get older there will be more options.

"It's not the best community, but for the future it will be a lot better because of the project. When you look at the social unrest, people on benefits, drugs and all that... this programme has brought something new and different for the kids – something that's not running around the streets causing mayhem."

Elizabeth Martin has a grandson who plays the double bass – "bigger than he is". "The mothers are so proud of their kids," she said. "The wee tears will be in my eyes on Thursday night."

A report commissioned by the Scottish government found that all the parents of pupils in the Scottish Sistema felt their child's confidence had improved as a result of their involvement, and more than 90% felt that their child was happier.

What makes the Scottish Sistema different from other music education schemes in Britain, according to its director, Nicola Killean, is the fact that it is completely immersive.

"We have everything from baby classes to orchestral rehearsals," she said. The children involved play three times a week, for nearly three hours. It is also collective: "about being part of a community from the very beginning".

Unlike traditional European and north American music education, it does not focus on individual tuition: children play in an orchestra from the beginning.

Verónica Urrego, who teaches violin and viola in Raploch, and is herself a Venezuelan product of El Sistema, says: "We are not here just to teach them how to play an instrument, but also how to behave in a community, in a society.

"We have to give them the whole package – the discipline to behave in an orchestral rehearsal... It's not an extracurricular activity, it's a way of life," she says.

In Venezuela, the Sistema has grown organically as children grow up and feed back into the system. According to Dudamel, the orchestra can act as a microcosm of wider society. "It has changed not just the lives of the individuals involved – but also of their families, the communities around the children. And it changed because they have access to beauty; because they have access to sensitivity; because they have access to creativity; they have access to discipline. We are talking here about the elements of a good citizen."

26 June

Farewell to Lonesome George, who never came out of his shell

JOHN VIDAL

He was on Ecuador's bank notes and stamps, an evolutionary remnant, a money-spinning tourist attraction and an icon of international conservation. No one knew if he was gay, impotent, bored or just very shy. But he is thought to have been about 100 years old and in his prime when he died on Sunday at the Charles Darwin research centre in the Galápagos Islands, although the giant tortoise known as Lonesome George and commonly called the "rarest animal on Earth" may in fact have been far older – or much younger.

In the 40 years he spent in a field on Santa Cruz Island, having been relocated from Pinta Island in 1972, the 200lb, 5ft-long animal showed little interest in either man or other tortoises. He mostly ignored the female company provided to encourage him to breed, kept his 3ft scraggy neck down in the long grass, and only responded to his keeper, Fausto Llerena, who runs a tortoise breeding centre.

"The park ranger in charge of looking after the tortoises found Lonesome George, his body was motionless," said Edwin Naula, head of the Galápagos National Park. "His lifecycle came to an end."

George was found near a water hole, but no one knows how or why he died, and evolutionary scientists are still baffled by his life in the volcanic Pacific islands 1,000km off Ecuador that inspired Darwin's theories on evolution and which are now a global laboratory for conservation.

The last known representative of the giant Galápagos tortoise subspecies *Chelonoidis nigra abingdoni* had every reason to shun humanity, however. His relatives were exterminated for food or oil by whalers and seal hunters in the 19th century, and his habitat on Pinta was devastated by escaped goats. George possibly has relations on neighbouring Isabela Island, but it is more likely his whole subspecies is now extinct – the end of what is probably a 10m-year-old line.

On Monday, scientists who had spent time with George recalled his peculiar ways. "George was the last of his kind. He had a unique personality. His natural tendency was to avoid people. He was very evasive. He had his favourites and his routines, but he really only came close to his keeper Llerena. He represents what we wanted to preserve for ever. When he looked at you, you saw time in the eyes," said Joe Flanagan, the head vet of the Houston zoo, who knew George for more than 20 years.

Scientists' attempts to get George to mate with other giant tortoises from the Galápagos Islands and to eventually repopulate Pinta all failed and were often comical. Artificial insemination did not work, nor did a $10,000 reward offered by the Ecuadorean government for a suitable mate. In the 1990s, Sveva Grigioni, a Swiss zoology graduate student, smeared herself with female tortoise hormones and, in the cause of science, spent four months trying to manually stimulate him – to no avail.

In 2008 and 2009 George unexpectedly mated with one of his two companions, but although two clutches of eggs were collected and incubated, all failed to hatch.

Henry Nicholls, author of Lonesome George: The Life and Loves of the World's Most Famous Tortoise, reported that George was irresistibly attracted to the late Lord Devon's wartime helmet, presumably because it resembled the shell of a young tortoise. Even after being put on a diet, the celibate tortoise with the scraggy neck, who could have been expected to live until he was well over 200, remained obstinately alone.

Conservation scientists on Monday said George was important because he symbolised both the rapid loss of biodiversity now taking place around the world, and provided the inspiration to begin restoring it in places like the Galápagos Islands. "Because of George's fame, Galápagos tortoises which were down to just a few animals on some islands have recovered their populations. He opened the door to finding new genetic techniques to help them breed and showed the way to restore habitats," said Richard Knab of the Galápagos Conservancy, which is running giant tortoise breeding programmes with the Ecuadorean government.

In 1960, 11 of the Galápagos Islands' original 14 populations of tortoises remained, and most were on the point of extinction. Today, around 20,000 giant tortoises of different subspecies inhabit the islands and most of the feral goats have been eradicated.

But George will be sorely missed for financial reasons, too. As the star of the islands and an icon of global wildlife, he helped attract 180,000 money-spinning visitors a year to the archipelago. He is likely to become a conservation relic and will probably be embalmed and displayed – alone still.

Summer

3 July

You've been bankered

ADITYA CHAKRABORTTY

We don't know each other, but I want to offer you a deal: You each give me £20,000. And that's it. What do you get in return? Well, it's a fair question but I can't even promise to pay it all back. But let me assure you of this: your hard-earned cash will keep me in the style to which I'm accustomed. And that's got to be good for all of us. So I'm sure you'll agree that 20 grand is an absolute bargain. Indeed, I would call it a once-in-a-lifetime offer; only I can't promise not to come back again.

You've probably guessed that the transfer I'm talking about has already happened. Each man, woman and child in Britain has already handed over £19,271. And our money has gone to the banks. According to the IMF, the British stuck £1.2 trillion behind the finance sector. Read that again: well over a trillion pounds in bailouts, and loans and state guarantees on bankers' trading. In just a few months, and with barely any public debate, every household subbed £46,774 to the City. A sliver of that money eventually went unused; as for the remaining hundreds of billions, we have no idea just how much we'll get back – or when.

There ought to be a verb for this kind of involuntary donation. For true accuracy, it should only come in the passive voice. We could call it: to be bankered. "What happened to the British in the early 21st century?", a future historian will ask. "Poor sods," her colleague might reply. "I'm afraid they got totally bankered".

Twenty grand each is the sum I've looked out for in the coverage of the latest banking scandal; in vain, of course. But what gives this latest market-rigging story such force is that it was carried out by a financial system that taxpayers were bankered into near-penury to prop up. And we did so in the belief that saving banks was vital to the public interest. But you haven't heard much about the public interest in what will inevitably be dubbed the Lie-bor scam. Instead, the political and media industries have typically treated the rogue bankers as a tale of personal greed or market failure.

So it is that the Daily Mail calls for market-rigging bankers to be banged up. That David Cameron and George Osborne talk up the need for an investigation of how benchmark lending rates are set. As for Ed Miliband, he'll doubtless carry on seeking an inquiry into "the culture of banking" with the same manner he always affects when discussing capitalist crisis: looking like a faintly peeved vicar who has just leafed through the Financial Times and discovered that Bad Things are happening in the cosmos. All of these demands are partly justified – and all ultimately miss the point. Where they are obviously right is in recognising that what's come out in the last few days really is a scandal. Through tampering with lending rates, financiers at Barclays and elsewhere distorted everything from how much home-owners paid on their tracker mortgages to the deals struck by pension funds purely to pump up bank profit margins and their own bonuses. The lawsuits for Barclays alone are likely to cost billions.

Against that, the punishment meted out to Bob Diamond's company barely figures. The £290m fine slapped on it by regulators is tax-deductible, making it equivalent to just 13 days' profit. In any case, the bill will be paid by shareholders, rather than traders or senior management. Even the chucking overboard of chairman Marcus Agius smacks of a firm doing the least it can, and hoping it doesn't have to do any more. Not a hint yet of any punishment for Trader C and Manager E and the rest of the

Summer

millionaire looters pinging around those internal emails. They cling on to their bonuses and their anonymity, which means they can carry on taking telephone-number salaries in the City.

But it's here that the various stories can't be contained in their respective boxes. The Mail's scapegoating of Cap'n Bob and the Bollinger crew doesn't fit with officials' warnings that this particular mess will not stop at Barclays or RBS – but will grow bigger by the week. Likewise, you can see why Cameron and Osborne would want to contain any fallout from this crisis, which is why they formally announced an independent inquiry into the way in which Libor is fixed, alongside a more nebulous inquiry into industry standards.

About time, too. Yet market manipulation is only the most jaw-dropping example of the corporate rampaging that caused the financial crisis. Early in the crisis, politicians, regulators and commentators discussed this recklessness as being largely about the selling of dodgy assets to other consenting financiers. But as time has gone by what's become clearer is that British banks have behaved in just as predatory a fashion whether dealing with the vulnerable or powerful.

Into the first category fall family butchers, high-street electrical shops and up to 28,000 other small businesses who, it was officially ruled last week, had been force-fed over-complex and expensive financial products. So too do the individual account-holders who were mis-sold billions in insurance they didn't need and which hardly ever paid out. As for the second category, well, even ministers aren't above the occasional poke in the eye; earlier this year Barclays was forced to close two tax-avoidance schemes worth at least £500m. That time, Diamond didn't offer to forfeit his bonus – but shot off a missive to MPs about the "unnecessary damage... placed on Barclays' reputation". So in a sequence of events reminiscent of the Wall Street crash of 1929, the same industry that brought you a financial crisis, a double-dip recession and the greatest economic misery in decades is now vomiting up scandal after scandal. Shot through these iniquities is a high-handed sense of being above the law. It's obvious in the blatancy with which Barclays went about rigging interest rates even at the height of the crisis while taxpayers were bailing it out with subsidies and guarantees. And it's here that Miliband's explanation runs out of road, too. Because this isn't just an everyday story of ordinary banking folk constantly hatching schemes to pervert markets, morality and the course of justice. In his call for a public inquiry, the Labour leader is desperate to restrict the role of politicians in the financial boom and bust to a mere walk-on part. But in the Libor scandal and elsewhere, the real picture is of an industry allowed to run riot by their regulators and governments.

As far back as 2008, the Wall Street Journal was running front-page pieces, beginning: "Major banks are contributing to the erratic behaviour of a crucial global lending benchmark". Yet neither the British Bankers' Association (which is in charge of setting Libor), nor any state regulator stepped in. More than that, the Financial Service Authority (FSA) has referred to "a telephone conversation between a senior individual at Barclays and the Bank of England during which the external perceptions of Barclays' Libor submissions were discussed." As the conversation was relayed through Barclays, the FSA observes, staff "believed mistakenly" that they had the thumbs up from Threadneedle Street to carry on lying.

What's clear is that politicians of both major parties sanctioned, even encouraged, the recklessness of the banks. Just a few months before Northern Rock fell over, Gordon Brown told financiers, "This is an era that history will record as a new golden age for the City of London." In 2006, Ed Balls, then-City minister declared, "Nothing should be done to put at risk a light-touch, risk-based regulatory regime." Such hostages to fortune surely explain why the two Eds would rather focus the spotlight on the City than widen it out to take in Downing Street.

Yet Labour ministers are not the only culpable parties. Last December Cameron stormed out of a Brussels summit that threatened to put extra restrictions on the City. He did it, he said, to protect the "national interest". The most generous spin you can put on this is of prime ministerial foolishness. This, you might say, just shows how far finance has convinced the British establishment that its special pleading somehow fits hand in Hermès glove with the national interest.

More than enough evidence shows that what bankers want is either no use to the rest of us, or positively harmful. Finance doesn't create jobs: in fact, the number of people directly employed by banks and others has remained almost flat at 1m. As Manchester University's Centre for Research on Socio-Cultural Change (Cresc) points out the taxes paid by finance between 2002 and 2008, during the boomiest boom in human history, came to only £193bn – and were immediately wiped out by the upfront costs of the banking bail-out.

Most of all, banks fail to lend to the real economy. And I'm not just trotting out the old line about how crisis-stricken financiers aren't giving loans to recession-hit businesses. I mean that they haven't been lending to the productive part of the economy for years. In March 2008, just over three-quarters – 76.2% – of all bank and building-society loans went either to other financial firms or on property for mortgages. Less than a quarter – 23.8% – went to what you might call the productive part of the economy – non-financial businesses.

You will be delighted to hear that things have improved in the crisis. This March, the proportions of loans taken by finance and property slumped all the way to a trifling 74.7%, while non-financial firms took a whopping 25.3%. And manufacturing got just 2.5% of all loans – even though it still makes up around 10% of the economy. Some of you might look at those figures and ask exactly how far our bankers have reformed themselves during the crisis. The rest, no doubt, are grateful for the huge and beneficial changes being made by the coalition and its "march of the makers".

Given how far banking fails to serve our own national interest, let alone live up to its own propaganda, we need a better explanation of why politicians are so willing to give it another chance, then another chance – all with 20 grand from each British resident with no strings attached. There's the revolving door between government and the City, which enables Tony Blair to leave No 10 and be chauffeured straight into a £2.5m a year part-time job with JP Morgan. Or the research showing how today's Tory party gets half its funding from the finance industry.

Most of all there is evidence of how the City retains its stranglehold on economic policy. The same coalition government that likes to promise a "rebalancing" of Britain's economy is even now generating schemes to keep the banks flush with billions – but couldn't guarantee an £80m loan to Sheffield Forgemasters.

Or there's the fact that, nearly five years on from the collapse and subsequent nationalisation of Northern Rock, British taxpayers have still not been provided with a comprehensive review of the causes of the financial crisis. One of Barack Obama's first acts as US president was to commission the Financial Crisis Inquiry Report, a 600-page document that was reviewed in the New York Review of Books as "the most comprehensive indictment of the American financial failure that has yet been made". What's the nearest British equivalent? The Bischoff report commissioned by Alistair Darling in the wake of the crisis, which looked into the long-term outlook for finance. Totting up the career histories of the authors of this government-sponsored review, the Cresc team calculated that three-quarters of their combined working lives had been spent either at a bank or in a closely-related field. The comparison is laughable. Without review of how the UK ended up in this mess, or reform beyond the narrowly technical proposals made by the Vickers Commission (40% of whose authors were ex-bankers), we are doomed to repeat the same mistakes again and again. Indeed, the evidence is that London is already gaining the reputation of being the SpivZone of international financial markets. At a hearing in the US last month into how JP Morgan lost up to $9bn in the UK in derivatives trading, congresswoman Carolyn Maloney commented: "It seems to be that every big trading disaster happens in London."

This is surely where the pressure from the Libor scandal needs to be directed. Miliband is right to demand a public inquiry. But rather than a nice, compact affair that can be swept under the ministerial carpet, any investigation needs to understand how to reform the finance sector so that crises like these don't recur; and so that banks actually work in the public interest rather than hire propagandists to pretend they do. Because in the end, financial reform is not about technicalities, but about politics: deciding what role banks should play in an economy, and what kind of economy we want. And just as the Leveson investigation has unpicked the toxic intimacy between the Murdoch empire and the political classes, so any inquiry into finance needs to expose the strength of its grip on our politics.

In the wake of the Lehman's collapse of 2008, there was much talk about how the relationship between state and finance would be changed in the public interest. Those efforts were effectively killed off by the finance lobbyists and, if we're honest, the unpreparedness of progressives in Britain to seize the opportunity. The Libor scandal offers a second go at the same argument. We either have it out this time, or we run the risk of repeating 2008. Only next time, the British might need to cough more than 20 grand each. A lot more.

3 JULY

We don't like the sound of Fifty Shades of Grey

MICHELE HANSON

I ask Rosemary if she's heard of Fifty Shades of Grey. "Only because its cover's been changed," says she. "Then it did rather well." So it did, but why?

We don't like the sound of it. Even When Harry Met Sally was a bit much for Rosemary, but she did rather like Molly Bloom, thinking about having a lovely time at the end of the BBC's non-stop Ulysses. That was a rather high-class bit of porn, and it lulled Rosemary happily to sleep. "Nothing rude happened, of course," said she.

Fielding wasn't half so delicate. "Oh, you mean the wank book," said he rather coarsely. "What's it like?" I don't know, I admit. I haven't read it. "You can't criticise it then."

Oh yes I can. I've read excerpts. I'm tremendously broadminded. I've read Fanny Hill, Casanova's diaries, and The Joy of Sex, with its mimsy drawings of people doing odd things with only their boots on, and I've even read one of those Black Lace books, which was rather bizarre, I thought, with the heroine covered in grease and tied naked to benches in odd positions. I couldn't quite work them out.

And disappointingly, when offered a chance of escape and freedom with a sensitive, caring and handsome slave, she chose to stay with her bossy, greasing, flogging, tremendously wealthy master, the Prince. What a let down to women everywhere.

"It's a searing indictment of capitalism," says Fielding. "A chap with a helicopter and basement full of whips is bound to be loaded. My friend went out with someone who longed to be tied up and lashed. It wore him out, doing all that lord of the castle routine. In my day, erotica came from Paris. But now you can just read it at the dentist."

So you can. Personally, I worry about where the world is going, sensation-wise. When we've finished being tortured, punished, pierced and stuck with metal, tattooed, trussed up and dressed only in a light coating of oil, what do we do for fun next? I think I'll stick to the piano. Metaphorically, of course, and fully dressed.

4 JULY

The Shard has slashed the face of London forever

SIMON JENKINS

We are shocked by the news from Timbuktu. The Islamists are at it again, smashing the medieval shrines and mosques of the desert city, as they did the buddhas of Afghanistan. They claim these jewels of African heritage offend sharia law. Unesco calls the destruction "a tragedy for all humanity", and a prosecutor at the international criminal court calls it a war crime.

Perhaps they are right. As with the RAF bombing of Dresden, Stalin's dynamiting of Moscow churches and the bulldozing of old Peking, the wilful destruction of beauty in the name of progress offends civilised sensibility.

So what of Thursday's bombastic celebration of the Shard's arrival on the London skyline? It too has drawn Unesco's ire for intruding on the Tower of London and Parliament Square. It will boast its hugeness with lights and lasers, and publicists will dismiss its critics as fuddy-duddies and aesthetes, proclaiming Shards for all time as angels of growth.

I suffer from having found London's skyline a thing of beauty. The views from Parliament and Primrose hills, from the parks and from bridges over the Thames offered a vista that allowed the eye to spread, with no part dominating the whole. Even St Paul's did not crush its neighbours but floated above them at just twice their height.

The eye has no such freedom now. From across the London basin it must rest on the Shard. Its architect, Renzo Piano, claims that his creation "is not about arrogance and power" but intended "to celebrate community... surprise and joy". Besides, it is so high "it will disappear into the sky". Architects have never been happy bedfellows with the English language. As for the tower's developer, Irvine Sellar, he suggests that his building is indeed about arrogance and power. He wants it to cry, "This is London, this is the Shard." Now, he says, "we can kick sand in the face of the Eiffel Tower".

This egomaniacal architecture echoes the tower's political backers, Ken Livingstone, John Prescott and Boris Johnson, who equate phallic prominence with civic prowess. They are in thrall to the Shard's Qatari financiers, who are said to see it as "non-pecuniary soft diplomacy". One Gulf expert explained that "if someone invades a country that has the highest skyscraper

Summer

in London, then surely the UK should come to the rescue". The Shard is thus an adjunct of Tony Blair's foreign policy, a cure for erectile dysfunction.

This tower is anarchy. It conforms to no planning policy. It marks no architectural focus or rond-point. It offers no civic forum or function, just luxury flats and hotels. It stands apart from the City cluster and pays no heed to its surrounding context in scale, materials or ground presence. It seems to have lost its way from Dubai to Canary Wharf.

The Shard was furiously opposed by local people, and by historic buildings and conservation authorities. It was pushed as a symbol of Britain's love affair with financial bling at the turn of the 21st century, with "iconic" celebrities and the eff-you greed of arbitrage. It was allowed to go ahead by Yorkshire's John Prescott as a single-finger gesture in the face of wimpish southerners.

There is no case for buildings like this on grounds of urban density. Their space ratios make them costly and inefficient to service. Any Londoner knows there are thousands of acres of unused and underused land within the M25 awaiting the high-density, low-rise building preferred by the property market.

Some people find the Shard beautiful. I am sure I would in the Gulf, as I admire the Burj Khalifa tower. But Bermondsey is not Dubai. Nor is this just a matter of one person's opinion against another's. It is the destruction of one for the other's gain. There are not two rooms in this visual realm, just one. There are plenty of places for Sellar and Piano to play their games. Why must they tip paint over my Canaletto?

The Shard shows money trumping planning. Let one rise high and there is no case against another. The argument that London's skyline should be an open market failed in its attempt to build over Hampstead Heath in the 19th century and to demolish Piccadilly Circus and much of Whitehall in the 20th. But it took courageous fighting against precisely the arguments deployed by the Shard's apologists.

Would they or their imitators now demand the right to build a shard on Blackheath, or in Kensington Square? If not, why not? Is it that the locals there are rich, whereas in Southwark they were poor? Or do we agree that there is something called beauty in townscape, but that Sellar and Piano claim the right to determine it for themselves.

The truth is that we have lost the ability to articulate what is beautiful for the purposes of development control. While the small man cannot touch a door frame, the big one can do what he likes, no holds barred. The clutch of permits awarded by Prescott and Livingstone is about to yield a forest of towers behind the National Theatre, behind the Festival Hall, over Waterloo station and at Vauxhall, where a tower is already looming over Pimlico. The precedent is set. I cannot see how a planner can now refuse further shards.

The Thames is to become a ditch of cash running through a canyon of glass, San Gimignano re-engineered as Blade Runner. This is planning in the age of Barclays, an oligarchy of wealth, a financial fanaticism every bit as selfish and destructive as the religious fanaticism of Timbuktu. But there is a difference. Timbuktu's shrines can and surely will be rebuilt. The Shard has slashed the face of London for ever.

5 JULY

Higgs boson: It's unofficial! Cern scientists discover missing particle

IAN SAMPLE

There comes a time in a scientist's life when the weight of evidence can no longer be ignored. That moment came today for physicists at Cern, near Geneva, home of the Large Hadron Collider, who announced overwhelming evidence for the obscure but profoundly important Higgs boson, the particle that sparked the greatest hunt in modern science.

In presentations given to a packed auditorium at the laboratory on Wednesday morning, and webcast around the world, the leaders of two research teams, who worked independently of each other, said they had spotted a new particle amid the microscopic flashes of primordial fire created inside the world's most powerful atom smasher.

Cern stopped short of claiming official discovery of the Higgs boson, even as many physicists conceded the evidence was now so compelling they had surely found the missing particle.

Formal confirmation of the discovery is expected within months, though it could take several years for scientists to work out whether they have found the simplest kind of Higgs particle that theories predict, or part of a more complex picture: for example, one of a larger family of Higgs bosons. The discovery of more than one kind of Higgs particle would open the door to an entirely new realm of physics.

"Is it a Higgs boson or not? Well, it has been found using techniques tuned for the Standard Model Higgs. A different object might have stepped in, but it is quite unlikely in my humble opinion," said Tommaso Dorigo, a scientist on the CMS experimental team at Cern. The Standard Model Higgs boson is the most simple proposed version of particle.

The queue for the auditorium left some physicists struggling for a seat to hear the announcement. Those inside broke into applause when Peter Higgs, the 83-year-old father of the particle, entered the room. "Cern should really build a larger auditorium. The present one is nice and cosy, but it is embarrassing and sad to see many distinguished colleagues queueing up at five in the morning knowing that they have a slim chance to get a seat, after working for 20 years on finding the Higgs boson," said Dorigo.

Scientists and engineers at the lab, many exhausted from working round the clock in recent weeks, clapped and whistled as Joe Incandela and Fabiola Gianotti, the respective heads of the Large Hadron Collider detector teams called CMS and Atlas, presented their results for the first time. Both teams saw the particle, which has a mass of around 125 to 126 GeV, about 130 times the mass of a proton.

"It's hard not to get excited by these results," said Cern research director, Sergio Bertolucci.

The lab's director general, Rolf Dieter Heuer, said: "We have reached a milestone in our understanding of nature." He later added: "As a layman I would now say I think we have it" – meaning the Higgs.

They have worked hard and long for this day. The particle, which is unlike any other known to exist, was proposed 48 years ago, when physicists worked on the laws of nature with pen and paper instead of the sleek, high-end laptops they carry around today. The hunt has spanned decades and occupied thousands of researchers from tens of countries. For some, this has been their life's work.

There is never a bad time for good news, but Cern will be relieved to have made the breakthrough before the machine shuts down for almost two years at the end of 2012, when engineers move in to carry out work for the accelerator to run at its full design energy.

The discovery of the Higgs particle ranks as one of the most important scientific advances of the past 100 years. It proves there is an invisible energy field that pervades the vacuum of the known universe. This field is thought to give mass to the smallest building blocks of matter, the quarks and electrons that make up atoms. Without the field, or something like it, there would be no planets, stars, or life as we know it.

While scientists work to understand the new particle, the discovery raises a quandary for the Nobel committee that must now decide who deserves credit for the work. Traditionally, Nobel prizes go to no more than three people, but six physicists published papers on the theory in 1964, and others laid important groundwork beforehand or developed the theory later. Peter Higgs at Edinburgh University was the first to point out in 1964 that a new particle, the eponymous boson, was a by-product of the mass-giving field. That was a crucial step, because it gave scientists a smoking gun to hunt for in their experiments. One of the original gang of six, Robert Brout at the Free University in Brussels, died last year. The others are Francois Englert from Belgium, Tom Kibble from the UK, and Dick Hagen and Gerry Guralnik in the US.

Peter Higgs said: "I am astounded at the amazing speed with which these results have emerged. They are a testament to the expertise of the researchers and the elaborate technologies in place.

"I never expected this to happen in my lifetime and shall be asking my family to put some champagne in the fridge."

According to the theory, all of the particles in the newborn universe were massless and hurtled around at the speed of light. But one trillionth of a second after the big bang, the Higgs field switched on, turning the vacuum of space into a kind of cosmic glue. Some particles feel the Higgs field more than others. The quarks that make up atomic nuclei feel a lot of drag from the field, and become heavy for subatomic particles. Others, such as electrons, feel less drag and gain much less weight. Particles of light, called photons, feel no drag at all, and so remain massless and keep moving at the speed of light. To find the Higgs particle, physicists at Cern sifted through the subatomic debris of more than 1,000 trillion proton collisions inside the Large Hadron Collider. Occasionally, these collisions might create a Higgs boson, which immediately disintegrates into more familiar particles. To spot the boson, the scientists have to look for unusual excesses of the particles it decays into, which appear as bumps in their data.

Particle physicists use a "sigma" scale to rank the certainty of their results that ranges from one to five. One and two sigma results come and go and are often no more than statistical fluctuations in the data. A three sigma result counts as an official "observation", but five sigma is usually needed to claim a discovery, amounting to less than a one in a million chance that it is wrong. Evidence for the Higgs boson has risen sharply in the past seven months. In December, the Atlas and CMS teams at Cern reported what appeared to be hints of a Higgs particle weighing about 125 gigaelectronvolts (GeV), roughly 130 times heavier than a proton. On Wednesday, that evidence became overwhelming. The Atlas team reported a particle at 126.5 GeV with a confidence of five sigma, while the CMS team found a particle with a mass of 125.3 GeV with a 4.9 sigma confidence.

At the end of the announcement, the room erupted into a standing ovation of whoops, cheers and whistles. Peter Higgs reached for a tissue and wiped a tear from his eye.

John Ellis, who has worked at Cern since the 1970s, said the discovery will open up a new era in particle physics. "There is no doubt that something very much like the Higgs boson has been discovered. The strengths of the signals observed independently by CMS and Atlas are completely convincing, and they are supported by data from the Tevatron experiments CDF and D0. Now the emphasis will shift to verifying the properties of the particle that has been discovered: does it have spin zero? Does it couple to other particles proportional to their masses? The discovery will open up a new era in particle physics, as we look for deviations from the properties expected in the Standard Model, and for other physics beyond the Standard Model that might be connected, such as the nature of dark matter."

Bill Murray, a physicist at Cern, told the Guardian: "I've had a bottle of champagne on ice for a long time. I'll be cracking it open tonight."

23 JULY

A dream comes true – now it's got to be Games gold

BRADLEY WIGGINS

Bradley Wiggins became the first British cyclist to win the Tour de France. Afterwards he spoke to William Fotheringham.

There is a set of railings, about six or eight of them, just before the entrance to the Place de la Concorde, about a kilometre from the Tour de France finish on the Champs-Élysées. I stood on those railings with my brother and my mum on 25 July 1993 watching the Tour de France go past.

It all went by in a flash, but I spotted Miguel Indurain in the yellow jersey – about to win his third Tour in a row – and Gianni Bugno in the rainbow jersey of world champion.

It was my first sight of the Tour. We'd come over from London for the weekend, gone up the Eiffel Tower the day before, then watched the Tour come into town on the Sunday. I remember thinking how big it was, how huge it was, seeing the riders whizzing past. I never imagined that 19 years later I'd be coming down there in the same position as Indurain.

It sounds cliched, but it's the stuff of childhood dreams really. It's what I've dreamed of for 20 years but I never dreamed it could become reality.

A lot of riding up the Champs-Élysées is goose-pimple stuff. When you come on there the roar, even when you finish last in the Tour, is the same for everyone. But coming on in the yellow jersey surrounded by the guys who have put me there, with all my family there waiting for me – well, I won't swear but...

It's very difficult to sum up what I'm feeling in words. The thing that's struck me most over the last 12 hours or so is just what it means to other people around me, like my personal photographer breaking down in tears in my room, and my mechanic in tears as well: you just think hell, it's not just me who's gone through this, everyone else around me has lived it too.

That's quite a nice feeling, that you can have that impact on someone. So I'm almost the last person to soak it up and know what it feels like. And I guess that will happen over time. A lot of it is relief. It's a little bit like when I won the Olympics for the first time in 2004.

It's almost a kind of disbelief that this is happening; it's little things like seeing the front page of L'Équipe, with my picture on it in the yellow jersey. You don't realise it's you on there. It's strange. And there are messages like the one I had from Sir Chris Hoy: it's humbling to hear praise of that kind. The biggest accolade is respect from your peers. They are people I look up to. So it blows you away a bit. In the medium-term, I want to go on until the end of the season, at this stage I want to keep going. My job is to ride a bike and that's what I like doing: going out on my bike, and training.

In the short term, it's gold or nothing in London now, if I'm 100% honest. We have prepared for this for a long time. We always knew I would be chasing the win in the Tour, and that after that I would be going for the win in the time trial in the London Olympics, so we planned for this happening, although we weren't taking it for granted by any means. Everything is in place for the next goal.

I've just a done a world-class time trial, on Saturday, averaging a ridiculous amount of power after three weeks of bike racing and two really tough Pyrenees stages, a 222km stage on the Friday at a 44km per hour average speed with a lead-out in the finale, and then I still did that on Saturday.

I was already thinking about the Olympics on Saturday. It's realistic to think I can win that now. I've made so many improvements in my time trialling this year. A year ago when I was beaten by Tony Martin at the worlds [the UCI Road World Championships] by 1 minute 15 seconds, I thought I was probably just going to get a medal. But I've certainly closed the gap now, if not gone past him. It's going to be another tough race but a very realistic chance of gold. So physically, you'd think not a lot's going to change in nine days. If anything, I'm going to be fresher. And once you start thinking in those terms, that you're so fit and you've trained for the demands of the three weeks and you've actually got three days off in between the road race and the time trial, it shouldn't be a problem. I will do the road race, but I don't envisage anything other than working 100% for Mark Cavendish.

An Olympic athlete can't envisage doing the Tour de France 10 days before the biggest race of their life, a marathon or whatever, but racing is what we do as professional cyclists, and we do so many races during the year that actually having nine days off amounts to a holiday. Physically, nothing changes – if I did that time trial yesterday in nine days' time, I'm going to be in the ballpark.

That's why I flew out of Paris on Sunday night to a secret location, so I can get on with riding my bike for the next couple of days, in peace and quiet with no motorbikes around me taking photographs and getting in the way. Coming off the back of this, it will kind of add the hundreds and thousands on the cake. You could say the icing is on it. We've just got to put the little cherry on top.

I've set a precedent now for performances. I can't sit and say I'll be happy with a silver, or happy with a bronze. It's got to be gold now.

And he won an Olympic gold medal in the cycling time trial nine days later

28 July

Olympic Games opening: Irreverent and idiosyncratic

MARINA HYDE

If a thought bubble had appeared above the shire horse's head, it would have read: "And they claim reason is what separates them from the animals..." Long before the Olympic cauldron was lit by seven teenage athletes, you had to salute the livestock stars for obliging their human overlords in a brilliantly irrational night, which saw the stadium rock to an LED-assisted version of the Beveridge report, Her actual Majesty do a skydiving sketch with James Bond, and Fiji arrive to the Bee Gees, all watched over by some of the leading lights of the global arseoisie.

Tonight was Britain's opportunity to speak directly to the world, and – as befits a nation that declines to learn other languages – it did so in English. An architect of Beijing's ceremony once said that event had served Chinese food for the foreign palate, but Danny Boyle's banquet felt as deliciously indigestible to global tastes as Marmite or jellied eels. I loved it. We can't be worrying about how it went down in Moscow or Madagascar. I'm still reeling that a country that can put on a show that hilariously bonkers is allowed nuclear weapons.

Olympic opening ceremonies make the most sense when staged by totalitarian states wishing to announce their imminent global primacy. The quintessential ones are the Nazis in 1936 and Beijing in 2008, in which China basically cowed the world with an insane display of manpower, muscular creativity and technical wizardry. They beat me at "hello". By the time those drummers had finished, they might as well have projected ALL YOUR ECONOMIES BELONG TO US into the night skies.

For a post-imperial power in the twilight home of international life, as Britain is, an opening ceremony is more poignantly challenging.

"How can one make a pattern out of this muddle?" George Orwell wondered of this country in his wonderful essay England Your England, written during the Blitz – a bombardment that featured, along with geese, suffragettes, Bowie, Brunel, the Archers, and weatherman Michael Fish's failure to forecast the

1987 hurricane. Boyle's answer to Orwell's question seemed to be that one can't really, and that's the best thing about the place. He embraced the muddle.

There were moments of subversive lucidity, exemplified by the joyously moving section featuring dancing nurses, which got much of the stadium to spontaneously cheer the NHS. Last year, Boyle and co successfully lobbied David Cameron for an increase in the ceremonies' budget, raising the amusing possibility that the PM effectively greenlit the funds for the piss to be taken out of his policies. Perhaps he'll get his own back by claiming it technically counted as extra spending on the health service.

As for his fellow dignitaries, they were corralled in a surprisingly open section of the stadium, making it possible for your correspondent to stand directly in front of serried ranks of VIPs – 2ft in front of Prince Andrew and his daughters, in fact – and watch them watching the build-up. HRH's attempts to engage one in banter were naturally rebuffed, though the temptation was to inquire of him: "Now, where are the *real* horrors sitting?"

For while it was the best of folks, it was also the worst of folks. Gazing stonily down on a parade of athletes, about whose dreams and sacrifices this entire extravaganza is supposed to be, were some absolute shockers. Taking gold in the Biggest Scumbag in the Stadium event was probably the Bahraini prince, on whose directives athletes are reportedly tortured, flanked on the podium by Rwanda's Paul Kagame and Prince Andrew's brutal mate from Azerbaijan.

So for all the irrepressible excitement about London's Games, a night such as this should not usher in two weeks of uncritical reverence. There must be room for distaste, but especially giggles.

In the aforementioned essay, Orwell said of the goosestep that it was not used in England "because the people in the street would laugh", and for the next fortnight to pass off in truly

British style, the sort of culturally ingrained irreverence that Boyle celebrated here tonight is required.

The greatest trick the IOC ever pulled was convincing people that laughing at any aspect of its machinery is somehow unpatriotic. The sport's the thing – much of the circus around it should be giggled at. For instance, Lord Coe telling the BBC that he really thought all of Britain's history had been leading up to this moment. (Is his lordship going a bit cuckoo? Quite understandable at this stage of his heroic effort, but worth keeping an eye on.)

As for the latest target of British irreverence, I can't say for sure that Mitt Romney didn't join in with Paul McCartney's Hey Jude singalong. But I imagine he reckons the Beatles were "not really that good". After tonight's idiosyncratic triumph, the nation can probably live with the failure to enchant him.

6 August

Usain Bolt takes 100 metres Olympic gold – this time even faster

ANNA KESSEL

The world had wondered: openly, loudly, some may even say rudely, if Usain Bolt was ready. There were rumours of injury, speculation over his commitment to training, worries over his wavering form, suggestions that the triple world record holder might even be psychologically damaged – from last year's false start in the world championships final, from the car crash in June, from his defeat at the hands of his training partner Yohan Blake in Kingston, Jamaica, just five weeks ago. But when that gun went in the 100m final Bolt delivered one almighty response to anyone who had dared to question him, dared to dream of beating him.

Crossing the line in an Olympic record of 9.63sec, the 25-year-old became the first man to defend an Olympic sprint title since Carl Lewis in 1988. Legend? Job done. What did Bolt have to say to the doubters? "I have nothing to say," said the two-times Olympic champion. "I said it on the track. All they can do is talk. I said when it comes to the championships it's all about me." Did he ever doubt his own ability? "I was slightly worried about my start, so I sat in the blocks a bit, but I executed and that was the key. My coach said, 'Stop worrying about your start, your best race is at the end.'"

The Jamaican had to work hard for a victory in which a record seven out of eight men ran under 10 seconds but once Bolt had made up the deficit of his awkward start and drawn level alongside the four fastest men in the field it was easy for him to pull away. At 50 metres Bolt was already going away, just as his compatriot Asafa Powell dropped back, hit by injury. From thereon in the win, although tight, never looked in doubt.

Yohan Blake, the 21-year-old world champion who had twice inflicted defeat on Bolt in recent weeks, was left fighting the two Americans alongside him to take silver. He needed to equal his personal best of 9.75 to do it. On the line Justin Gatlin timed his dip perfectly to snatch bronze from his team-mate Tyson Gay in 9.79 – a miraculous return to the sport for the 2004 Olympic champion who served a four-year suspension after testing positive for a banned substance in 2006. At the finish both Powell, the former world record holder who has never won a global title, and Gay, the second fastest man in history who has never won an Olympic medal, appeared devastated.

Bolt's victory was emphatic and, as the evening had progressed, it had looked ever more likely. In those last few minutes on the warm-up track Bolt and Blake provided an image reminiscent of Bolt's demeanour before his 100m victory in Beijing four years ago.

Joking about together, as though back on the training ground at their Kingston track, they were as relaxed as anyone can be ahead of such a momentous event. Playful as ever, Bolt had toyed with the TV camera that spied on them, leaping left and then right, in and out of vision with seemingly boundless energy as though the fact that he was about to attempt to defend the first of his Olympic titles was not even on his mind. In Beijing, so the story goes, he had been the same, rolling about on the floor, play-fighting with his agent.

Earlier in the evening, in the semi- finals, Bolt had already begun to turn on the speed. Crossing the line in 9.87, the third fastest semi-finalist, Bolt wagged his finger as if to say: did you doubt me? Now you know the answer. Like a knife through butter, Bolt had run easy, languid, assured, as soon as he turned on the accelerators the competition, including Britain's Dwain Chambers, fell away unable even to hang on to his coat tails. Of all the semi-finalists, it was Bolt who looked the most comfortable. That was the giveaway. There lay the hint of what was to come. Not the time as such but the manner in which he won. Glancing right and left before leisurely crossing the line, Bolt was back in his formidable stride.

The performance lay in sharp contrast to his first-round performance on Saturday morning that had kept onlookers guessing. The Jamaican had run the slowest winning time of all seven heats, only 10.09. The Americans blasted their way out of the blocks and powering to record speeds – first Gatlin in 9.97, and then 23-year-old Ryan Bailey in 9.88. Set against that background one could not help wondering if Bolt might be missing a trick. Some accused him of playing a poker game; others simply believed that he was not up to the job. Either way there was reasonable doubt, and a final medal prediction looked difficult to call.

With Jamaica celebrating 50 years of independence, the national anthem already having rung out around the stadium during the medal ceremony for Shelly-Ann Fraser-Pryce's 100m victory, it was a Jamaica sprint double.

Wrapped in the green, black and gold of the Jamaican flag, Bolt and Blake performed their victory lap, the older athlete paying tribute to the younger man. "He works harder than me," Bolt said of the youngster known as "The Beast". "He will do better next time because he was a little bit stressed this time." Bolt's legacy may prove to be far more than simply securing his own status as a legend. He may well have secured a golden future for generations of Jamaican sprinters.

Usain Bolt also won gold medals in the 200 metres and the 4 x 100 metres relay

11 August

Mo Farah runs into history

RICHARD WILLIAMS

Mo Farah can skip the cryosauna, the one in which liquid nitrogen takes the room temperature down to −200F. This time the

Summer

tiny tears in his muscles can be left to repair themselves. Instead he can enjoy the warmth of what is left of this Olympic summer, soaking up the balm of a nation's adoration.

On Saturday Farah, who came to Britain from Somalia as a refugee at the age of eight, won the 5,000m to add to the 10,000m gold medal he captured a week ago on the Super Saturday when gold seemed to rain down from the east London skies on to British athletes.

On that night he had ended 116 years of failure by generations of British athletes to win a long-distance Olympic gold. Now he has done it twice, once again defeating competitors of the highest class with a performance that required the expenditure of every last scrap of his physical and mental resources but, in the end, brooked absolutely no argument.

Thanks to Bradley Wiggins, Jessica Ennis, Greg Rutherford, Charlotte Dujardin, Nicola Adams, Sir Chris Hoy and a host of others, Britain is not short of sporting heroes just now. But it is hard to avoid the instinctive feeling that Farah, who was rescued from temptation in his teenage years by a perceptive PE teacher, stands *primus inter pares* as the symbolic figure of London's inordinately successful and joyous Games.

What he achieved had been done by only six men in history: Hannes Kolehmainen of Finland exactly a century ago, Emil Zátopek of Czechoslovakia in 1952, Vladimir Kuts of the Soviet Union four years later, Lasse Viren in 1972 and again in 1976 – a double double that Farah might feel inclined to emulate in Rio in four years' time – followed by two Ethiopians, Miruts Yifter in 1980 and Kenenisa Bekele in Beijing. Now the British runner is the magnificent seventh.

Brendan Foster, who tried the same double himself 40 years ago and can be assumed to know whereof he speaks, called it the greatest feat in the history of British athletics. That is some claim, but it would take a brave voice to dispute it after the 29-year-old Farah set the Olympic stadium rocking for the second time in eight days.

It was a race that started like a gentle jog to pick up the Sunday papers and ended in an absolute maelstrom of a sprint. A field of 15 offered danger from all sides, from three Ethiopians, two Kenyans, the Kenyan-born Bernard Lagat, who now runs for the United States, Lopez Lomong, born in Southern Sudan but also now running for the US, Hayle Ibrahimov, an Ethiopian who now represents Azerbaijan, and Abdalaati Iguider of Morocco. But no one was willing to make the early pace, which suited the fast-finishing Farah just fine.

Isiah Koech of Kenya led them through the first 1,000m in 2min 55sec, which made it seem like a stroll. The progress to 2,000m was even slower, with Lomong at the front. In the third kilometre two of the Ethiopians, Yenew Alamirew and Dejen Gebremeskel, moved to the front, with Farah carefully manoeuvring himself into position behind them.

Suddenly the pace, which had been inconsistent, was raised. The Ethiopians accelerated, followed by Ibrahimov and the third Ethiopian, Hagos Gebrhiwet. A 60-second lap started to shake out the also-rans from the contenders, and the Kenyan pair of Koech and Thomas Longosiwa took station behind the Ethiopians. Farah stayed cool, but quickly moved up and with four laps to go he slid back into the order of precedence behind Alamirew and Gebremeskel.

With three laps to go, and the pace holding up, he slipped into second behind Gebremeskel. After another 62sec lap he made his move, going to the front as the field straightened on to the back stretch. Had he gone too early? At 600m his training partner, the tall American runner Galen Rupp, came up on to his shoulder, presented a more formidable obstacle to any competitor who fancied attacking with a run round the outside as they came into the finishing straight and approached the last lap.

A week earlier Rupp had also run in support of the man with whom he shares a coach, the Cuban-born former marathon champion Alberto Salazar. On that occasion Rupp was rewarded, to Farah's delight, with an unexpected silver medal. This time, however, he was sacrificing himself, giving his friend a buffer against the first wave of assaults.

At the bell they began to come, Rupp falling back as Farah ploughed on at the head of a group of six, all with their own schemes and dreams about to be fulfilled or shattered.

The 24-year-old Longosiwa was the first to challenge, and the most persistent, coming round the outside of Gebremeskel with his arms flailing wildly.

The full-throttle sprint to the line started 250m out and was agonising to watch as each athlete put every sinew to the test. But that was where Farah's extra burst of acceleration, the "second kick" he has been working on for the last year, enabled him to hold them all at bay and finish two metres ahead of Gebremeskel, with Longosiwa in the bronze medal position.

Watched by his wife, Tania, who is expecting twins, and daughter, Rihanna, Farah came home in triumph, twice a hero and many times blessed.

27 August

Since Neil Armstrong's small step space flight has lost its glamour

MARTIN REES

The first arrival of earthly life on another celestial body ranks as an epochal event not only for our generation, but in the history of our planet. Neil Armstrong was at the cusp of the Apollo programme. This was a collective technological effort of epic scale, but his is the one name sure to be remembered centuries hence.

Armstrong spent years as a test pilot, but he didn't seem a daredevil; indeed his demeanour more resembled a stolid civilian airline captain. He described himself as a "nerdy engineer", and it was as a professor of engineering that he quietly spent his later life.

Apollo 11 landed on the moon only twelve years after the launch of Sputnik, and only 66 years after the Wright brothers' first flight. Had the pace been sustained there would by now be human footprints on Mars. But the moon race was an end in itself, driven by the urge to beat the Russians; there was no motive to sustain the huge expenditure.

The images of Earth's delicate biosphere, contrasting with the sterile moonscape where the astronauts left their footsteps, have become iconic for environmentalists: these may indeed be the Apollo programme's most enduring legacy.

It is now 40 years since Harrison Schmidt and Eugene Cernan, the last men on the moon, returned to Earth. To the young, this is all ancient history. They learn that America landed men on the moon just as they learn that the Egyptians built the pyramids, but the motivations seem almost as bizarre in the one case as in the other; the outdated gadgetry and "right stuff" values portrayed in films and news clips of the period seem as antiquated as those of a traditional Western. Manned spaceflight has lost its glamour – understandably so, because it hardly seems inspiring, 40 years after Apollo, for astronauts merely to circle the Earth in the space shuttle and the International Space Station.

We depend on space technology for communications, weather forecasting, mapping, position-finding and so forth quite apart from the science it has given us. But this doesn't need astronauts.

Close-ups of the Martian surface, and of Jupiter, Saturn and their moons, have beamed back pictures of varied and distinctive worlds. In the coming decades, the entire solar system will be explored by flotillas of unmanned craft. Indeed, it is realistic to expect robotic fabricators, building large structures, or perhaps mining rare materials from asteroids.

But will people venture back to the moon, and beyond? The need weakens with each advance in robots and miniaturisation. But deep space still beckons as a long-range adventure for – at least a few – humans.

Perhaps the Chinese will embark on a prestigious space spectacular. For this, a return to the moon would not be enough. To repeat Neil Armstrong's feat, 50 years later, would hardly proclaim that China had achieved parity with the US. They would surely aim to trump Apollo by heading for Mars.

But would humans on Mars serve a purpose beyond mere prestige? There's no denying that an observant geologist might make startling discoveries that Nasa's recently landed Curiosity rover would overlook. But the current cost gap between manned and unmanned missions is huge.

This is partly because Nasa has become constrained by public and political opinion to be too risk-averse. The space shuttle's two failures in its 135 launches were national traumas in the US, though that is a risk-level that astronauts would willingly accept.

Indeed Neil Armstrong, who landed the tiny Eagle module with the aid of no more computer power than we have in a washing machine today, rated his odds of a safe touchdown as no better than 50/50. And that wasn't the scariest risk: the rockets that blasted them off on the return trip could have failed. Indeed, staff of the president, Richard Nixon, had prepared an alternative speech for him to give if Armstrong and Buzz Aldrin had been stranded and perished on the moon.

Future expeditions to the moon and beyond will only be politically and financially viable if they are cut-price ventures, spearheaded by individuals with the right stuff of the Apollo astronauts, prepared to accept high risks – perhaps even "one-way tickets". They may be privately funded adventurers. The SpaceX company led by the entrepreneur Elon Musk has successfully sent a payload into orbit and docked with the International Space Station.

It is foolish to claim, as some do, that emigration into space offers a long-term escape from Earth's problems. Nowhere in our solar system offers an environment even as clement as the Antarctic or the top of Everest. Nonetheless, a century or two from now, small groups of intrepid adventurers may be living independent from the Earth. Whatever ethical constraints we impose here on the ground, we should surely wish such pioneers good luck in genetically modifying their progeny to adapt to alien environments: the post-human era would then begin. Neil Armstrong, the quiet hero, would then indeed have prefigured "one giant leap for mankind".

Neil Armstrong died on 25 August aged 82. Sir Martin Rees is the Astronomer Royal.

27 August

Martine Wright: From 7 July victim to Paralympic athlete

SANDRA LAVILLE

The Olympic dream for Martine Wright was one shared by thousands the moment London was announced as the host of the 2012 Games – a chance to be in the stadium when the world's top sportsmen and women stepped on to the track. But life intervened and this week it will be as an athlete, not a spectator, that her dream will be fulfilled.

For Wright there is a symbolism to her role as an athlete representing ParalympicsGB that she finds hard to dismiss as one of life's strange coincidences. On the night London was announced as the winning city, she celebrated with friends from work, before making her way home late that night, gripped in the euphoria of the time. Her late night turned into a late morning, and she rushed to work, departing from her usual routine by jumping on to a Circle Line train as the doors were about to close. It was there that her future collided with the murderous intentions of Shehzad Tanweer, one of four suicide bombers who struck that day, ending the party for Wright in a blinding white flash which engulfed the carriage and left her mangled in the wreckage.

She lost both her legs above the knee, and had to undergo many operations before her condition was stable enough to begin the long task of learning to walk again on prosthetic limbs.

"I definitely cannot ignore the fact that the day before I lost my legs I was celebrating that London had won the Olympic bid," she said. "The last thing I was reading on the tube in the newspaper was about the Olympics." This symbolism has been accentuated, she believes, by other signals along her path to the Paralympics.

Her team's training courts both drew her back to the places which dominated her life in the aftermath of the bombings. One was behind the Royal London hospital, where surgeons had carried out the multiple operations that saved her life. The second was opposite Queen Mary's hospital in Roehampton, where she learned to walk again in an exhausting and painful process that lasted many months.

When the team embarked on their first international tour two years ago, they boarded a plane for Oklahoma on 7 July – the anniversary of the bombings; and a few weeks ago as Wright stood at the top of City Hall to hear her name included in the first women's Paralympic sitting volleyball team, she looked across the river and found herself standing directly opposite her old offices in Tower Hill – her thwarted destination on the day of the attacks.

"There's definitely something. I don't know whether it's spiritual or it's fate, but I really truly believe that I was meant to do this journey," she said.

"I find I cannot ignore all these arrows or pointers that have led me to where I am now and made me think that somehow I was always meant to do this."

Today she smiles as she talks of the goal which has driven her for the last two years – to represent her country as an amateur athlete whose exuberance and pride seems to embody the epitome of the Olympic spirit.

"I'm in a very different place now than when I last spoke to you," she said of our meeting seven years ago. "I feel lucky to be in this place. I have had so many opportunities and life is good."

To have survived the bomb attack might have been enough for some people, but for her the years since seem to have been

Summer

marked by a determination and defiance to fully exploit the life she nearly lost on the Circle Line train at Aldgate.

Taking on a new sport, excelling in it and being picked for the Paralympic team has been the story of just the last two years.

She also married Nick, the boyfriend who along with her parents, and two siblings, spent 48 hours searching London hospitals for her in the aftermath of the attacks; and she had a son, Oscar, who has just turned three.

She earned her pilot's licence after winning a Douglas Bader Scholarship for disabled people and spending three months in South Africa, she has been skiing and done a parachute jump. In the midst of it all, she has been outspoken about the length of time it has taken to fully compensate victims of the bombings, and supported calls for a public inquiry into the 7 July attacks.

It was three months after giving birth to Oscar that Wright felt there was something else she needed to fulfil in her life. "I had opportunities to do lots of stuff – flying, skiing, we had moved to Hertfordshire, found a bungalow, pretty much knocked it down and started again when I was pregnant.

"So I'd redone my house, I'd had Oscar and I wanted to do something for me. To be honest I was missing that drive and ambition that I got from work, but I knew I didn't want to go back into marketing."

Maggie, her physiotherapist, mentioned games for amputees that were taking place at Stoke Mandeville hospital, so Wright decided to take part.

She tried wheelchair tennis, which she liked, but felt it was too solitary. "So I tried sitting volleyball and thought: 'Gosh, I really like this.'"

Sitting volleyball developed after the second world war as a sport that injured soldiers could play. It is the only Paralympic sport that is played sitting down and does not involve wheelchairs.

Wright joined a London club which practiced behind the Royal London hospital – where surgeons put her back together when she was wheeled in as an unrecognisable victim of the attacks. A few months later she was asked if she wanted to join the first women's team and agreed immediately.

After an Olympic Games which has drawn criticism for excessive commercialism and the inclusion of professional sports like tennis and football, the makeup of the GB women's sitting volleyball team seems refreshing.

All but one are amateurs, who have never played competitive sport at the national level before. "You get established Paralympic sports like basketball where people have played since they were 10.

"We've only really been playing for the last two years and that's what makes us so unique as a team and so diverse," she said.

"We have maybe got a stronger spirit as a result of all having our own lives and then suddenly coming into it."

Meeting and training so intensely with a group of women, all of whom have had their own particular traumas or challenges to overcome, has also given Wright confidence, she said.

"With all of us girls together suddenly you are talking to people who understand that one day you are someone and suddenly the next day you are someone else. It's really healing and gives you a confidence boost. You are suddenly in a room full of people where it's not just me – and you are saying to each other: 'Well how did you get through that?'

"It is what makes our bond so strong."

For the last few weeks all her time has been taken up with intensive training for the Games. She spent two weeks in Loughborough training up to 30 hours a week, and the team flew to Hungary and Russia for pre-Olympic matches before moving to a holding camp in Bath on 20 August and then three days later into the Paralympic Village.

Exciting as it has been, she has missed her family, and her son, who will be in the audience cheering her on. "Nick has taught him to shout: 'Go mummy go' and 'win mummy win,'" she said.

This year, in the midst of all the activity, the seventh anniversary of the attacks came and went more gently perhaps than in the years before, a sign that she is no longer defined by what happened to her.

"The first five years was really, really tough but it's been seven years and things do get normal," she said. "What I found in the beginning was those memories of how you used to do things were there, and that was really hard to cope with. I don't think about those memories now. I just do things differently."

She puts the easing of the trauma, and the mellowing of the memories down to the passing of time, but only in part.

"I'm doing something that is absolutely amazing, that I would never ever have done, as a result of going through the most traumatic day of my life and nearly dying, and thank God I didn't die," she said.

"I think in my head it is this reasoning that helps me. There was nothing that I could have done to stop what happened that day, it was going to happen and it was going to happen because – maybe – I was always meant to be where I am today."

The GB women's sitting volleyball team did not win a medal

2 September

Ellie Simmonds blazes a record trail

OWEN GIBSON

As she drove to the Olympic Park, Ellie Simmonds looked up at the giant advertising billboard that looms over it bearing her face and the legend "Take the Stage". She did: energised by the deafening roar of the giddy crowd, Simmonds dramatically retained the 400m freestyle S6 title that catapulted her to fame as a then unknown 13-year-old in Beijing four years ago.

Much has changed since then, but if she was feeling the pressure of being the face of these Games, it did not show. She not only narrowly beat her new US rival, Victoria Arlen, as she overhauled her lead in the last 60m, but seized back the world record from the American in a time of 5min 19.17sec.

In the call room before the race, the pair had resolved to "put on a show" for the rowdy 17,500 spectators outside. That Simmonds smashed Arlen's world record by more than five seconds and the American finished just a second behind shows the extent to which they did so.

Simmonds trailed Arlen until 60m and turned for home 0.8 ahead of an opponent who remained something of an unknown quantity. As Simmonds touched the pad, emotions – "excited, happy, relieved" – came tumbling out and she dissolved into tears.

"I gave it everything and that last 50m just killed me. I had no regrets and I just gave it my all. I'm on the edge of the world right now," she said. "She was with me and on that last 50m I gave it everything. It was so tough, one of the toughest races of my life."

Summer

London 2012's chairman, Lord Coe, had already paid tribute to the atmosphere in the Aquatics Centre, suggesting it has been even louder than during the Olympic Games thanks to the quality of the "home town" performances. He was borne out, as a capacity crowd roared their appreciation for the British poster girl. "It gives you a home advantage, it gives you an extra buzz," she said. As Simmonds came out to race, she took one of her earphones out to take in the roar of the crowd.

In one of the two events in which she won gold in Beijing, when she became the youngest ever Briton to win a Paralympic title, Simmonds beat her long-standing Dutch rival Mirjam de Koning-Peper and Arlen, who appeared from nowhere to take both her world records this year.

They raced either side of Simmonds, who was in lane four. After 100m, Simmonds was narrowly fourth but she began to move through the gears on her third length and turned at 150m just behind the leader Arlen. Those two – the titleholder and her challenger – then stretched away from the pack.

From the ParalympicsGB House in a Westfield office block where its medal winners will celebrate their achievements, a billboard bearing a huge image of Simmonds dominates the skyline. "It really inspired me, and made me think I wanted to do it for my country and for all the people who have supported me," Simmonds said.

It is testament to how far she, and the Paralympics, have come that she is as marketable as any other British athlete across this extraordinary summer. With that increased profile comes added pressure.

But just as Jessica Ennis, the face of the Olympics, rose to the occasion on the opening Saturday of those Games so Simmonds seemed to thrive as the noise levels rose. Like Ennis, she acknowledged its effect: "I felt I had a lot of pressure on me going into the race, because people expected me to get the gold medal and that wasn't the case with Victoria on the scene."

Arlen, who had spent the last week with the threat of reclassification hanging over her, recorded a personal best. She said "the best person won" and that the pair had driven one another on. They will renew their rivalry in the 100m and 50m freestyle. "She's a sweetheart. I'm very happy for her, especially as it's her home turf," said Arlen.

Since she shot to prominence by winning the S6 100m and 400m freestyle gold medals in Beijing, Simmonds has won the BBC Young Sports Personality of the Year award and become the youngest person to receive an MBE from the Queen. Her form has fluctuated, but the 400m freestyle remained her most consistent event and she appeared to have peaked at just the right time as she approached the Games.

Simmonds has achondroplasia, a form of dwarfism, and swims in the S6 category. In swimming, as in most Paralympic sports, classifications are "functional" and based on the impact an impairment has on a particular event – which is why swimmers with outwardly different impairments may be grouped together.

After recording a personal best in the heats – surprising herself – she recorded a time of 5:24.64 that was 18 hundredths of a second outside the world record when she expected to swim closer to 5:30. Simmonds was visibly pumped up for the final on this huge occasion and said that she felt "really good".

Summer

12 SEPTEMBER

Ivan Lendl's stony façade cracked as Andy Murray realised his dream

KEVIN MITCHELL

If there is one facial movement Ivan Lendl finds excruciating, it is that upward of curl of the mouth that spreads into what might loosely be described as a smile. When it is accompanied by an ever-so-slight moistening of the eyes, Old Stone Face is hurled into a maelstrom of embarrassment.

All of that happened in New York on Monday night. He couldn't help himself. He stood in Andy Murray's box, positioned like a royal enclosure, raised slightly above the Arthur Ashe Court on which Murray had just created tennis history – and lost it. "That was definitely a smile," Murray said.

The man who had guided Murray to his first grand slam title in just nine months was rightly proud, but the biggest struggle for him was to contain his emotions. This fighting of sentiment is part of his core philosophy of life, one he has imparted to the Scot, whose psyche has dangled on thin string for so long.

But Lendl is never tempted to live a late career as a coach through Murray. He won eight grand slam titles himself. He's done it all already.

"Well, that's why I came on board," he said later, "to help Andy win. He has won two big ones [an Olympic gold medal, where he beat Roger Federer in straight sets, then this US Open, where he ground down Novak Djokovic], it's a fantastic year, I'm very happy for Andy. It's a great achievement for him and let's hope he can continue, and rack up many more.

"I'm 52 years old. I've been away from tennis for 14 years. I don't look at myself as a tennis player, it's somebody that's... it's so long ago, I don't even think about it. I said the goal was for Andy to win majors and he had two fantastic tournaments this year and I'm very happy for him."

Yet some things will remain locked away. Asked what was the most important improvement he had brought to Murray's game since they started working together before the Australian Open in January, he bridled, a fall-back position.

"I'm not going to discuss that. He still has a career to go, he still has to play matches against these guys and, if I tell you what we worked on, what we planned to work on, if I dissect any of the matches, I'm giving away stuff. And, as you saw, the margins are so small that giving away something which would help somebody with two points in the match would be suicidal."

That's why Murray hired Lendl. He brings hard-headedness to the job, a work ethic and calculating approach that Murray can identify with. While others fretted towards the end of an extraordinarily physical struggle against Djokovic, Lendl stayed calm. Murray said later that detachment from the roaring atmosphere transmitted itself to him on the court.

Lendl said: "He started looking, in my mind, better than Novak half way through the fourth set. I thought then there was a chance Andy could come back in the fourth as well. He was a bit unlucky on some big points; Novak played very well on some big points and the fifth set was in front of us."

He agreed, after a quibble about the nature and purpose of the question, that Murray could win more titles. "I thought that when we started, yeah."

Asked if he was surprised how quickly they had gelled as a team, with a slam title to show for it after only nine months, Lendl gave it the full Czech stare: "I think your memory is very short. Or you have selective memory. Or it's just short. Both Andy and I were saying, 'Give us six to nine months'. Do the math. You can help somebody, obviously, in a very short period of time, however, it takes longer than that to help more than that, for things to set in. You cannot do that in one week, you cannot do that in one month and, hopefully, we're not anywhere near where Andy can get."

And the next stage of the grand plan? "I'm not going to talk at all about the details. Again: listen to my words." But he was happy to expand on what had gone before. "We all know that it's a war out there. At some point it's very unlikely you're going to win a match in a blow-out. Especially against a guy like Novak.

"At some stage, it's going to come to who wants it more or how badly do you want it. I don't want to say that Novak didn't want it – you British guys, I have to be very careful with. So, how bad do you want it? What price are you willing to pay? And who can execute under extreme pressure? It's just a war out there. You've seen both of those guys: they are totally spent."

Lendl said the simple lesson Murray learned at Flushing Meadows was what it is like to win a slam. "I wasn't there for the Olympic final. We talked over the phone almost every day and so on but Andy has been maturing very nicely as a player, as a competitor and as a person. And as you mature, you become more comfortable in these situations.

"The more of them you are in, the more comfortable you feel. To me, one of the most important matches of the year, maybe the most important, was his loss to Novak at the Australian Open. Because that was a war, just like tonight. And that has given him the belief that he can hang with these guys. It has also shown him what it takes him to win so it doesn't catch him by surprise."

Was there anything he discovered about Andy that surprised him? "No," he said, "except that his sense of humour, maybe, is as sick as mine." And, with that, an unequivocal grin played across his weathered, knowing face.

10 SEPTEMBER

Our summer of love

EDITORIAL

Just the victory parade to go, and then Britain's summer of love will be over. London 2012, the capital's greatest party in living memory, is done. At the risk of using up the entire annual quota of Guardian editorial schmaltz in one go, this past month it feels as if most of us have been (as Boris Johnson would have it) cropdusted with serotonin, the happiness hormone. The Olympics held the country rapt but, against all expectations, the Paralympics made them feel like a mere warm-up act. From July's opening ceremony to the festival of flame, the venues have been packed and the TV audiences, national and global, have broken all records. There has surely been no comparable event in this country since the coronation nearly 60 years ago.

The athletes are the most obvious but far from the only factor in this success. In a world of professional sport where every aspect is commodified, the Olympic ideal is extraordinarily resilient. A handful of the global superstars – Usain Bolt and now Mo Farah – have enhanced their personal value, but most have driven

Summer

themselves relentlessly for the glory alone. So they are interesting not as, say, some abstract transfer deal with a gambling habit, but as individuals who, like all true heroes, might be any one of us. The Paralympics have overlaid this already astonishing substance with their personal tales of sudden grief and disaster overcome – although their particular triumph has been to make us disregard altogether the athletes' disabilities and shift the focus to their capacity to compete and win. Or to lose. For every victory there are a score of defeats, where the years of sacrifice have turned to ashes. These are more accessible tales, and the more telling. If sport can be said to have a moral purpose, it is that it can show it is worth more to try and fail than not to try at all, and the devastation and the fortitude of the losers is more moving even than the easier joy of the victors. The irresistible human stories of the past weeks have simply erased the scepticism of the previous seven years.

Of course, if you have £9bn to spend on a party, surely only a dolt could fail. But a single day of the widely anticipated public transport chaos or of fractious queues or malfunctioning lavatories would have soured the event. Instead, the least attractive aspects of London 2012, the ZiL lanes and the Visa-only policy and McDonald's and Coca-Cola as purveyors of sustenance to a sporting nation, were smothered not only by the competition but by the ocean of good humour fostered by the joviality of the volunteers, the inspirational architecture and the attention given to the natural landscape (with apologies to those who had to move to make room for it all).

Now it is all about the legacy. Some things that once seemed improbable may now be within reach. Boris Johnson really could be in Downing Street within the decade, where perhaps the experience of being suspended on a zip wire might inform his attitude to the frequent failings of public transport policy towards people in wheelchairs. Seb Coe has become an interesting candidate for mayor. More substantially, there is the promise on the local economic legacy, of regeneration of homes and recreation of jobs, and there is the equally important promise to translate the amplified passion for watching sport into an equal passion for doing it.

But there is more. Danny Boyle's description of Britishness as something that is as much an achievement of its ordinary citizens as it is of empire and monarchy was exactly right for the festival of sport that followed because both are reminders of what the state can achieve. Britain's athletes have been the beneficiaries of what amounts to an industrial policy for sport, millions channelled through expert organisations to find and train stars. London 2012 itself was initiated, orchestrated and largely funded by the state. It was a collective national effort, where successive governments of different political persuasions stuck to a common policy and showed just what, with imagination and ambition, can be done.

23 SEPTEMBER

Obama counting on massive ground campaign to win Iowa's electoral votes

EWEN MacASKILL IN DES MOINES

Rick Wilkey knocked on the door in the affluent neighbourhood of West Des Moines, Iowa. Four years ago, when the Barack Obama campaign volunteer talked to voters about the candidate's hope-

and-change message, he was greeted with yelps of excitement. This time, it's very different.

The man who opened the door looked disdainfully at Wilkey and his bright-red "Fired Up" Obama shirt, a souvenir from the 2008 campaign. Wilkey got only slightly into his introduction – "I am from the Obama campaign..." – before he was cut off. "I want you to leave my property immediately. I hate that son-of-a-bitch," the man said, before closing the door.

It is hard work being a volunteer in the swing states where the Obama and Mitt Romney teams are grinding it out district by district, street by street. With six weeks still to go to the election, the focus is shifting to the ground game: which side is going to prove better at getting its support out.

And in Iowa, that is shaping up to be a more closely fought contest than expected. It is one of eight swing states that could help decide the election. The most recent poll, by Rasmussen, gives Obama a two-point lead, while one by NBC/WSJ last week had him up by eight. Both campaign teams on the ground describe it as tight.

Obama and Romney are devoting serious amounts of time and resources to the state. The president has made eight trips this year, including a three-day bus tour, unusual for an incumbent. Romney, since the end of the Republican primaries and caucuses, has been here eight times. Last Monday, both vice-president Joe Biden and his Republican challenger Paul Ryan were campaigning in the state.

All this is extraordinary in a state that can contribute just six electoral college votes as the candidates aim to get the 270 required for victory. But for Romney, who has failed to overturn Obama's national poll lead or to break through in any of the major battleground states, winning Iowa is crucial.

For Obama, part of the reason is his emotional attachment to the state. It provided the launch pad for his White House bid, first with his surprise caucus victory over Hillary Clinton, in January 2008. In November that year, in the White House race, Iowa again delivered for him, giving him a huge 9% majority over Republican John McCain.

And the grassroots strategy that delivered victory last time is what gives Obama the edge over Romney now. The Democrat won Iowa in 2008 with a game plan that established a network of offices across the state, a mixture of paid staff and volunteers that dwarfed the efforts of Clinton and later McCain. In addition, his team created a sophisticated data bank to identify supporters. The offices behaved like community centres, inviting various demographic groups to come in to discuss their problems.

In 2012, the Obama campaign has 67 offices round the state, more than in 2008, and has an estimated 120 full-time, paid staff, as well as thousands of unpaid volunteers such as Rick Wilkey. Romney has only 13 offices and fewer staff: 25 full-time employees in the headquarters in Urbandale and at least one in each field office.

Wilkey works out of Obama's West Des Moines campaign office, a rented space in shopping mall. Inside, amid the maps and coffee cups, is a portrait of Obama as Superman and a calendar listing the days remaining to the election.

Wilkey, a 72-year-old former Des Moines city manager and businessman, is a precinct captain, as he was in 2008. He co-ordinates the weekly meeting with other volunteers to discuss canvassing and manning the phone-banks. He saw the inauguration of JFK in 1961 and was inspired, but that marked the end of his political involvement until he met Obama early in 2007.

He is not among the disillusioned. "I still support Obama, even more strongly than I did, because the choices are more stark, because his opponents are Romney and Ryan," he said.

Summer

Wilkey, who puts in between 10 and 15 hours a week, added: "I think the most important thing is getting the ground vote out. There are 2,000 precincts in Iowa. In 2000, Gore won by 4,000: that is an average of two votes per precinct. In 2004, Bush won by 10,000 votes: that is an average of five. These small margins show the importance of precinct level organisation."

He spent three hours canvassing in and around 57th and 58th street, in West Des Moines. He said he had not found any "enthusiasm gap" among Democratic supporters.

He had a list of 46 homes where he hoped there would be potential Democratic voters. About two-thirds were not at home. Of the 14 homes where he received a response of some sort from the people inside, seven people said they will vote Obama, six Romney, four declared they were undecided and one would not say.

One of the undecideds was Ron Myers, 68, who was working as a handyman after losing a senior job in publishing. He backed Obama last time but will not make up his mind until the final week. One of the issues for him is the size of the national debt, which tends to be one Republicans become more upset about than Democrats.

Among the Obama supporters was Terri Lentz, 57, a speech language specialist, who thinks he deserves more time in office. "I do not think Obama has had enough time to make the changes he has to, to clear up the Bush mess," she said.

Then she added: "I am hoping Obama wins but I do not think it is a slam dunk by any stretch."

Index

Abdel-Aziz, Abdel-Jalil 37
Abdel-Karim, Raja 126, 127
Abreu, José Antonio 239
Abuja 57
Accra 47–9, 56–7
Action 223–4
Adams, Nicola 275
Addounia TV 123
Adnan (in Syria) 120–1
Adonis, Andrew 159
A4e 233
Africa:
    enforced economic reforms in 53
    rising population of 51–2; *see also individual countries*
After Etan (Cohen) 190
Agius, Marcus 250
Ahmad, Abu 126
Aitkenhead, Decca 157
Akers, Sue 140–1, 143
al-Jazeera 123
al-Qaida 124
Alamirew, Yenew 276
Aldrin, Buzz 280
Ali, Mohammed 164
Ali, Muhammad (formerly Cassius Clay) 62
Allen, Lily 67
Ambridge 191–2
Amnesty International 75
Anderson Walsh, Paul 91
Andrew, Prince 270
Aniwa, Marilyn 52–3, 54

Anonymous 43
apartheid 61–5, 88, 137
Apollo 11 278
Apple 15–24
    iPad 22
    iPhone 21–2, 23
    iPod 20–1
    iTunes 20
    Jobs's absence from 19
    Lisa 18
    Macintosh 18, 20
apple crumble 144
Arab Spring 39
Archers, The, see Ambridge
Argentina 223, 224
Argos 233–5
Argyropoulou, Sofia 224
Arlen, Victoria 286, 287, 288
Armstrong, Neil 278, 280
Arnold, Matthew 102, 103
Arthur, Charles 15
Assad, Bashar al- 3, 120–1, 124–5
    see also Syria
Assad, Hafez al- 121
Associated Press 37, 79
Atkins, Humphrey 94
Atos 120
Ayresome Park 99

Baazis, Cherifa 165
Babyface 138
Bacharach, Burt 138
Badasi, Delali 54
Baggini, Julian 156

Bailey, Ryan 274
Bakeer, Salem 39
Ball, Cllr Tony 33–4
Balls, Ed 158, 165, 207, 252–3
banks:
    crisis concerning 249–56
    Europe's, under-capitalised 210
    and loans to real economy 253–4
    see also financial crisis; Libor
Barclays 250, 251–2
    interest rates rigged by 252
    tax-avoidance schemes closed by 251
Barlow, Eddie 63
Baron Cohen, Sacha 161
Bashford, Tony 139
Bassam (in Syria) 122
Bates, Stephen, last *Guardian* day of 7
BBC Young Sports Personality of the Year 288
Bear (at Occupy London) 43
Beatles 271
Bebb, Thomas 114–20 *passim*
    heart attack suffered by 120
Begum, Mahmoona 167
Behring, Wenche 173, 174, 177
Being Bobby Brown 138
Bekele, Kenenisa 275
Bell, Andy 112
Bell, Steve 96, 158
Benjamin, Alison 158
Bennett, Alan 226
Bentham, Jeremy 229
Bergh-Johnsen, Jonas 204
Berlusconi, Silvio 213
Bertolucci, Sergio 262
Biden, Joe 295

Big Brother 87
    see also Celebrity Big Brother
Big Noise Orchestra 238, 241
    see also Sistema Scotland
Birbalsingh, Katharine 172
Bischoff report 251–2
Black Power 163
Blair, Tony 29, 226–7
    £2.5m part-time job of 254
Blake, Yohan 272, 273
Blitz (second world war) 128
Boar 157
Bodyguard, The 138
Bolt, Usain 271–4, 292
Borat 161
Born Free 75
Bouckaert, Peter 37, 38
Boycott Workfare 235, 236
Boyle, Danny 269, 270, 294
Bradford West byelection 164–8
Breivik, Anders Behring 171–8
    online "manifesto" of 174, 175, 176, 177
Breivik, Jens 171–8
Breivik, Tove 173, 175, 177
Breivik, Wanda 175, 176, 177
Brezhnev, Leonid 145–6
Brighton & Hove Bus and Coach Company 149
British Bankers' Association 252
British Heart Foundation 233
Broadbent, Jim 92, 93
Brout, Robert 263
Brown, Bobby 137, 138
Brown, Gordon 92, 199, 209, 252
Browning, Robert 131
Buffett, Warren 104
Bugno, Gianni 266
Bulley, Michael 193
Bunting, Madeleine 155

Burdon, Ian 100
Burkina Faso 52
Burrell, Paul 226
Bush, George W. 297
Byfield, Rosemary 75
Byfield, Stefan 75

Cable, Vince 199
Calpac 237
Cambridge University 105–13
Cameron, David 29, 95, 198, 199
    and banks 250, 251
    on Gaddafi's death 38–9
    and Olympic budget 270
    summit walkout of 253
Cameron, Samantha 197, 198
Captive Animals Conservation Society 75
Carlisle, Sam 44
Carlos, John 162–3
Carroll, James 157
Cartoon Museum 96
Cartwright, Tom 64
Carvel, Bertie 71
Carvel, John 71
Castle, Barbara 94
Cavendish, Mark 268
Cazeneuve, Bernard 179
Celebrity Big Brother 168
    see also Big Brother
Cellcrypt 30
CERN 261–5
Cernan, Eugene 278
Chad 52
Chambers, Dwain 273
Chambers's Encyclopaedia 152–3
Charity Commission 168
Charles Darwin Research Station 243
Charles I, King 131

Charles, Prince of Wales 128, 227
Chekhov, Anton 188
Chi Chi 75
Children's Encyclopedia 152–3
China:
    and Kim Jong-il death 77
    pandas from 72–5
Ching Ching 75
Chirac, Jacques 180
Cholmondeley, 7th Marquess of 198
Christmas Carol, A (Dickens) 131
Churchill: The Struggle for Survival 1945–60 (Moran) 95
Churchill, Winston 95, 128
    sketches by 107–8
Cityitis 200
Clark, Alan 95
Clark, Natasha 157
Clarke, Ken 198
Clay, Cassius (later Muhammad Ali) 61–2
Cleese, John 200
Climate Camp 43
Clinton, Hillary 147, 295–6
Cloake, Felicity 155, 156
Clockwise 200
Close Protection UK 230–1
Coe, Lord (Sebastian) 163, 271, 286, 293
Cohen, Lisa R. 190
Collins, Wilkie 131, 133
Colman, Olivia 92
Comte, August 102
Conservative Party, finance-industry funding of 254
Cook, Tim 17, 19
Cooke, Alistair 12
Cooper, Yvette 165

Cowell, Simon 135, 136
Cringely, Robert X. 20
Critchley, Simon 101
crosswords 156–7
Crouch, Peter 100
Cultural Olympiad 238
Cutler, Nick 108

Dahl, Roald 70
Daily Mail 66–7, 140, 163
    and bankers 250
    Lawrence suspects labelled "murderers" by 86
Daily Mirror 93
Daily Telegraph 140
Dale Farm, Travellers evicted from 31–6
Darkwah, Felicia 50–1
Darling, Alistair 206, 254
Darwin, Charles 243
David (at Occupy London) 43
Davies, Lynn 162
Davis, Clive 136, 138
Davis Cup 161–2
de Botton, Alain 101–4
Delhi, traffic in 25–8
Delury, John 78, 79
Desmond, Pascal 25
Deutschman, Alan 17
Dhou, Mansour 37
Diamond, Bob 250, 251
diamond jubilee 228–32, 237–8
    stewards for 230–2
Diana, Princess of Wales 128, 226, 229
Dickens, Charles 131–3
    characters of 131–2
Diderot, Denis 102
Disney 19
Djokovic, Novak 289, 290, 291

Dmitrienko, Maria 161
Dobson, Gary 85
Dolby, George 133
D'Oliveira, Basil 61–5
Dorigo, Tommaso 262
D'Orsay, Count 133
Dowler, Bob 68
Dowler, Milly 68
Dowler, Sally 68
Dowling, Tim 160
Downton Abbey 94
Drance, Matt 15, 21–2
Drifters, The 136
D'Souza, Lady 198
du Preez, Frik 61
Dudamel, Gustavo 239, 242
Dujardin, Charlotte 275
Duncan (at Occupy London) 43

Edinburgh zoo 72–5
Egypt, uprisings in 127
Ekaub, Emmanuel 53
El Sistema 239–40, 242
Elizabeth II, Queen 197–9, 225–30, 237–8
    diamond jubilee of, *see* diamond jubilee
    golden jubilee of 229
    and interviews 225–6
    jewellery worn by 4, 198
    and Olympic skydiving sketch 269
    poll shows support for 229
Ellis, John 265
Encyclopaedia Britannica 151–5 *passim*
encyclopedias 151–5
Englert, François 263
Ennis, Jessica 275, 288
Équipe 266–7

Ethiopia 52
euro:
   future of 205
   and Greece, *see* Greece
   Lagarde's mission to save 207
European Football
   Championships (Euros) 161
European Organisation for
   Nuclear Research (CERN)
   261–5
Evans, Paul 156

Faith of the Faithless, The
   (Critchley) 101
Falklands war 93, 158
Falun Gong 75
Farah, Mo 274–7, 292
Farah, Rihanna 277
Farah, Tania 277
Federal Bureau of Investigation
   (FBI) 143
Federer, Roger 289
Ferdinand, Rio 201
Field, Mary-Ellen 68
Fifty Shades of Grey (James) 256–7
financial crisis 130, 214, 249–56
   see also banks
Financial Services Authority 252
Fish, Michael 269–70
Flanagan, Joe 244
Fletcher, PC Yvonne 39
Flitcroft, Garry 67
Forster, John 131, 133
Foster, Brendan 275
Fox, Dr Liam 28–30
France, Hollande becomes
   president of 178–84
Francis, Cummings 238
Franco, Gen. Francisco 162
Franklin, Aretha 136

Fraser-Pryce, Shelly-Ann 274
Free Tibet 75
Freemantle, Simon 55
French grammar 193–5
Further Maths Network 110

G4S 233
Gaddafi, Muammar 36–9
   death of 36, 37–8
Gaddafi, Mutassim 38
Gaddafi, Saif al-Islam 39, 214
Galápagos Conservancy 245
Galápagos National Park 243
Galápagos tortoises 243–5
   see also Lonesome George
Galloway, George 164–8
   on *Celebrity Big Brother* 168
Galtieri, Gen. Leopoldo 92
Garbo, Greta 226
Garnham, Neil 67
Gascoigne, Paul 67
Gascoigne, Sheryl 67
Gates, Bill 16–17, 18–19
   on Jobs 16
Gatlin, Justin 272, 273
Gay, Tyson 272–3
Gearing, Jay 44
Gebremeskel, Dejen 276, 277
Gebrhiwet, Hagos 276
Geithner, Timothy 206
Ghana 47–58
   Accra 47–9
   census, in (1948) 49
   independence of 50
Ghazzawi, Razan 127
Gianotti, Fabiola 262
Gibbon, Edward 101–2
Gilmore, Alec 160
Gilmore, Enid 160–1
Glancey, Jonathan 24–5

Glasgow Herald 69
Glen, Iain 94
Glover, Barbara 69
God Is Not Great (Hitchens) 104
Golding, William 12
Goldsmith, Zac 156
Gómez-Angulo, Juan Antonio 162
Goodhew, Duncan 163
Goodman, Clive 143
Google 21
Gorbachev, Mikhail 188
Gore, Al 297
Gove, Michael 30
Grant, Hugh 66
Granta 96
Greece:
    economy of 205, 208–9, 213, 217–24
    "governed by a group of gangsters" 223
Greene, Graham 101
Greene, Patricia 192
Greenwood, Alice 167
Greenwood, George 167
Grieve, John 87
Griffiths, Kim 119
Grigioni, Sveva 244
Guardian:
    enduring ethos of 8
    extent of 8–9
    Golding's comments on 12
    and *NOW* phone-hacking affair 65–6
    open weekend of 6, 155–61
Guralnik, Gerry 263
Gypsy Council 35

Habermas, Jürgen 102
Hagen, Dick 263
Hague, William 77
Halpern, John 156
Hammond, Philip 29
Hardman, Robert 228
Harley, John Pritt 133
Hayes, Julie 150
Heart of Midlothian FC 139
Heath, Edward 92
Hedges, Chris 130
Hehir, Joe 194
Hepburn, Katharine 226
Herald and Times Group 69
Heuer, Rolf Dieter 262
Higgs boson particle 261–5
Higgs, Peter 262, 263, 264
Hirst, Damien 214–17
Hitchens, Christopher 104
Hitler, Adolf 211, 218
Hobsbawm, Eric 96
Hoggard, Simon 158
Hollande, François 178–84, 205
Holloway, Richard 240
Houston, Cissy 136
Houston, Whitney 135–8
Howell, Rob 71
Howells, Ros 89–90
Hoy, Chris 267, 275
Huddersfield Town FC 99
Hughes, Simon 159
Hulse, Carl 2
Human Rights Watch 37, 78
Hussain, Imran 166–7
Hussain, Naweed 166
Hussein, Yasser 165

I Look to You 138
"I Will Always Love You" 138
I Will Always Love You 138
Ibrahimov, Hayle 276
Icarus 219
Iguider, Abdalaati 276

I'm Your Baby Tonight 137
Indurain, Miguel 266
International Monetary Fund (IMF) 205–14 *passim*, 249
International Olympic Committee 63
International Space Station 279, 280
iPad 22
iPhone 21–2, 23
iPod 20–1
IPPR 237
Iraq War 165
Irish Republican Army (IRA) 39
Iron Lady, The 91–5
iTunes 20
Ive, Jonathan 17

Jackson, Michael 137
Jacovides, Alex 220–1
Jacquier, Gilles 123
James, Clive 163
Jeffers, David 195
Jia Jiansheng 74
Jibril, Mahmoud 38
Jobs, Lisa 18
Jobs, Steve 15–24
   cancer suffered by 23
   leaves and returns to Apple 19
   staff loyalty and devotion to 17
   tributes to 15–16
Johnson, Boris 199, 258, 293
Jones, Phil 193–4
Jones, Tom 163, 164
JP Morgan 254, 255
Just Whitney 137

Kagame, Paul 270

Karbo I, King 56
Karbo III, King 55–7
Kavanagh, Trevor 140
Kazakhstan 161
KCNA 76, 79, 80
Keeler, James 112–13
Kelly, Dennis 70, 71
Kelly, Wayne 58–60
Kennedy, John F. 91, 296
Khan, Chaka 136
Khan, Imran 86–7
Khan, Jemima 66
Kibble, Tom 263
Kiely, Sophia 70
Killean, Nicola 242
Kim Il-sung 79
Kim Jong-il 76–80
Kim Jong-un 76–7
King Jorbie Akodam Karbo I, King 47
Kinnock, Neil 93
Kirkdale Community Centre 118
Knab, Richard 245
Koech, Isiah 276
Kolehmainen, Hannes 275
Koning-Peper, Mirjam de 287
Koranteng-Addo, Cecilia 54
Korle Bu hospital 47, 48, 49
Kuts, Vladimir 275
Kuwait, World Shooting Championships in 161

labour, unpaid 230–7
   see also diamond jubilee: stewards for
Lagarde, Christine 204–14
   Guardian interview of 221
   on UK economy 213
Lagat, Bernard 276
Lancaster, Stuart 163

Landor, Walter Savage 131
Large Hadron Collider 261–5
Lasseter, John 19
Law, Jude 67
Lawra 47, 55–6, 57
Lawrence, Doreen 86, 87, 89–90
Lawrence, Neville 86, 87, 89–90
Lawrence, Stephen 5, 85–91
Le Foll, Stéphane 181
Le Roux, Piet 62
Leech, John 133
Leese, Sir Richard 201–2
Lehman Bros 255
Lendl, Ivan 289–92
Lentz, Terri 297
Les Misérables (*Les Mis*) 70
Letter from America 12
Leveson Inquiry 65–9, 139–43, 255
Lewis, Carl 272
Libor 250–1, 252, 255–6
   see also banks
Libya 36–9
   Misrata 38
   National Transitional Council 37
   Sirte 37, 39
   Tripoli, celebrations in 38
   uprisings in 127
Lisa (Apple computer) 18
Littlejohn, Richard 140, 155
Litvinenko, Alexander 148
Liverpool City Council 114, 118–19
Liverpool Into Work 119
Liverpool, unemployment in 114–20
Livingstone, Ken 258
Llerena, Fausto 243
Lloyd, Peter 89

Lloyd, Phyllida 91, 93, 94
Lockerbie 39
Lomong, Lopez 276
London:
   Bishop of 129
   7/7 bombings in 281–2
   Shard's effect on skyline of 257–60
Lonesome George 243–5
   tourist attraction 245
Lonesome George (Nicholls) 244
Long, Joanna 235
Longosiwa, Thomas 276, 277
Lucas, George 19
Lucy (at Occupy London) 43

McBride, Betty 233
McCain, John 296
McCann, Gerry 68–9
McCann, Kate 68–9
McCann, Madeleine 68–9, 188
McCarthy, Kathleen 33, 36
McCartney, Paul 271
McFaul, Michael 147
Machiavelli, Niccolò 101
Macintosh 18, 20
Maclean, Steve 42
Maclise, Daniel 133
Macpherson, Elle 68
Macpherson Inquiry 85–6, 88–9
   see also Lawrence, Stephen
Macready, William 133
Magoche, Chantelle 241
Magoche, Taf 241
Mail on Sunday 66
Major, John 29
Makdissi, Jihad 124
Mali 52
Malik, Shiv 231
Maloney, Carolyn 255

Malt, Henry 65
Manchester City FC 200–4
    FA Cup won by 201
    United's derby with 202
Manchester United FC 200, 201, 203
    City's derby with 202
Manchester University Centre for Research on Socio-Cultural Change (CRESC) 253, 255
Mandela, Nelson 88
Manet, Édouard 216
Maniatisan, Thanasis 222
Manos, Stefanos 223–4
Marie Claire 69
Mars 279
Martin, Elizabeth 241
Martin, Tony (cyclist) 267
Mason, Fr Dan 35
Matar, Ghayath 122
Mather, Andrew 203
Matilda 70–1
Matthews, Ken 162
Medvedev, Dmitry 146
Merkel, Angela 220
Microsoft 16–17, 18–19, 21
    Windows 19, 22
    Zune 21
midget gems 97–101
Miliband, David 159
Miliband, Ed 165, 199, 250, 252, 255
Milios, John 218, 220
Miller, Sienna 67
Milligan, Spike 96
Minchin, Tim 70, 71
Mirren, Helen 226
Mitterrand, François 178, 179–80, 183

Mladic, Ratko 5
MobileMe 17
Moir, Jenny 194
Monti, Mario 211, 213
moon landings 278–9
Moore, Brian 163
Moran, Lord 95
Morgan, Abi 93, 94
Moscow State University 187–8
Moscow zoo 74
Mosley, Alexander 68
Mosley, Max 68
Moss, Kate 225
M25 149–51
Mudar (in Syria) 124
Muhammad, Abu 123
Mulcaire, Glenn 142
Murdoch, Rupert 3, 140, 143
Murphy, Jim 30
Murray, Andy 289–92
    first grand-slam title of 289
Murray, Bill 265
Musil, Robert 213
My Love is Your Love 138
Myers, Ron 297

Nader (in Syria) 123
NASA 279–80
Nash, Paul (athlete) 61
national anthems 161–4
National Bank of Greece 223
National Missing Children's Day 190
Naula, Edwin 243
Nelkon, Philip 59–60
New Tang Dynasty Television 75
New York Review of Books 254
New York Times 151, 189
News Corp 143
    see also Leveson Inquiry

News of the World:
    and D'Oliveira 64
    and phone hacking, *see*
        Leveson Inquiry
Newsnight 231
NeXT 19
Nicholls, Henry 75, 244
Nietzsche, Friedrich 102 in Guardian
Niger, rising population of 52
Nigeria, rising population of 52
Nikita (at Occupy London) 46–7
Nixon, Richard 280
Nokia 21
Norman, Don 23
Norris, David 85
North Korea 76–80
    "human rights hell on earth" 78
Northern Rock 252, 254
Norway shootings 171–8

Obama, Barack 254, 294–7
    on Jobs 15
Obed, Prof. Samuel 49–50
Occupy London 5, 40–7, 128–30
    football team of 41–2
    general assembly of 45
    silent gestures used during 45
Office of Fair Access 107
O'Hare, Margaret 193–4
Oliver, Gary 58–60
Olympic Games (1936, Berlin) 269
Olympic Games (1964, Tokyo) 162
Olympic Games (1968, Mexico City) 63, 162–3
Olympic Games (1980, Moscow) 163
Olympic Games (1988, Seoul) 272
Olympic Games (2004, Athens) 266
Olympic Games (2008, Beijing) 269, 286, 287, 288
Olympic Games (2012, London) 148, 162, 267, 268–77, 292–4
    announcement of 281
    brutal dictators at opening of 270
    cultural events ushering in 238
    opening of 6, 268–71; *see also* Paralympic Games
One Show, The 46
Orton, Sheena 118
Orwell, George 269, 270
Osborne, George 30, 206, 214
    and banks 250, 251
    Paralympic booing of 11
    and unpaid labour 236
Ovett, Steve 163
Oxford University 107

Packer, Ann 162
Paddick, Brian 141, 142–3
Paltrow, Gwyneth 195–6
pandas 72–5
Papademos, Lucas 211
Papandreou, George 220
Paralympic Games (2012, London) 281–5, 286–8, 292–4
    Osborne booed at 11
    see also Olympic Games
Pardkh, Sal 204
Parker, Dai 163–4
Parker, Dorothy 192, 226
Parkinson, Cecil 94–5

Parks, Geoff 110
Parliament, State Opening of 197–9
Partington, Richard 105, 106–7, 109
Parton, Dolly 136
Paternoster Square, London 40
Paterson, Sandy 153–4
Patz, Etan 188–9
Patz, Julie 189, 190, 191
Patz, Stanley 189, 190–1
Payne's Army and Navy Drops 99
Pears Cyclopaedia 152, 153
Perez, Tom Rodriguez 41–2
Perry, Grayson 157–8
Petrov, Leonid 80
Philip, Prince, Duke of Edinburgh 198
Piano, Renzo 4, 258, 259, 260
Pickles, Eric 65
Pickett, Wilson 136
Pimlott, Ben 229
Pixar 19
police, Tasers used by 31–2, 32–3
Pollock, Graeme 61, 62, 63, 64
Pollock, Peter 63
population:
    in Africa 51–2
    of Ghana 47–58 *passim*
    UN's warning concerning 51
Porter, Tiffany 162
Positive Bradford 167
Poundland 235
Powell, Asafa 272–3
Prescott, Lord (John) 141, 142, 231
    and Shard 258, 259
Preston Bus Station 24–5
Preston, Peter 11
Private Eye 93

Professional Footballers' Association 142
Pullen, Nigel 149–50, 151
Putin, Vladimir 3, 145–8

Qashoush, Ibrahim 121
Qasim, Wail 42
Qatar 123
Qin Gang 72–3, 74
Queens Park Rangers FC 200

Raffy, Serge 182
raisins 143–5
Ramos, José 190
Rand, Mary 162
Randy (at Occupy London) 43
Raploch 238, 239, 240–1
Rawlings, Flt Lt Jerry 54
Rea, Chris 149
Reagan, Ronald 95
Reid, L.A. 138
Reilly, Cait 235
Religion for Atheists (de Botton) 101–4
Respect 165, 167
RIM 21
Rima (in Syria) 120–1
Roberts, Alfred 94
Roberts, Hugh 73, 74
Robertson, Cathy 160
Robinson, Smokey 135
Rock and Roll Hall of Fame 138
Rocksavage, David (7th Marquess of Cholmondeley) 198
Roe, Insp. Trevor 33
Romney, Mitt 271, 295
Rooks, Dickie 99
Rooney, Wayne 201
Roth, Kenneth 78

Rowling, J.K. 67
Rowson, Martin 158
Royal, Ségolène 180, 183
Royal Zoological Society 73
Royle, Joe 200
Rubin, Gerry 139
Rubinstein, Jon 20
Rupp, Galen 276, 277
Rusbridger, Alan 157, 159, 160
    and Bates's leaving 7
    in old *Bedside Guardian* 12
Rushdie, Salman 5, 196
Russia 145–8
    Britain's relations with 147
    bureaucracy in 184–8
Rutherford, Greg 275
Ryan, Paul 295

Saatchi Gallery 216
Saddam Hussein 168
St Paul's Cathedral:
    cleaning bill for 129
    Dickens's description of 132
    German bombs survived by 128
    myths surrounding 128
    occupation near, *see* Occupy London
Salazar, Alberto 277
Salmond, Alex 73
Sandwell and West Birmingham Hospitals NHS Trust 233
Sarah (at Occupy London) 42, 45–6
Sarkozy, Nicolas 179, 182, 184
Sawyer, Diane 138
Scarfe, Gerald 97
Scargill, Arthur 92
Schiller, Phil 17
Schmidt, Harrison 278

Scott, C.P. 8
Scott-Heron, Gil 100
Scrabble 58–60
Scriberia 158
Scruton, Roger 101
Sculley, John 18
Searle, Ronald 95–7
Second Coming of Steve Jobs, The (Deutschman) 17
Seetec 233–4
Sellar, Irvine 258, 259, 260
Semtex 39
Sendak, Maurice 5, 195–6
Serco 233
Shaaban, Buthaina 124
Shakespeare, William 131
Shard 4, 257–60
    furious opposition to 259
    political backers of 258
    see also Occupy London
Sheffield Forgemasters 254
Sheffield United FC 97
Sheridan, Candy 35–6
Sheridan, Cornelius 35
Sheridan Margaret 35
Sheridan, Mary 32–3, 34
Sheridan, Nora 32
Sheridan, Richard 35
Shirky, Clay 159–60
Shuttleworth, John 97
Simmonds, Ellie 286–8
Simón Bolívar Symphony Orchestra 239–40
Singh, Marsha 165
Sirte 37, 39
Sistema Scotland 239–42
Skinner, Dennis 165
Small, Cllr Nick 118
Smith, James 150
Smith, Tommie 162–3

Index

Smitheram, Brett 60
Socialist Workers Party 43
South Africa, and apartheid 61–5, 88, 137
South Uist 81–2
space exploration 278–80
space shuttle 279, 280
Spencer, Pete 100
Sputnik 278
Srebrenica 5
Stalin, Joseph 146
Stanfield, Clarkson 133
State Opening of Parliament 197–9
Statham, Darren 203
Steadman, Ralph 97
Steinberg, Ellis 200, 201
Steiner, George 101
Stephen Lawrence Centre 89–90
   see also Lawrence, Stephen; Macpherson Inquiry
Stephens, Mark 20
Stone, Dr Richard 88
Strauss-Kahn, Dominique 180–1, 206
Straw, Jack 89
Streep, Meryl 91–4
Sturgeon, Nicola 73
Suleiman, Fadwa 125
Sun 140, 141
Sutton Trust 108
Swarbrick, Andrew 24
Syria 120–7
   deepening economic plight of 125
   sanctions on 125–6
Syriza 218, 220

Tangtastics 99
Tanweer, Shehzad 281

Tasers, at Dale Farm 31–2, 32–3
Tate Modern 215
Taylor, Gordon 142
Tesco 236
Thabang, Maggie 63
Thatcher, Carol 92, 94
Thatcher, Denis 92, 93
Thatcher, Margaret 91–5, 163
   and Liverpool 115
   M25 opened by 151
Tian Tian 72–5
Times 140
Today 231
Toland, John 101
Tolstoy, Leo 133
Tomorrow's People 231, 232
top-up fees 107
Tour de France 265–7
Travellers, Dale Farm eviction of 31–6
Trierweiler, Valérie 183–4
Tsafendas, Dimitri 62
Tsigos, Dimitris 222, 223
Tsipras, Alexis 220
Tunisia, uprisings in 127

UCI Road World Championships 267
UK Uncut 43
unemployment 114–20
Union for African Population Studies 52
United Nations, population warning of 51
United States of America:
   Financial Crisis Inquiry Report of 254
   and Kim Jong-il death 77
   missing children in 191; *see also* Patz, Etan

presidential election in
    294–7
sanctions on Libya imposed
    by 125
unpaid labour 230–7
    see also diamond jubilee:
    stewards for
Urrego, Verónica 242
US Open Tennis Championships
    289–91
Utøya shootings 171–8

Varoufakis, Yanis 219–20, 224
Vatikiotis, Leonidas 223
Verwoerd, Hendrik 62
Vickers Commission 255
Victoria, Queen 228
Villemot, Dominique 183
Vimto Book of Knowledge 153
Vincent, Jane 167
Vine, Jeremy 231
Viner, Katharine 158
Viren, Lasse 275
Voltaire 101
von Rospach, Chuq 17
Vorster, John 64

Wall Street crash 251
Wall Street Journal 252
Warburton, Lynn 204
Warchus, Matthew 71
Waring, Frank 62
Warwick, Dionne 136
Warwick University 157
Watson, Alan 69
Watson, Diane 69
Watson, Jim 69
Watson, Margaret 69
Way of the Panda, The (Nicholls) 75
Werrity, Adam 28

Westland crisis 93
Westminster Abbey 128
Weston, Mark 151
White Cube 215
Whitelaw, Willie 93
Whiteley, Jackie 166
Whitney 137
Whitney Houston 137
Wiggins, Bradley 265–8, 275
Wilkey, Rick 294–5, 296–7
William, Prince, Duke of
    Cambridge 227
Williams, Alex 202–3
Williams, Elaine 46
Williams, Phoenix 46
Windows 19
Winfrey, Oprah 138
Wired 18
work schemes 230–7
World Shooting Championships
    161
Worthington, Frank 99
Wozniak, Steve 18
Wren, Christopher 130
Wright, Martine 281–5

Xerox 18

Yang Guang 72–5
Yates, John 142
Yeru, Anthony 58
Yeru, Stella 57–8
Yifter, Miruts 275
Yonhap 77
York, Archbishop of 130
Young, Janet 94

Zátopek, Emil 275
Zeegen, Maurice 194
Zune 21